Paddy Hopkirk says:

'Sooner or later, every car owner faces the ruinous cost of servicing, maintaining and repairing his car. That's why more and more car owners are turning to DIY methods as the <u>only</u> way of slashing motoring costs.

PITMAN'S ALL-IN-ONE motoring books are written by professional motoring writers who understand car owners' needs.
The books have been specially designed to give <u>all</u> the information needed, in clear diagrams, trouble-shooting charts, photographs and easy-to-follow text, making it easy for DIY car owners to keep costs of motoring at rock bottom.

Whatever the car owner's approach to home servicing – whether as a novice or an expert – PITMAN'S ALL-IN-ONE motoring books offer him <u>for the first time</u> a combined maintenance handbook and workshop manual – all the DIY car owner needs to get the best out of his car.'

The attractive, compact lines of the hatchback are shown to advantage here. This is the GLS model, with sports-type road wheels

The counterbalanced tailage of the estate can opens through a wide angle to allow unobstructed access to the roomy load compartment

The Chevette E four-door saloon, one of the lowest-priced models in the range, but still well-equipped and attractively trimmed

All-in-one
book of the
Vauxhall Chevette

Staton Abbey

A maintenance,
fault-tracing and home
workshop manual

Covering the 1256 cc
Hatchback
Saloon
Estate car

Pitman Publishing

PITMAN PUBLISHING LIMITED
39 Parker Street, London WC2B 5PB

Associated Companies
Copp Clark Ltd, Toronto · Fearon Publishers Inc, Belmont, California
Pitman Publishing Co. SA (Pty) Ltd, Johannesburg · Pitman Publishing
New Zealand Ltd, Wellington · Pitman Publishing Pty Ltd, Melbourne
Sir Isaac Pitman Ltd, Nairobi

First published in Great Britain 1977

ISBN 0 273 01010 7

Reproduced and printed by photolithography and bound in
Great Britain at The Pitman Press, Bath

Contents

This partly-sectioned view of the hatchback shows many of the features which have made the Chevette an outstanding success

Acknowledgements

Special thanks are due to Vauxhall Motors Ltd, for providing information and advice during the preparation of this book, and for permission to reproduce some of the illustrations from the Service Training manuals for the Chevette, which can be obtained from Vauxhall dealers or from Vauxhall Motors Ltd, at Luton, Beds.

Among the other firms to whom thanks are due are:

Automotive Products Company Ltd
Champion Sparking Plug Company Ltd
AE Edmunds Walker Ltd
Girling Ltd
Holt Products Ltd
Joseph Lucas Ltd
Zenith Carburettor Company Ltd

The greatest care has been taken to check and cross-check the information and servicing data, but liability cannot be accepted for errors or omissions, or for changes in specifications that are sometimes introduced by a manufacturer during the production run of a model.

Part one

1 Before you begin
How this series was planned

Are you a dedicated do-it-yourself enthusiast—or an owner with only limited practical experience, forced by continually rising costs to maintain and repair your car at home?

Whatever your approach to home servicing—whether as a novice or as an expert—the handbooks in this series have been tailored to meet your needs and abilities. Each forms a combined, all-in-one maintenance handbook and home workshop manual, with the emphasis solidly on the practical aspects of the work.

We introduce you to your car, advise you how to vet a used example, tell you how to get it through the Ministry test and take you progressively through preventive maintenance, trouble-shooting, servicing, repairs and overhauls.

We have made the workshop manual chapters as comprehensive as possible, while bearing in mind the less than ideal conditions under which the average owner must usually carry out repairs and overhauls. But it must be accepted that some jobs are outside the province of the home mechanic; they call for the use of special workshop tools and equipment and—in many cases—for special skills.

Botched-up repairs can be dangerous and we feel strongly that owners should not be encouraged to do work which might entail safety risks.

How this book is arranged

In Part One you will find an in-depth study of the models covered, together with information on servicing and preventive maintenance. We take the logical view that it is better to avoid trouble than to try to put it right after it has developed.

Even the most meticulous maintenance, however, cannot guarantee freedom from faults, so we have included in Part Two a comprehensive set of trouble-tracing charts which should enable you to pin-point a trouble quickly and accurately.

If your car is due for the Ministry test, the tips that we give should enable it to pass with flying colours. Many cars fail quite unnecessarily, due to faults which could have been put right by a practical owner.

While still on the theme of putting your car in tip-top condition, we tell you how to tackle rust and bodywork blemishes and how to restore a showroom shine.

The remainder of the book forms a concise home workshop manual, covering all the jobs that can be safely tackled without the need for elaborate equipment, and supported by comprehensive specifications and data tables.

The practical aspects

We have tried to anticipate your difficulties and to give practical pointers and advice where necessary. For example, would it be quicker and cheaper to fit a new or fully-reconditioned part instead of stripping and repairing a worn component? When should the help of a specialist repair firm be enlisted? We give you the pros and cons (and the economics) of these problems, to help you to make the correct decision.

Time is often a vital factor and we have included in the workshop manual chapters what we think are some realistic times for the more important jobs and major operations. We have erred on the generous side, bearing in mind the needs of the novice, but it would be wise to allow an additional safety margin to take care of unexpected snags. The times that we suggest, therefore, will not necessarily agree with those that may be quoted by a dealer, who has a well-equipped workshop and racks full of expensive special tools.

Finally, we have broken down the servicing and overhaul instructions into simple step-by-step sequences which are exceptionally easy to follow and should give a beginner the confidence to tackle fairly ambitious work.

Where there are snags, we don't hesitate to say so. And where special service tools and other equipment are needed, we list them.

As for the work itself, that is—literally—in your hands. We hope that we shall have helped to make it a little easier.

2 Getting to know your car
Facts and figures

When pre-release stories about the Vauxhall Chevette began to appear in the press, the rumour was that this new, compact Vauxhall would be a British version of a truly international General Motors design — the so-called T-car — which would also be built in the USA, Brazil, Germany, Japan and Australia.

Like most rumours, this had a basis of truth, but when the Chevette was announced at the Geneva Motor Show in March 1975 it became evident that the only common feature of the various models was the floorpan — an intricate, expensive pressing — and the running gear, which included the suspension, brakes and rear axle.

Opel in Germany were responsible for the design of these parts, but engines and gearboxes which were already available in the various countries were slotted into this basic layout, together with a fairly high proportion of other local components.

An important difference at that time, however, was that the Vauxhall Chevette body took the form of an attractive two-door hatchback, with a wide, lift-up rear window and a folding rear seat, in contrast to the conventional saloons produced in the other countries. Later the hatchback design was adopted for the American version of the Chevette (launched in 1976) and also as an additional model in the German Opel Kadett range and for other General Motors overseas territories.

Although the Chevette hatchback was an immediate success, however, it soon became evident that a conventional two-door or four-door saloon, with a large lockable boot, would be required by many buyers and in January 1976 the saloon version of the Chevette — very similar in design to the Opel Kadett but using a Vauxhall engine and gearbox and with the distinctive Vauxhall sloping bonnet nose — made its appearance. It was perhaps predictable, too, that in order to reach as wide a potential market as possible the hatchback and the saloon should be joined in June 1976 by a Chevette estate-car version.

The engine

The three models share the same basic mechanical specification and previous owners of Vivas will be reassured to find the well-tried Viva 1256 engine and gearbox installed in the Chevette.

Progressively developed over the years, these power units have a reputation for trouble-free running and ease of maintenance. In the Viva they are notable for their liveliness and their good pulling power — but not unfortunately, for smoothness and freedom from fuss when revving hard.

It is difficult to believe that the same engine is installed in the Chevette, however. Improved engine mountings and better sound-proofing result in a notably smooth, quiet power unit. Combined with a low level of wind noise and road noise, this makes the Chevette a very relaxed car at motorway cruising speeds.

The maximum power (58.5 bhp DIN) is produced at 5000 rpm and the maximum torque or pulling power (68 lb ft) at the relatively low speed of 2600 rpm.

A themostatically - controlled, vacuum - operated heated-air intake for the carburettor — as fitted to later Viva engines — supplies air to the carburettor at a reasonably constant termperature, thus enabling more economical carburettor settings to be used for part-throttle running. When the throttle is opened fully, however, cold air is supplied, allowing full power to be developed. Revised ignition distributor settings and wide plug gaps are used to suit the leaner mixture provided by the carburettor. The result is a very modest fuel consumption, even when using the lively performance that is available.

The transmission

The only black mark earned by the Chevette is a fault which has been carried over from the Viva: the transmission vibration which occurs in the 25-30 mph range when the engine is pulling hard in top gear. This causes an unpleasant body boom, more prominent in the hatchback and the estate than in the saloon model, which encourages one to change down to third gear when the lusty torque of the engine would otherwise make top gear a perfectly usable ratio.

The four-speed gearbox itself, however, has always been notable for a precise gearchange and the clutch provides a sweet, smooth take-up. If it judders, there must be something amiss with the clutch itself, or possibly with the propeller shaft or the rear axle.

The latter, as mentioned earlier, is an Opel design and is unusual nowadays in incorporating a long torque tube which encloses the rear part of the split propeller shaft, the forward end of the tube being located in a rubber-mounted bearing in a housing which is bolted to the underside of the floorpan. This design allows the rear axle to have a large range of vertical movement without the risk of the propeller shaft striking the bodywork.

The forward propeller shaft, however, is of the type so common today which has non-replaceable universal joints. When a joint becomes worn, or if it fails prematurely, there is no option but to replace the complete front propeller-shaft assembly.

The suspension and steering

The coil-spring suspension is an Opel design which has already earned an excellent reputation in the Kadett. It is, perhaps, set-up with the emphasis rather too much on handling as opposed to comfort, and can give a rather joggly ride at low speeds on rough roads, but when rough surfaces are taken at speed the combination or variable-ratio springs, a Panhard-rod location for the rear axle, anti-roll bars at front and rear and sensitive rack-and-pinion steering, provide a much smoother ride and first-class controllability. The Chevette is, in fact, essentially a driver's car, nimble, responsive and sure-footed.

The brakes

Disc brakes are used at the front and self-adjusting drum brakes at the rear. A vacuum-operated servo ensures that only modest pedal pressures are needed, and a pressure-regulating valve in the rear pipeline reduces the risk of the rear wheels locking prematurely under panic braking conditions.

The system also complies with modern safety requirements in having a tandem master cylinder which operates separate front and rear hydraulic circuits, so that if pressure should be lost in one circuit, reasonable braking power will still be available.

At the same time a warning lamp on the instrument panel will be illuminated. This lamp also lights-up when the handbrake is applied with the ignition switched on, providing both a test to make sure that the warning lamp circuit and bulb are operating correctly, and a reminder to the driver not to drive off with the handbrake applied.

The bodywork

In the design of the Chevette the manufacturers have taken particular care to eliminate, as far as possible, any potential water and mud traps, which are usually the focus points for the start of rust and corrosion. In addition, particularly vulnerable panels are zinc-coated and zinc-rich primer is used on other exposed sections. This, combined with bituminous undercoating and the injection of water-repellent wax into the hollow sections of the body-shell, should help to keep the dreaded rust-bug at bay.

Model line-up

Now for a list of the most important dates in the development of the various models. Remember, however, that sometimes changes are made gradually during the production-run of a car, as parts become available on the assembly line. Also, the completed cars often spend some time in the factory compound awaiting collection, followed by a further waiting period in dealers' showrooms before they are sold. So the date of registration is not always a guarantee that a modification has been incorporated.

There is, of course, the other, brighter side of the coin: keen owners often modify used cars, bringing them into line with later specifications – a useful bonus for a subsequent buyer, but it does emphasize that one must treat the 'official' modification dates with some reserve!

1975. Chevette announced in March at Geneva Motor Show, but not available until May. Hatchback-style two-door body, with opening rear window. Front-mounted 1256 cc Viva engine, clutch and gearbox, driving the rear axle through a propeller shaft and a torque-tube assembly. Coil-spring suspension all round, independent at the front and with the live rear axle located by trailing arms and a Panhard rod. Dual-circuit servo-assisted front disc brakes, self-adjusting drum rear brakes. Divided hydraulic circuit with pressure-regulating valve. Rack-and-pinion steering. Radial-ply tyres, alternator and a high standard of equipment for price range even on basic model. L model had better trim, opening rear quarter windows and other improvements.

1975, November. Hatchback GL model announced, with still further improved trim and equipment, including sports road wheels with 175SRx13 radial-ply tyres, underriders at front and rear, carpeted lower door trims, map pockets, central console and tray, under-bonnet lamp and other items not fitted to the basic and L models.

1976, January. Limited production run of hatchback Chevette E. Still well-equipped but minus a heated rear window. No carpeting on the rear seat-back and load area. Fitted with 5.60x13 cross-ply tyres.

1976, April 26 onwards. Specification of Chevette hatchback models from chassis No. 128321 revised. Changes mainly affected interior trim. Models now designated Chevette L, GL and GLS – roughly equivalent to previous Chevette basic, L and GL cars but with detail differences in trim and equipment between the various models.

1976, June. Chevette saloon models introduced, in addition to hatchback range. Two-door and four-door saloons available in E (Economy), L and GL versions. Top-of-the-range GLS model available only as a four-door saloon. Mechanical specifications as for hatch-back models.

1976, September. Chevette estate car announced. Mechanically similar to hatchback and two-door saloon models, but with large top-hinged rear door.

3 Vetting a used car
How to detect or forestall trouble

There must always be some element of risk when buying any used car — but you can shorten the odds against you by carrying out a really thorough check, as suggested in this chapter, before concluding the deal.

If you already own a Chevette, a similar check will enable you to decide what work will be needed to put it into tip-top condition.

Fill in an inspection record, on the lines shown on page 18, as you go along. This will help later when summing-up the condition of the car and planning the work to be done.

If you are in the market for the cheapest Chevette in the used car range, remember that a standard Chevette or Chevette E may have been sold originally to a fleet owner and is therefore like to have had a somewhat harder life, and to have covered a much higher mileage, than most privately-owned examples. It is best to look for an L, GL or GLS model, if your budget is sufficiently elastic.

Begin with the bodywork

Take a tip from the motor trade and pay particular attention to the condition of the bodywork. Repairs to rusty or damaged panels, if they are beyond simple home remedies, can be very expensive.

Early Vauxhall Victors and Vivas acquired an unfortunate reputation for rusting but Vauxhall Motors quickly got the message and later models were much less prone to this trouble. When the Chevette was being developed, therefore, particular care was taken to eliminate mud and water traps and a very thorough rust-proofing process was adopted. As a result a Chevette should not pose any real corrosion problems unless it has been badly neglected.

It is best to have the vehicle raised for inspection on a lift, however, or at least on wheel ramps or on axle stands, so that the underbody can be carefully inspected.

Apart from checking for rust, pay special attention to the safety points mentioned on page 12.

Engine condition and performance

We can now turn our attention to the mechanical components, beginning with the power unit. The Viva engine used in the Chevette has earned an excellent reputation for reliability and freedom from minor troubles.

Unless the car has covered a very large mileage, therefore, inspection can be confined to looking for such obvious faults as oil and water leaks, smoke from the exhaust and suspicious noises when the engine is revved-up — check with the engine both hot and cold — followed by a test run during which any misfiring, knocking and lack of power should be evident.

If the engine is quiet and reasonably smooth, but seems to be down on power, a 6000-mile service may be all that is need to restore the normal liveliness.

A rattling noise from the front of the engine is probably caused by a loose timing chain. An automatic tensioner is fitted, but if this has reached the limit of its adjustment, renewal of the chain is a fairly big job, as it is necessary to remove the engine. The same applies if new pistons, piston-rings, connecting-rod or crankshaft bearings are required, as the sump is not usually removed with the engine in the car. For details see Chapter 9.

Above all, don't be tempted — or persuaded — to ignore a noisy timing chain. If it jumps the teeth on the sprockets, serious engine damage can occur.

Jot down your observations on your check sheet and at the end of the test compare your notes with the symptoms listed in Trouble-shooting Charts 1-5.

At the end of this chapter we give some typical performance figures for the various models, of which the acceleration times are probably the most useful in providing an indication of overall efficiency.

The maximum speeds in second and third gears should not be held indefinitely owing to the risk of damaging the engine. In normal driving, of course, one would change up at lower speeds.

If the car cannot reach the figures quoted, the engine is below par. Faults such as weak valve springs, sticking or burnt valves, retarded ignition timing or inefficient sparking plugs or contact-breaker points, must be suspected.

It is difficult to estimate an acceptable fuel consumption figure accurately, the critical factors being the road and traffic conditions, the load carried, the tyre pressures, and above all, the manner in which the car is driven. All the performance figures, in fact, can only be regarded as fairly representative averages, and allowance must be made for possible speedometer errors.

The transmission

The clutch and synchromesh gearbox have proved to be relatively trouble-free — again, we have previous experience of these units in the Viva to go on. The action of the clutch should be smooth. If it slips or does not free completely, resulting in difficult gear-changing, first check that the adjustment of the operating cable is correct — a point which is sometimes overlooked in these days when so many clutches are self-adjusting.

The only trouble which seems to occur to any extent in the Viva is breakage of the clutch cable, so this is a possible fault in the Chevette. Renewal is not difficult but is a somewhat time-consuming job.

If the gearbox is rather noisier than the average, this is not necessarily a sign of impending trouble. The opinion in the trade is that the life of the gearbox may be somewhat less than that of the engine. If a car has covered more than about 40 000 miles, a particularly careful check should be made on the condition of the gearbox. It is sometimes difficult to cure a 'zizz' from the gear lever, but this is annoying rather than serious.

Check the drive-line for 'clonks' when the drive is taken up and when opening and closing the throttle. These are most likely to be caused by worn propeller shaft universal joints, but excessive play in the rear-axle gears cannot be ruled out. The comments in Chapter 2 concerning drive-line vibration and the need to replace the complete front prop shaft if the universal joints are worn, should be borne in mind when testing the car. The propeller shaft is quite a costly item.

The Opel rear axle used in the Chevette does not usually give trouble, but check the inner sides of the brake backplates for signs of oil leakage from the drain hole at the base of each plate. Leakage here means worn axle seals, and possibly rear-wheel hub bearings also. As renewal of these parts is beyond the scope of the owner (see Chapter 14) a cure is likely to be fairly expensive.

Also check the rear of the gearbox extension and the nose of the torque tube casing for any signs of oil leakage. Renewal of the oil seal in the gearbox or fitting a new seal to the rear axle pinion shaft must be done in the approved manner — and should normally be carried out by a Vauxhall dealer.

Suspension and steering

As indicated in Chapter 2, the steering and roadholding of the Chevette are excellent — as might be expected, since the components are based on the Opel Kadett designs and Opels have earned a very high reputation as drivers' cars. The ride at low speeds on rough roads does leave something to be desired, however, and this should be taken into account during a road test.

Check the front suspension for any signs of oil or grease leakage from the ball joints and make sure that the rubber boots on the joints are in good condition. Worn joints will cause steering wobble.

Also check the rubber bushes at the other pivot points in the suspension. Worn or perished bushes will contribute to steering problems and can also cause brake judder.

The main characteristic of the steering is moderate understeer — a tendency to run outwards on a curve — but this should not be excessive and gives good straight-line stability.

The shock absorbers will be tired when the car has covered more than 30 000 miles and will be due for pensioning-off. Fitting new rear units is well within the scope of a practical owner and renewing the front dampers is not too difficult.

The brakes

The servo-assisted brakes should be smooth and progressive, giving excellent stopping power for moderate pedal pressures. If the rear wheels lock-up prematurely when the brakes are applied hard on a smooth road surface, the pressure-regulating valve in the rear-brake pipeline may not be operating properly. It is not an expensive job to put this right.

If the brakes seem to lack power under ordinary driving conditions or the steering pulls to one side, however, Chart 9 will help to pin-point the most likely causes. The automatic adjusters fitted to the rear brakes can sometimes slip and allow too much clearance between the shoes and the drums. Check these points, as described in Chapter 15, before assuming that more serious faults necessarily exist in the system.

The handbrake is — or should be — much more powerful than the average. It is capable of holding the car safely on a 1 in 3 or a 1 in 4 hill.

Typical average performance figures

Maximum speed in gears — mph

	1st	2nd	3rd	Top
Hatchback	30	49	77	92
Saloon	30	49	75	90
Estate	30	48	74	85

Acceleration (seconds) in top gear

	30-50 mph	40-60 mph	50-70 mph
Hatchback	12	13	15
Saloon	13	14	17
Estate	14	15	18

Fuel consumption

Hatchback	30-40 mpg
Saloon	30-35 mpg
Estate	29-34 mpg

4 Planned servicing
Preventive maintenance

Although we are living in the days of the horseless carriage, there is still some truth in the old adage that it is useless to lock the stable door after the horse has bolted! That is why, in this and other chapters, we emphasize the importance of *preventive* maintenance—the avoidance of trouble before it becomes serious, or can result in a roadside breakdown.

Your car instruction book specifies servicing at intervals which are determined either by the mileage that has been covered, or by the time that has elapsed, since the last service was carried out: after 3000 miles or 3 months, 6000 miles or 6 months, 12 000 miles or 12 months, and so on.

We are not too happy, however, about the modern tendency to specify servicing by time intervals, rather than by mileage. If the car is used mostly for shopping and for an occasional week-end run into the country, for example, the mileage will not accumulate very quickly. While the car is standing idle the contact-breaker gap or the tappet clearances will not be increasing, the brake shoes or pads will not be wearing away and other parts will not require the checks and adjustments called for in the maintenance schedule.

There is, however, another side to the picture which justifies—for some items—servicing on a time basis. For example, the engine oil will deteriorate much more quickly when short runs and frequent starts from cold cause excessive condensation of water and acids in the cylinders and sump. The tyres will almost certainly lose pressure, whether the car is running or standing unused and the battery will be subject to slow self-discharge. The brake fluid slowly absorbs moisture from the air and will need to be changed after 18–24 months. And, of course, the rust bugs will be happily munching away beneath your gleaming paintwork and—if you haven't taken the precaution of having extra rustproofing carried out by a specialist – making lacework of the vulnerable undercar components.

The maintenance schedule must therefore be approached in a certain spirit of compromise, depending on the sort of use that the car receives.

Vital checks

A major drawback of do-it-yourself servicing in the home garage is the tendency of most owners to ignore the underside of the car: a case of out of sight, out of mind, perhaps?

Don't be tempted to crawl under the car when it is supported only by a jack or by a pile of bricks, however. A pair of drive-on wheel ramps will usually give enough clearance, or the car can be taken to your neighbourhood dealer at least twice a year to be put on a lift or over a pit so that the whole of the underside can be thoroughly inspected at leisure. It is well worthwhile to pay for this service, if necessary, or to hire a self-service bay if a garage is operating this scheme in your district.

If the underside is coated with mud and filth, it will obviously pay to hose it down thoroughly, or better still, to have it steam-cleaned, before starting work. Garages which service commercial vehicles usually have steam-cleaning equipment, but the cost of the work, although well worthwhile, is not cheap.

Now for the vital check points:

First go over the whole of the underside of the car for any signs of flaking paint, peeling underbody coating, if this has been applied, and the beginning of rust. Pay particular attention to the sub-frames and the areas around the suspension mountings.

Check the brake pipes inch by inch for any signs of chafing, rust or pitting. A small corrosion pit can eat through a new pipe within two years, causing a pin-hole leak which may result in complete loss of brake fluid.

Check the flexible brake hoses for perishing, chafing and leakage from the unions.

There will probably have been some oil leakage from the engine and transmission units, but a heavy leak obviously calls for investigation.

Examine the inner walls of the tyres for cuts or splits. It is surprising how often accidental damage occurs on the inside wall of a tyre, rather than on the outside, where it would be immediately visible. While checking the tyres, look for any signs of rubbing against the body when the springs are fully compressed or when the front wheels are turned to full lock.

Check the exhaust system for rust, damage and leakage, and make sure that the supports are sound.

Finally, push, pull and shake all suspension and steering components vigorously, to show up any wear or loose attachments.

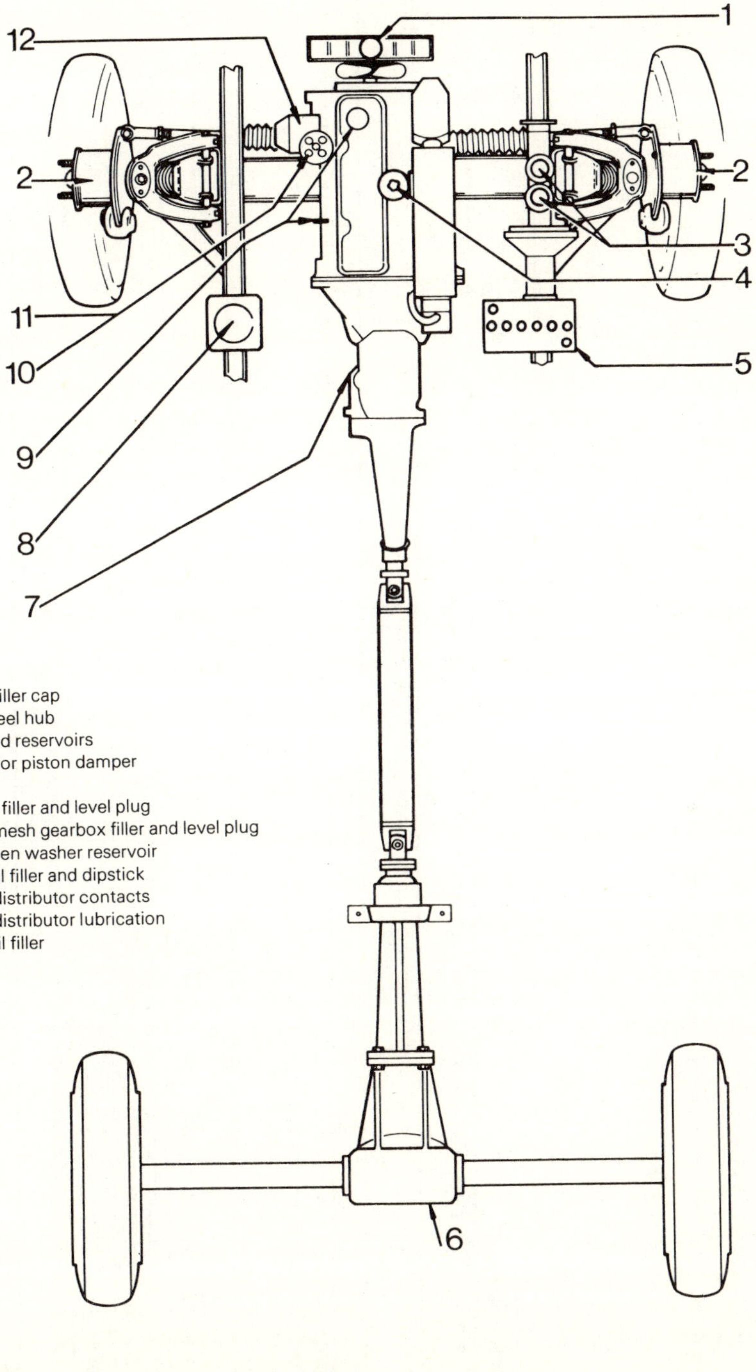

1 radiator filler cap
2 front-wheel hub
3 brake fluid reservoirs
4 carburettor piston damper
5 battery
6 rear-axle filler and level plug
7 synchromesh gearbox filler and level plug
8 windscreen washer reservoir
9 engine oil filler and dipstick
10 ignition distributor contacts
11 ignition distributor lubrication
12 engine oil filler

Fig. 4.1 Top-up, fill-up and lubrication points which require attention during routine maintenance

Maintenance summary

This chart has been arranged to show at a glance the frequency with which the various jobs must be done. The items which make up a complete service can thus be identified and the work spread over several week-ends, if necessary. Remember that the columns are cumulative: the 3000 mile jobs must be repeated at 6000 and 9000 miles, the 6000 mile service at 12 000 miles (plus the jobs in the 12 000 mile column), and so on

	Weekly or before a long journey	Every 3000 miles (5000 km) or 3 months	Every 6000 miles (10 000 km) or 6 months	Every 12 000 miles (20 000 km) or 12 months	Every 24 000 miles (40 000 km) or 2 years
Vital safety checks					
Wheels and Tyres Check tyre pressures when cold. Watch for signs of uneven wear. Check tightness of wheel nuts	●				
Brake Fluid Reservoir Check level of fluid (this is a precautionary check only – topping-up should be required only at long intervals, unless a leak has developed in system)	●				
Brakes Check pedal travel; adjust brakes if necessary. Inspect brake pipes and hoses for leakage		●			
Brakes – Preventive Check Check thickness of linings. Check operating cylinders for leakage. Blow out dust. Check thickness of disc-brake friction pads. Check handbrake adjustment. Check pipes and flexible hoses for chafing. Renew all flexible hoses and rubber seals in braking system after 40 000 miles (65 000 km) or 3 years in service			●		
Wheels Remove road wheels, wash and examine for possible damage			●		
Exhaust System Check for corrosion, leakage and security of attachments			●		
Lighting System Check headlamp beam alignment, lamp glasses for cracks, side, tail and indicator lamps for blackened bulbs, rusty contacts and water in lampholders		●			
Lubrication					
Engine Check oil-level and top-up if necessary (check daily if engine is worn and also when refilling with fuel on long run)	●				
Engine Drain oil and re-fill sump. Renew oil-filter element			●		
Gearbox Check oil level			●		
Rear Axle Check oil level			●		
Ignition Distributor Lubricate			●		
Front-Wheel Bearings Dismantle hubs, inspect bearings, lubricate and adjust					●
Oil-can Lubrication Apply a few drops of oil to throttle linkage, handbrake linkage, door, boot and bonnet locks and hinges			●		

Servicing and adjustments

Radiator Check water-level and top-up if necessary	●				
Cooling System Check condition of hoses, and for leaks. Check tension of fan/generator driving belt				●	
Cooling System De-scale, flush and refill. Check operation of thermostat. Have strength of anti-freeze solution checked with a hydrometer (this should be a regular autumn service)		●			
Battery Check level of liquid in cells		●			
Windscreen Washer Reservoir Check level of fluid. Add special anti-freeze solvent in winter		●			
Engine Check valve tappet clearances. Adjust if necessary			●		
Engine Clean breather hose			●		
Carburettor Top-up piston damper with oil, check damper piston for freedom. Check slow-running adjustments		●			
Carburettor Air-cleaner Renew pleated-paper element.			●		
Carburettor Warm-air Intake Check action of sensor and vacuum motor			●		
Carburettor Clean float chamber. Check piston and diaphragm			●		
Fuel Pump Check pump and clean filter if necessary				●	
Sparking Plugs Clean; check gaps and re-set if necessary			●		
Ignition System Fit new sparking plugs and new contact-breaker points. Preferably do this at 10 000 miles (16 000 km)				●	
Ignition Distributor Clean or renew contact points and adjust gap. Clean distributor rotor and cap. Check timing. Preferably have system checked with electronic test-tune equipment.			●		
Clutch Check free movement of pedal and if necessary adjust			●		
Steering and Front Suspension Check bellows on rack-and-pinion unit for splits or leakage. Check steering and suspension joints for damaged grease-retaining gaiters and wear.			●		
Steering and Front Suspension Have front-wheel alignment and steering geometry checked with special equipment			●		
Steering Column Check condition of flexible coupling and tightness of bolts			●		
Front Wheel Bearings Check for leakage of grease, excessive end-play and noise when wheel is rotated				●	
Wheels Change from side to side at front and rear. Grease wheel studs. Have wheel balance checked			●		
Braking System Drain fluid from system, flush, refill and bleed-off air. This should be done every 2 years if mileage is less than 24 000 miles (40 000 km) in this period. See also 'Vital safety checks'					
Brake Servo Fit new servo air filter every 36 000 miles					
Electrical System Clean and tighten battery terminals. Check operation of charging system, starter motor, lights and instruments			●		
Starter Motor Check condition of brushes, commutator and pinion drive assembly					●
Road Test Give car a thorough road test and carry out any adjustments required. If possible, have final check made with electronic test-tune equipment and check compression in cylinders. After test, check for oil, fuel, fluid or grease leaks at all plugs, flanges, joints and unions			●		

Your basic tool kit

The items listed below will be needed for routine servicing. More specialized tools can be added, as necessary, when repairs and overhauls are undertaken and a list of these is given at the beginning of each workshop manual section.

Special tools tend to be rather expensive, but you may be able to hire them from your local Vauxhall dealer. The most frequently needed items, such as extractors, however, can normally be purchased from car accessory shops and these are usually cheaper than the 'official' service tools. Alternatively, there may be a shop in your neighbourhood which hires-out tools at reasonable charges.

A basic tool kit for routine servicing and minor repairs should include –

- Set of open-ended or ring, or combination spanners, plus socket spanners with extensions and preferably a universal joint and a ratchet handle. AF and metric sizes will be required, plus $\frac{15}{16}$ in. and 1 in. AF sockets (or box spanners) and a set of AF hexagonal Allen keys, including $\frac{5}{16}$ in. and $\frac{9}{16}$ in. sizes
- Selection of screwdrivers, including two sizes for cross-head screws
- Large and small adjustable spanners
- Self-locking adjustable spanner (Mole wrench type)
- Side-cutting and pointed-nose 6 in. pliers
- Set of feeler gauges
- Sparking plug gap-setting tool
- Tyre pressure gauge
- Tyre tread-depth gauge
- Engineer's hammer (ball pane)
- Soft-faced hammer (with hide, plastic or copper faces)
- Fine carborundum stone
- Wire brush
- Centre-punch, scriber and marking paint
- Inspection lamp

A good tyre-pressure gauge is essential. Garage-pressure gauges are not always as accurate as they should be; and pressures should always be checked with the tyres *cold,* which is obviously impossible if the car has to be driven to a garage or if pressures are checked during the course of a journey.

A tread-depth gauge is an inexpensive item which will enable you to keep a check on the rate of wear of the tyres and will also indicate when they are due for replacement. The official regulation in Britain calls for 1 mm of tread over three-quarters of the width of the tread pattern, around the complete circumference of the tyre, but it is much safer to change the tyres when the treads are worn down to a depth of 2 mm.

An electrical drill is, perhaps, something of a luxury, but the way in which it can speed-up a surprisingly large number of jobs, particularly if it is provided with the usual range of accessories, such as wire brushes for decarbonizing the cylinder head, a grindstone and a lambswool polishing mop, renders it a really worthwhile investment for an owner who carries out any appreciable amount of work.

Turning the engine when making adjustments

The most usual way of turning the engine when a manual gearbox is fitted is to remove the sparking plugs (in order to relieve the compression in the cylinders and allow the engine to turn easily), engage top gear and then push the car backwards and forwards.

Alternatively, it is usually possible to turn the engine by pulling on the fan belt. The fan blades, incidentally, rotate freely because they are driven by a viscous clutch, but even if this were not the case it is bad practice to turn any engine by means of the fan blades. Probably the best plan, however, is to use a spanner on the crankshaft pulley retaining nut.

Some garage mechanics operate the starter motor for a few seconds at a time, but this method is only justifiable as a time-saver, to obtain approximately the correct position of the flywheel. Final adjustments must be made by one of the methods just described, since accuracy is essential when setting the ignition timing, or adjusting the valve clearances.

Workbench and vice

A workbench will be needed for any jobs that are done on components that have been removed from the car, but it is quite possible to make do with a stout kitchen table, which can often be picked up cheaply at an auction. If any but elementary servicing is carried out, a vice will be needed. This can often be obtained quite cheaply from a surplus equipment shop.

Working beneath the car

If an inspection pit is not available, a pair of drive-on wheel ramps will also be needed, or a pair of adjustable axle stands. These have the advantage of leaving the wheels free to rotate and are more useful than ramps when carrying out overhauls. On the other hand, when servicing it takes only a minute or two to drive the front or rear wheels on to a pair of ramps, whereas both sides of the car must be jacked up to allow stands to be placed below the jacking points.

Finally we must repeat – never be tempted to work beneath the car when it is supported only by the jack or by an insecure pile of bricks.

Part two

5 Trouble-shooting
Systematic diagnosis

The risk of an unexpected breakdown must obviously be greatly reduced by regular servicing. The work described in Chapter 4 can therefore be described as *preventive* maintenance in the best sense of the word; it aims at detecting or forestalling trouble before it becomes serious. Most faults, in fact, can be traced back to neglect at some stage. Dirt, lack of lubrication or incorrect adjustment are the most frequent culprits.

When devising the special trouble-shooting charts in this section, we had in mind mainly the practical owner, who often has to trace a fault without the benefit of a voltmeter, an ammeter, a vacuum gauge, a cylinder compression-pressure gauge or a simple stethoscope. These useful aids to diagnosis are usually conspicuous by their absence when the car breaks down miles from the home base!

The aim has been to produce a set of charts which will encourage a logical process of elimination. Inspired guesswork (intelligent intuition?) will sometimes get results, but systematic investigation will usually be less time-consuming in tracking-down obscure faults—although there are, of course, occasions on which the possibility of a particular fault can be assumed with a fair amount of certainty.

Take the case of a normally well-behaved engine that refuses to fire from cold after the car has been parked in the open during a spell of damp, misty weather, for example. Condensation on the high-tension leads, ignition coil, distributor, and sparking-plug insulators is almost a certainty, and a spray with one of the water-repelling aerosol fluids, or a wipe with a dry cloth, will usually be all that is needed to restore normal starting.

Similarly, if an engine runs well, but is a brute to start from cold, suspect too weak a starting mixture. Make sure that the mixture control is operating properly and that the petrol pump is delivering plenty of fuel. If the engine is reluctant to start when hot, on the other hand, check for an over-rich mixture. In either case, if the carburation seems to be satisfactory, the ignition system should be checked-over, following the step-by-step charts in this chapter.

Now a word as to how to use the trouble-tracing charts.

By reading vertically down the column, under the various symptoms, the most likely causes of the trouble can be picked out and eliminated one by one. Alternatively, by reading horizontally across the chart, a combination of different symptoms will often point pretty conclusively to one particular fault which is causing the trouble.

In some cases, these charts cover alternative types of equipment. To find out which items apply to your model, consult the Specifications and Overhaul Data at the end of this book.

Preventing trouble and restoring performance

There is a great deal to be said for carrying out a systematic inspection of the car at regular intervals—say, every 5000-6000 miles—in order to detect any incipient trouble and to correct any faults which may exist.

A ten-point check and tune-up to restore engine efficiency is outlined on page 19. A suggested routine for a more thorough check of the whole car is given in the fault-tracing and condition report sheet. If these checks are conscientiously carried out and any necessary adjustments are made, they will restore 'new car' performance on a vehicle that is in reasonably good mechanical condition. Any major faults which are present, such as loss of engine compression, and transmission or similar troubles, will, of course, require attention as soon as possible.

An inspection record of this type has, in itself, a number of advantages. Not only does it ensure that no item is overlooked, but it also enables the general condition of the car to be assessed at a glance. If completed systematically at each inspection period and filed for reference purposes, it will serve as a guide to the reconditioning required and as a check on the performance of each item.

When made out for the first time, as with a newly-purchased used car, the chart is almost certain to reveal defects that might otherwise have been unsuspected and that might have developed into major troubles.

Inspection record

Vehicle make and year ______
Capacity or horse power ______
Reg. number ______
Speedometer reading ______
Date of inspection ______

Engine and accessories
Compression
Tappets: clearance; noise
Valve gear: noise; cover gaskets
Timing gears or chain: noise; backlash
Cylinder head: nuts; gaskets
Manifolds: securing nuts; gaskets; air or gas leaks
Driving belts: fan; dynamo; accessories
Water pump: leakage; effectiveness
Radiator: water level; leakage; filler cap; condition of core; shutters; relief valve; overflow pipe
Oil leaks: crankcase; pipes and unions; timing covers; main bearings; drain plugs
Oil filters
Engine mountings

Carburettor and fuel pump
Jets
Float chamber level
Cold starting device: interconnecting linkage thermostat; dashboard control
Fuel pump: effectiveness; delivery pressure
Filters: carburettor; petrol pump; air cleaner

Ignition system
Contact breaker points: gap; condition
Rotor: condition
Distributor cap: cleanliness; cracks; tracking
Timing control: manual; centrifugal; suction operated
Coil and wiring: efficiency; condition of high and low tension wiring; support
Sparking plugs: gap at points; condition of points and insulators; washers

Electrical system
Dynamo or alternator: charging rate
Dynamo brushes and commutator: burning or pitting; chatter and sparking
Dynamo or alternator drive: condition of belt, tension
Voltage regulator
Ammeter: accuracy
Battery: acid level; specific gravity; voltage of each cell; connections; corrosion

Lights
Headlamps: focus and alignment; condition of reflectors
Side lamps
Tail lamps
Stop lamp
Other lamps: ignition warning; interior; trafficators
Switches and fuses

Electrical accessories
Windscreen wipers: efficiency; noise; condition of blades
Indicators
Starter: efficiency; condition of pinion and fly-wheel teeth
Horns
Interior heater
Defroster
Radio

Steering
Lost motion
Stiffness
Front axle alignment: toe-in; castor and camber angles
Swivels and bushes
Front hub bearings
Steering linkage and joints

Suspension
Springs: condition
Shock absorbers: effectiveness; fluid leaks; security of attachments
Torque reaction rods or cables: adjustment; security of attachment

Brakes
Pedal travel
Condition of rods or cables
Hydraulic system: fluid level; leakage from pipe lines, choked pipes, air in system
Handbrake: adjustment; condition of ratchet
Servo mechanism: vacuum servo; pipe lines

Bodywork
General appearance
Windows: winding controls; glass; channels
Doors: alignment; buffers; locks; check straps
Sunshine roof: operation; water leaks
Seats: condition of springs; adjustments
Bumpers: condition; attachments
Tool kit
Fire extinguisher, safety belts

Transmission
Clutch: adjustment
Backlash: in universal joints; in back axle; in gearbox
Rear axle: leakage

Wheels
Rims: buckling; rust
Wheel nuts: tightness; condition of studs; splines on knock-off wheels

Tyres
Pressures
Tread wear
Condition of sidewalls
Valves and caps

Road test

Engine
Ease of starting
Oil pressure when hot
Idling
Acceleration
Maximum speed
Fuel consumption
Oil consumption
Engine temperature
Exhaust: noise, restriction; smoke
General noise, fumes

Clutch
Slip
Fierceness
Spinning
Unusual noises

Propeller shaft
Vibration
Noise

Gearbox
Noisy gears
Synchromesh operation
Preselector operation
Vibration on gear lever
Gears jumping out of mesh

Instruments
Functioning
Accuracy

Suspension
Comfort
Roll on corners

Brakes
Power
Balance
Smoothness
Judder or squeal
Binding

Back axle
Noise on drive
Noise on overrun
Noise on corners

Steering
Positiveness
Castor action
Wander
Road shocks at steering wheel

Ten-point engine check and tune-up

The ten-point check on engine efficiency described in this section carries the principle of preventive maintenance, already outlined in Part 1, a stage further.

The object of an engine tune-up at an intermediate stage is to check deterioration: to restore the keen edge of engine efficiency, with a bonus in the form of improved performance and better fuel consumption. A good time to carry it out would be between the 5000-6000 miles services.

1 Electrical check

The effectiveness of the ignition system depends on sound electrical connections throughout the low-tension and high-tension wiring. Check them systematically, starting at the battery terminals and the earthing strap, and working via the ignition switch to the low-tension terminals on the ignition coil, and from there to the terminal on the side of the ignition distributor.

Check the security of the high-tension leads in the distributor cap and coil by lightly tugging them. Bear in mind that modern carbon-trace ignition cables usually have a life of about two years. After that, misfiring is increasingly likely. A new set of leads will often rejuvenate an engine.

2 Check carburettor and manifold flange nuts

The nuts must not be loose but must never be overtightened—particularly the carburettor flange nuts—owing to the risk of distorting or cracking the flanges, a fault which is a common cause of air leakage into the induction system, resulting in a weak mixture, misfiring and difficult starting.

3 Clean the carburettor filter (when fitted) and the float chamber

Traces of sediment or water in the float chamber can upset the carburation and cause misfiring.

4 Fuel pump check

If the fuel pump does not deliver its maximum output when the engine is operating under full-throttle, continuous high-speed conditions, fuel starvation may cause severe exhaust-valve burning and possibly piston failure. If in doubt, have the pump checked by a garage, using a special flow-test rig.

5 Check the ignition distributor and contact-breaker

Peak efficiency cannot be expected if the contact-breaker points are dirty, badly pitted or incorrectly gapped. Distributor checks are covered in the section dealing with the ignition system.

6 Check the ignition timing

Again refer to the section dealing with the ignition system. The correct ignition timing is critical, affecting both performance and fuel consumption.

7 Remove and check the sparking plugs

The plugs are a good guide to running conditions, as shown by the colour illustrations in this chapter. Clean them if necessary and re-set the gaps. Carry out a compression check (below) before refitting them.

8 Compression test

The compression check gives a reliable indication of the efficiency of the valves, piston rings and cylinder bores. A compression gauge is not expensive. The simple type which combines a compression gauge with a tyre-pressure gauge will give reliable readings.

Bring the engine to normal running temperature. Remove all the sparking plugs and wedge or tie the throttle fully open. The compressions should be recorded at normal cranking speed which must remain constant throughout the test, so the battery must be well charged.

Make a note of the number of pulsations required to obtain a maximum gauge reading for the first cylinder tested. The same number of crankshaft revs should be used when testing the other cylinders.

When the first set of readings has been recorded, repeat the tests with approximately a tablespoonful of engine oil injected into each cylinder. Higher readings may now be obtained on some or all of the cylinders, indicating that the oil has sealed any leakage past the piston rings that was occurring during the first tests.

Any remaining differences between the maximum pressures recorded for the individual cylinder which exceed about 10lb per sq. in. are probably due to leakage past the valves (possibly due to wrong valve clearances). It is also possible that the cylinder head gasket is leaking, but this would normally cause overheating and, in some case, misfiring.

9 Check carburettor idling adjustments

Refit the plugs and adjust the carburettor idling speed and mixture strength. These adjustments are fully described in the chapter dealing with the carburettor and fuel system.

10 Road test

Carry out a thorough road test as described in the section which deals with vetting a used car. Record the figures and file them for reference when the next tune-up is carried out. 'Before and after' comparisons will then quickly show up any loss of efficiency and indicate the need for further action.

At-a-glance trouble-shooting chart 1

Engine faults - key chart

Symptoms

	Engine will not start	Starts but will not keep running	Stalls during normal running	Poor idling	Misfiring at all speeds	Not giving full power or revs	Fuel consumption excessive	Oil consumption excessive	Pinking or detonation	Over-heating, pre-ignition, running-on	Unusual noises
Carburation and Fuel System Chart 5	●	●	●	●	●	●	●		●	●	
Ignition System Chart 4	●	●	●	●	●	●	●		●	●	
Electrical System Chart 10	●										
Mechanical Faults Chart 2	●	●	●	●	●	●	●	●	●	●	●
Cooling System Chart 3						●	●	●	●	●	

First - Check your plugs

Normal
Nose lightly coated with grey brown deposits. Electrodes not burning unduly – gap increasing about .001 in. per 1000 miles. Plugs ideally suited to engine.

Carbon fouling
Deposits can short circuit the firing end. If recommended plug is fitted check for over-rich mixture, faulty choke mechanism or clogged air cleaner.

Oil fouling
Deposits can short circuit the firing end and this weakens or eliminates the spark. May be caused by worn valve guides, bores or piston rings or by running in an overhauled engine.

Overheating
Likely causes are overadvanced ignition timing, wrong grade of plug, use of too low octane fuel, weak mixture, or cooling system troubles.

At-a-glance trouble-shooting chart 2

Engine: mechanical faults and noise

Running conditions and probable causes	Noises: Tapping or clicking	Noises: Knock, tapping or light clatter	Noises: Clatter or knocking	Noises: Light clatter or chattering	Noises: High-pitched metallic tapping	Noises: Scraping noise	Noises: Knocking, rumbling or thumping	Noises: Lashing, rattling or grinding noise	Noises: Squeaks or whistles
Apparent source	Cylinder head or block	Cylinder head or top of block	Crankcase or front of engine	Cylinder head	Audible when acceler-ating	Cylinder block	Crankcase	Timing chain cover	Front of engine or near manifolds
Engine cold—worn pistons, rings, cylinder bores (piston slap)[1]		●							
Engine hot—worn little-end bearings[1]		●							
Engine hot, more evident when idling—worn camshaft bearings			●						
Valve-rocker clearances too great, worn valve-operating mechanism, bent push-rod	●			●					
Broken piston rings[2]	●					●			
Engine under load or when revved in neutral—big-end bearing wear[3]			●						
Engine under load and hot—'pinking' caused by pre-ignition or detonation[4]					●				
Crankcase, engine under load—main-bearing and/or crankshaft journal wear[3]							●		
Loose flywheel							●		
Occurring at high revs—valve-bounce (possibly weak valve springs)				●					
Loose or broken engine mounting							●		
Worn timing chain (when fitted). Defective chain tensioner								●	
Front of engine—loose crankshaft pulley or worn pulley key (can be mistaken for big-end bearing wear)			●						
Front of engine—worn, glazed or slipping fan belt. Worn or dry generator or fan bearings. Noisy water pump bearing or seal									●
Vicinity of inlet and exhaust manifolds—loose manifold bolts or nuts, or defective gaskets									●

1 Noise can be reduced or eliminated by shorting-out appropriate sparking plug

2 Badly-worn rings and grooves in pistons may also cause clicking

3 Usually accompanied by low oil pressure

4 Check that correct grade of fuel is in use. Also see Chart 1

At-a-glance trouble-shooting chart 3

Cooling system

This is a general chart covering water-cooled and air-cooled engines. All the items apply to water-cooled systems but only those marked with an asterisk affect air-cooled engines

Symptoms

* Overheating at normal atmospheric temperatures	* Overheating in very cold weather	* Engine slow to warm-up	* Engine does not reach normal running temperature	* Radiator needs frequent topping-up	**Probable causes**
●	●				* Fan belt – not correctly tensioned or broken
●				●	Radiator filler cap – not sealing properly, or wrong pressure rating
●	●	●	●		Thermostat – faulty or wrong rating
●	●				* Radiator or cooling fins – water or air passages clogged
●	●				Water passages in cylinder head or block – choked by deposits of lime, rust or sludge
	●				Radiator – frozen at base (no anti-freeze, or too low a concentration)
●	●				Water pump – inefficient or inoperative
●	●			●	Air-lock – in cooling system or heater
				●	Water hoses – leaking (check with engine revved-up)
●					Water hoses – perished, collapsed or obstructed by disintegrated linings
●	●			●	Internal water or gas leakage – caused by faulty cylinder-head gasket, cracked head or cylinder block
●	●			●	Local boiling in cylinder head – rust and lime deposits, filler cap pressure rating too low, or cap leaking
●					* Ignition faults – retarded timing, pre-ignition or detonation (see Chart 4)
●					* Carburation – faults causing weak mixture (see Chart 5)
●	●				* Brakes – binding (see Chart 9)
●					* Exhaust system – choked or damaged, restricting flow of gas
●	●				* Engine – assembled too tightly after overhaul

At-a-glance trouble-shooting chart 4

Ignition system faults

The faults in this chart are confined to the ignition system. Some of the symptoms may be caused by carburation, mechanical or cooling system faults. These are dealt with in Charts 2, 3, 5

Engine running symptoms

Engine will not start	Starts but will not keep running	Stalls during normal running	Poor idling	Mis-firing at all speeds	Mis-firing at high speed	Not giving full power or revs	Fuel con-sumption excessive	Pinking or detonation	Overheating, pre-ignition, running-on	Probable causes
●										Battery voltage too low – discharged or defective battery, resulting in heavy 'coil robbing' due to current drain by starter
●										Cold-start coil circuit (when fitted) defective
●	●	●	●	●	●	●	●			Low-tension circuit – faulty ignition switch, loose connections, faulty earthing strap (engine or battery to frame)
●	●	●	●	●	●	●	●	●	●	Sparking plugs – wrong gap, dirty or worn-out
			●	●	●	●	●	●	●	Sparking plugs – wrong type fitted
●	●	●	●	●	●	●	●	●	●	Contact-breaker points – dirty or pitted, wrong gap, incorrectly assembled, sticking open
			●	●	●	●	●			Contact-breaker – weak contact spring
●										Contact-breaker – broken spring
●	●	●	●	●	●	●	●			High-tension circuit – current leakage across coil, distributor cap or rotor: insulation cracked, dirty or damp
●	●	●	●	●	●	●	●			High-tension leads – poor contact at terminals, breaks in internal conductors, leads shorting to earth or to each other, faulty suppressors (when fitted)
●	●		●	●						Sparking plug leads – connected in wrong sequence
			●	●	●	●	●			High-tension polarity incorrect – ignition to coil low tension connections reversed
●	●	●	●	●	●	●	●			Distributor cap centre contact broken or sticking
●	●	●	●	●	●	●	●			Coil or condenser – open-circuit, short-circuit, intermittent faults
●			●	●	●	●	●	●	●	Static ignition timing – incorrect
			●	●	●	●	●	●		Centrifugal timing mechanism – not functioning correctly
							●	●		Vacuum timing mechanism – not functioning correctly
			●	●	●	●	●	●		Distributor – shaft bearing worn
				●	●	●	●	●	●	Distributor – wrong type fitted

At-a-glance trouble-shooting chart 5

Carburettor and fuel system

The faults in this chart are confined to the carburettor and fuel system. Some of the symptoms may be caused by other faults, which are dealt with in Charts 2, 3, 4.

Engine will not start	Starts but will not keep running	Stalls during normal running	Poor idling	Misfiring at all speeds	Not giving full power or revs	Fuel consumption excessive	Pinking or detonation	Overheating, pre-ignition, running-on	Probable causes
									Carburettor(s)
●		●							No petrol in float chamber – petrol tank empty, float needle valve sticking faulty fuel pump, filter clogged, petrol pipe obstructed, pipe union loose (see *Petrol Pump, Pipes and Tank*)
●	●								Mixture (choke) control not lowering jet fully (S.U. carburettor)
	●	●	●	●		●			Mixture (choke) control not returning to 'off' position
				●	●	●			Hydraulic damper needs topping-up (S.U. carburettor)
●	●	●	●	●	●	●	●	●	Carburettor suction piston sticking (S.U. carburettor). Choked jets (Zenith, Solex, Weber carburettors)
●	●	●	●	●	●	●			Carburettor flooding – float needle valve not seating, fuel pump pressure too high
●	●	●	●		●		●	●	Air leakage past carburettor or manifold flanges
●		●	●	●	●		●	●	Water or sediment in float chamber
	●	●	●	●	●	●			Idling speed and mixture adjustments incorrect
			●	●	●	●		●	Twin carburettors not properly synchronized
				●	●	●	●	●	Wrong jet needle, jet or piston spring fitted (S.U. and Stromberg carburettors). Wrong size of jet, faulty acceleration pump (Zenith, Solex, Weber carburettors)
	●	●		●	●				Carburettor icing-up internally (normal running restored when carburettor warms-up). See also *Air Cleaner*
									Petrol pump, pipes and tank
●		●		●	●		●	●	Electric pump – dirty filter, poor electrical connections, dirty contacts
●		●		●	●		●	●	Mechanical pump – dirty filter, air leak at filter cover flange
●	●	●	●	●		●			Electrical or mechanical pump – delivery pressure excessive
●	●	●	●	●	●				Fuel pipes – clogged, loose unions, vapour-lock in fuel pipe
●	●	●							Petrol tank – empty (fuel gauge may be giving wrong reading)
●	●	●	●	●	●				Petrol tank – air-vent obstructed, internal filter clogged
									Air cleaner
					●	●			Filter clogged, overdue for renewal
					●	●			Air intake not correctly positioned for summer or winter use or thermostatically-controlled flap not functioning properly (may cause carburettor icing in winter – see *Carburettor icing-up*)

At-a-glance trouble-shooting chart 6

Clutch and transmission

This chart deals only with manual transmissions. Automatic transmission torque converters and gearboxes are complex units and special test equipment, which is held by authorized dealers, must be used to diagnose faults in them

Clutch slip	Clutch judder or snatch	Rattle, knock or squeal from clutch	Difficulty in engaging gear	Jumping out of gear	Noisy gearbox	Rattle or buzz from gear lever	Rattle from transmission when idling	Knocking or clicking from front of car when cornering	**Probable causes**
			●						Air in clutch hydraulic operating system – needs bleeding (hydraulically-operated clutches)
●			●						Clutch adjustment incorrect
●									Clutch driven plate – worn, or oil on friction lining
		●							Clutch release bearing dry and due for renewal
	●								Clutch driven plate buckled during assembly
		●	●						Clutch release mechanism worn
	●	●							Clutch hub splines worn
				●	●		●		Gears and/or bearings worn
					●				Gear teeth chipped
			●	●		●			Selector linkage worn or damaged
						●			Gear lever pivot and linkage worn or needs lubrication
			●	●					Synchromesh mechanism worn
							●		Noise caused by transfer-gears on some front-wheel drive models – difficult to cure at idling speed, but careful carburettor adjustment helps
								●	Universal joints at outer ends of driving shafts worn and due for renewal (front-wheel drive cars only)

At-a-glance trouble-shooting chart 7
Suspension

This is a general trouble-shooting chart, applicable to most suspension systems using leaf springs, coil springs, torsion bars and also hydro-pneumatic systems (eg British Leyland Hydrolastics, Hydragas and other pressurized systems using gas and hydraulic fluid)

Symptoms

'Bouncy' ride – insufficient damping	Car too low at front and/or rear	Car sags to one side	Groaning or grunting from suspension	Squeak from front or rear suspension	Knock from front suspension	Knock from rear suspension	Rumble or whine from front or rear suspension	**Probable causes**
●	●	●						Weak or broken springs. Incorrect pressure in hydro-pneumatic system or loss of fluid
					●	●		Weak springs allowing suspension to hit bump stops
			●					Noisy damper valves in hydro-pneumatic system
						●		Broken check strap
●								Faulty shock absorbers or hydro-pneumatic unit
					●	●		Worn shock absorber bushes or loose mountings
				●				Squeak from rubber components – to cure, spray with silicone fluid or brush on brake fluid (*not* mineral oil)
						●		Worn bushes in radius arms or links
					●			Worn bushes in tie-bars, suspension arms or linkage
				●	●	●		Worn or incorrectly adjusted wheel bearings
							●	Worn, unlubricated or incorrectly adjusted wheel bearings

At-a-glance trouble-shooting chart 8

Steering and controlability

Excessive free movement at steering wheel	Car wanders, or 'oversteers' excessively	Car pulls to one side	Heavy steering	Wheel wobble or vibration at steering wheel	Rattle or knock from beneath front floor near passenger's feet	Knock from base of steering column	Probable causes
	●	●	●	●			Incorrect tyre pressures
	●						Rear tyre pressures too low
	●	●		●			Incorrect steering geometry and/or front-wheel alignment
				●			Tyres 'out of round,' or unbalanced tyres and wheels – have front and rear wheels balanced regularly
●	●	●		●			Worn or incorrectly adjusted steering and suspension joints and/or wheel hub bearings
●		●	●				Worn or incorrectly adjusted steering rack-and-pinion
			●				Distortion of column or rack-and-pinion unit caused by incorrect fitting
●	●			●	●		Loose bolts holding rack-and-pinion unit to bulkhead
●	●			●		●	Loose clamping bolt on steering column clamp or universal joint
					●		Worn bush in rack-and-pinion unit
			●		●		Lack of oil in rack-and-pinion unit – check condition of telescopic gaiters
	●	●	●				Accidental damage – have suspension and steering units checked by authorized dealer
		●		●			Braking system faults – brakes unevenly adjusted, faulty hydraulic system, oil or grease on linings, brake discs running out-of-true. See Chart 9
	●	●					Suspension faults causing insufficient damping, sagging to one side or incorrect suspension height at front or rear – see Chart 7

At-a-glance trouble-shooting chart 9

Braking system

This chart covers the most common faults in the full range of braking systems – all-drum, disc-and-drum and servo-assisted installations. When disc brakes or a servo are not fitted, the relevant items in the chart do not, of course, apply

Symptoms

Excessive pedal travel	Pedal feels spongy	Brakes lack power	Brakes bind or fail to release fully	Unbalanced braking – locking or pulling to one side	Brake judder	Brake squeal	Rapid wear of linings	**Probable causes**
●		●	●	●			●	Brakes incorrectly adjusted
	●	●						Fluid level in reservoir too low
	●	●	●	●			●	Rubber seals in hydraulic cylinders swollen
		●	●	●			●	Wheel cylinder or caliper piston seized
●	●	●		●				Leakage past seals in main or wheel cylinders, or from pipeline
	●							Internal fluid leak in servo (level in reservoir falls without visible external leak)
		●			●	●		Accumulation of brake dust in drums
		●		●			●	Badly-scored discs or drums
●					●	●		Worn wheel bearings
		●		●	●	●	●	Wrong type of friction linings fitted
●		●						Brakes 'fading' due to excessive use or wrong grade of linings
●		●						Brake fluid boiling in wheel cylinders – pump all fluid out of system, refill with correct fluid and bleed brakes
		●		●	●	●		Master-cylinder, wheel cylinder or caliper bolts loose
	●	●						Air in system – requires bleeding
	●	●						New linings or pads not bedded-in
●					●			Disc running out of true or drums distorted
		●		●	●	●		Water, oil or brake fluid on linings
		●	●					Servo defective
		●						Servo vacuum hose leaking or non-return valve faulty
			●				●	Pedal push-rod incorrectly adjusted
			●				●	Handbrake operating levers or cable guides seized with rust or mud – brakes remain on or partly applied
				●				Faulty rear-brake pressure-regulating valve
				●	●			Worn steering and suspension parts – see Charts 7 and 8

At-a-glance trouble-shooting chart 10

Electrical equipment

It has been possible to deal only with the broader aspects of electrical fault-tracing in this chart. Detailed diagnosis calls for the use of accurate instruments and a good deal of electrical know-how. It is best left to a qualified auto-electrician

Symptoms: Battery and Charging system				Starter motor		Lamps				
Battery cells need frequent topping-up with water	Battery apparently not receiving sufficient charge	Battery will not hold charge	Starter does not turn engine, or rotates it slowly	Starter runs but pinion does not engage with flywheel gear	Starter pinion jams in mesh of flywheel gear	Headlamps give poor illumination when correctly aligned	Brightness of lights varies noticeably with engine speed	Lights flicker	Bulbs or light units burn out frequently	**Probable causes**
			●	●		●	●			Battery discharged
	●	●								Battery electrolyte level too low or of wrong specific gravity
		●	●	●		●	●			Defective battery – sulphated or buckled plates
	●						●			Generator driving belt slipping
	●						●			Faulty generator
●	●						●		●	Charging regulator defective or incorrectly adjusted. Charging rate too high or too low
							●		●	Loose or high-resistance connections in charging circuit
						●		●		Loose or high-resistance connections in lighting circuits
	●		●	●			●	●	●	Corroded or loose battery terminals
			●	●		●		●		Poor earth-return connections
		●								Leakage of current in car wiring
			●							Faulty starter switch
			●	●						Poor connections in starter circuit
				●	●					Dirty or faulty starter pinion drive
					●					Worn starter pinion teeth on flywheel ring gear
			●							Faulty starter motor

6 Bodywork Defects

Dealing with dents, scratches and rust

One of the recurring themes in this book is 'Prevention is better than cure'. In Chapter 3 we emphasize the importance of making a careful check for rust. Here we are concerned with minimizing its effects. Neglect even a minor blemish, and you will find that rust can spread with alarming rapidity under the surrounding paintwork.

1 Dealing with scratches and chips

As shown in the first photograph, it is best to use a fine brush for touching-in small blemishes. If an aerosol paint spray is used it is difficult to confine the spray to a very small area. We give some notes on spraying larger areas at the end of this section.

Scrape any loose paint and rust from the area with the tip of a penknife blade, apply a rust-preventive, such as Zinc Plate, to the bright metal and then knife-on a thin layer of cellulose stopping, building up the level to slightly above the surrounding paintwork.

When the stopping is dry, rub it down with very fine wet-or-dry paper, used wet; with a smear of soap to prevent clogging. Then touch-in the area with the correct colour to match the surrounding finish.

Alternatively, your accessory shop may sell a card of special paint transfers which, when applied on a clean surface and rubbed down, produce an almost indetectable repair to a scratch or chip.

2 Removing dents

The second picture shows the sort of dent that can be dealt with at home by filling it with glass-fibre resin paste.

Rub down to bare metal, extending to about 2 in. beyond the edge of the dent, using 80 grit paper. Score the base and sides of the dent with a file or screwdriver to provide a key for the body filler, and apply this with a plastic spatula as illustrated until the level is above the surrounding metal.

If the dent is localized, it is usually a mistake to attempt to tap it out. The metal has probably been stretched, and too enthusiastic attempts at amateur panel-beating will turn the dent into a bulge—which must then be tapped back again so that the hollow can be built-up with body filler!

In the case of a large, shallow dent, however, the metal may simply have bulged inwards and can be

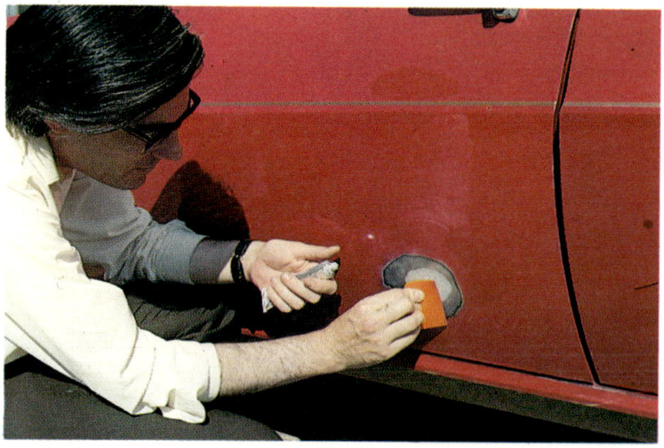

persuaded to spring out again by applying pressure to the inside of the panel. When the inner side cannot be reached – for example in a double-skinned section of the body – the simplest plan is to drill a hole at the centre of the dent, insert a self-tapping screw and pull the dent out by gripping the head of the screw with a pair of pliers, a self-locking wrench, or a claw hammer. The hole can then be filled with stopper, sanded down and touched-in. Another ploy that has proved successful is to ease a deflated football bladder between the two skins of the bodywork, pump it up and pop the dent out.

3 Rubbing down the filler

Here the filler is being rubbed down with progressively finer paper, after the paste has hardened, until a good finish is obtained, to prepare the surface for spraying as described in Sections 8 and 9.

4 Dealing with badly-rusted panels

The corroded metal must be ruthlessly cut away until sound, bright metal is reached. When rust has attacked the back of a panel this may mean that an innocuous-looking pimpled area is converted into a fairly large hole with ragged edges, as shown in the photograph. These must be tapped back with a hammer to about ¼ in. below the level of the surrounding paintwork.

5 Glass-fibre repairs

A typical glass-fibre kit is shown in this photograph. It contains a supply of glass-fibre mat, which is used to cover the damaged area, tissue and ribbon to repair smaller areas, resin, hardener and filler powder, and often a stippling brush, a stirring rod and a mixing bowl.

If the damaged area is a load-bearing one, the only safe repair is to have a patch welded in by a garage. You can then save money by filling and spraying the repaired area at home. If the part is unstressed, however, the sound edges should be tapped in until they are about ¼ in. below the surface of the surrounding metal and a glass-fibre patch can be applied.

6 Applying the glass-fibre mat

Here we show a piece of glass-fibre mat being applied to the damaged area. It is essential to follow the instructions which are supplied with each kit. The principle is to cut a suitably sized piece of mat, mix some resin and catalyst in the correct proportions, stipple the resin generously over the damaged area, apply the glass mat, thoroughly soak this with resin, and repeat the operation with a second layer of mat.

If the damage is fairly extensive, a sheet of perforated zinc can be used to reinforce the glass-fibre. When repairing a rusty hollow section, a self-foaming plastic can be poured into the cavity until it overflows from the

hole, quickly setting into a sufficiently rigid mass to provide a good support for the glass-fibre mat.

7 Preparing for spraying

When the resin has hardened, build up the external surface with the filler paste as shown in the picture.

Use coarse emery paper, an emery disc in an electric drill, or a Surform file to obtain the correct profile. Then rub down the surface with 180 grade wet-or-dry emery paper, used wet, to blend the repair into the surrounding paintwork, followed by light rubbing with 400 grade, again used wet, and preferably with a trace of soap, until a silky smooth surface can be felt.

8 Masking-off and spraying

Special masking tape can be obtained from garages and accessory shops. Never use ordinary cellulose tape, which will lift during spraying. Tape around the area to be sprayed, and attach sheets of newspaper to this tape with a second strip of tape, as shown.

Allow sufficient space to blend-in the new paint gradually. If you spray right up to the masking tape, the paint will build up along the edge of the tape and leave a ridge when it is removed.

Aerosol paint spray cans are ideal for small jobs, but first practise spraying on a sheet of metal or hardboard. Spray guns are more expensive and call for experience to obtain really good results.

Wash the prepared surface and allow it to dry before applying at least two coats of primer. Keep the spraying nozzle about 6-9 in. away from the surface, as shown in the photograph. Rub down each coat with 400 grade paper. The first colour coat can then be sprayed on, again followed by a light rub down, before the next coat is applied. Apply further light coats until a good finish is obtained.

Blend the spray into the surrounding paintwork. The colour of the new paint will usually change slightly as it dries and the true colour may not be obtained until a day or so has elapsed.

9 Blending and polishing

After the new paint has hardened thoroughly—allow at least a week for this—the surface can be polished and blended in with the old paintwork by using a mild abrasive compound. Liquid metal polish, or one of the 'cleaners' sold by the car polish firms for removing the stale outer film from the paintwork (such as Colour Cut) will produce a good finish.

7 The Ministry Test
Will your car pass or fail?

When you submit your car for the DoE test, the chances are about one in three that it will fail at the first attempt.

This is, of course, an average failure rate for all the cars tested in Great Britain. A more encouraging aspect is that an experienced tester will tell you that in many cases these failures need never have occurred. The faults could have been detected by a practical owner and should have been put right before the car was taken to the testing station.

The value of the test is that it is essentially a safety check. Think of it, if you like, as an expert second opinion on the efficiency of your servicing during the past twelve months, covering such vital points as the brakes, steering, tyres, seat belts and the lighting system. Approach it in this spirit and you will give your car the best chance of passing with flying colours.

In the space available here it is not possible to give a detailed, point-by-point summary of the requirements laid down in the comprehensive Ministry tester's manual (which is revised from time to time to include additional items) but it *is* possible to provide an overall picture of the sort of checks that you can carry out at home.

A surprisingly large number of cars do not get even as far as a detailed inspection. The tester may fail your car if he finds any of the following faults—

Failure of the horn, windscreen wipers and washers to work; stop-lamps which have broken or dirty lenses or faulty bulbs (when two lamps are fitted they must light up simultaneously); direction indicators which do not flash at the correct rate of 60–120 flashes per minute, or have a faulty indicator light; a rusty or perforated exhaust pipe or silencer; shock absorbers which are so worn as to affect the controllability of the car; and bodywork faults such as loose or broken seat mountings, a faulty door lock or bonnet catch, or damaged or torn sections which might injure other road users.

Before going further, you might ask yourself, 'If this were a car belonging to a stranger, would I be completely happy to drive it?'

It is also reasonable to expect a refusal if the underside of the car is so caked with mud and grime that the tester cannot easily examine it, or if you cannot produce a previous test certificate or the vehicle registration book as evidence of the age of the car.

It you have carried out the checks described in Chapter 3, however, have, preferably, filled in a condition report sheet on the lines suggested in Chapter 5, and have conscientiously carried out the regular servicing outlined in Chapter 4, you should be able to face the test with confidence and we can now turn to some of the detailed checks which can be carried out at home. These form, in effect, a 'dummy run' for the actual test itself.

Checking the braking system

Begin by checking the 'feel' of the brake pedal, with the engine running to operate the servo. A 'spongy' pedal, or the need to pump it to take up excessive travel, will call for immediate investigation. Refer to Chart No. 9 to diagnose the most likely causes and turn to Chapter 15 for advice on how to put them right.

Next get under the car, and with an inspection lamp go over the flexible hoses, every inch of the rigid pipelines and the unions. Look for cracks in the hoses, corrosion of the pipelines and seepage of fluid from the unions. Make sure that there is no risk of the hoses being rubbed by the front wheels on full lock and that none of the rigid pipes is in danger of being chafed where it passes close to the underframe or through an opening. Pay particular attention to the handbrake operating cables and rods, looking for frayed cables, worn pivots and clevis pins, and any signs of binding in the mechanism.

Seepage of brake fluid or grease from the wheel bearings on to the brake drums, backplates, discs and calipers will immediately be obvious and would be an equally immediate cause for failing the car.

Check the handbrake for excessive travel and make sure that the ratchet holds securely.

The tester will pay particular attention to all these points before carrying out a brake test. You will not be able to measure the efficiency of the brakes—the minimum is 50% for the foot brake and 25% for the handbrake—but by testing the brakes at about 30 mph on a smooth-surfaced, traffic-free road you should be able to detect any lack of efficiency or a tendency to pull to one side or the other, or to lock one wheel prematurely.

A final point: before handing the car over to the tester, make sure that the brake fluid reservoir has been topped-up to the correct level.

Steering checks

It is reasonable to suppose that you would not allow

your car to go for test if there was an obvious fault such as excessive lost motion at the steering wheel, tight steering, poor self-centring, a tendency to pull to one side or wheel-wobble. Apart from steering faults, one cannot rule out poor roadholding due to weak dampers or a generally tired suspension system.

Check through the symptoms listed in Chart No. 8 and then turn to Chapters 14 and 15 for the corrective action.

The Ministry inspection is not confined to the road test. The tester will raise the car on a lift, or place it over a pit and with the front wheels supported clear of the ground, will push, pull and tug at all the steering connections in order to detect worn joints or loose mountings.

You can forestall him by jacking up each wheel in turn, grasping it at the top and bottom and rocking it to show up excess play in the wheel bearings and in the hub-carrier swivel joints. There should be just perceptible end-play in the wheel bearings. Any excessive movement calls for investigation. Next spin the wheel and listen for grinding or rubbing noises which would indicate that the bearings are badly worn or are breaking up.

With both wheels lowered to the ground, get under the car and ask a friend to tug the steering wheel towards each lock in turn and release it, while you closely watch the steering joints for any signs of wear.

Nowadays, the joints are of the self-adjusting type, except where rubber bushes are used. It used to be said that if any slackness could be felt when the upper part of the joint was levered away from the lower part, replacement was indicated. Many modern joints, however, have a small amount of 'lift' when new, in order to increase their service life. With this type of joint, if the lower half can be raised by more than about 0.01 in. by exerting pressure with a lever pivoted against the inside of the wheel rim, renewal is probably necessary.

You may find that an eccentric type joint is fitted, however, which must be checked for wear by levering it *sideways* in relation to the ball-pin.

Obviously, accurate assessment of the amount of wear which is present calls for experience and that is why we recommend that the best check is to watch the joints while the steering wheel is tugged towards each lock and released. Sloppy joints will immediately show up under this treatment.

If the protective rubber boot on a joint is found to be damaged or displaced, the joint should be renewed as a safety precaution. The tester will probably condemn it, anyway.

The tyres

It should be obvious that tyres which are worn below the legal minimum of 1 mm of tread depth across at least three-quarters of the width of the tread, and around the whole of the circumference of the tyre, are potentially lethal and should not be found on a well-maintained car.

Not so obvious, however, are cuts or bulges on the inner walls of the tyres, or a damaged wheel rim which could cut the tyre or cause sudden loss of pressure. The tester will also look for uneven tread wear, which suggests steering or braking defects, and will immediately fail the car if he discovers an illegal mixture of cross-ply and radial-ply covers. If the tyres are of different types, the radials must always be fitted to the rear wheels. Obviously, it is best to avoid any mixture and stick to cross-plies or radials throughout.

Remember to check the spare wheel. The tester must assume that if you carry a spare you intend to use it if a puncture occurs, and it is therefore logical to fail the car if the spare wheel is fitted with a badly-worn or otherwise defective tyre, or one of the wrong type.

Bodywork condition

The tester will pay particular attention to the underside of the vehicle. Vital components in this respect are the underframes, stressed body sills, suspension mountings and the floor pans, especially where the seat mountings and seat belt attachments are bolted through.

Never be tempted to try to camouflage badly-rusted, stressed areas by glass-fibre repairs. An experienced tester will spot this immediately and will refuse to pass the car until a proper repair has been made by welding-in new sections.

The lighting system

The requirements laid down in the tester's manual can be summed-up in a few words: all the lights on the car which are required by the Construction and Use Regulations must be working properly and the headlamps must be correctly aligned so that they do not dazzle other drivers when dipped.

So far as the standard lighting system is concerned, therefore, all that you have to do is to check for a 'blown' bulb, a wiring fault, a poor earth contact or a faulty switch which prevents a light functioning, a cracked or missing lamp glass or a badly-rusted reflector.

It is not really practical to attempt to adjust the headlamp beams by aiming them at marks on a wall. There are too many sources of error and a proper check can be carried out so much more accurately by a garage, using an optical beam setter. If you have any doubts, have this check made before submitting the car for the test.

The seat belts

Finally, don't forget to check the seat belts and their mountings. The tester is justified in failing a car if he finds a loose or insecure mounting or a badly-frayed belt.

Part three

8 Strip, repair or replace?
Practical notes on overhauls

'Whip it off and fit a new one!' says the garage mechanic or a knowledgeable friend dogmatically when a fault develops in a component which calls for more than a minor repair — and with high labour charges in mind you may feel inclined to agree with him.

But is he giving you good advice? Does it always make economic sense, for example, to fit a service-exchange starter motor? The answer is probably 'No,' if all that is required is a set of new brushes and cleaning up the commutator — but the works-reconditioned component has been fully overhauled and *does* carry a guarantee!

In the case of an alternator, on the other hand, it is almost certainly best to fit an exhange unit. It is possible to change the alternator brushes, but testing the diodes and the charging regulator should be left to a qualified auto-electrician.

Where safety is involved we think it better to renew all doubtful items. The hydraulic components in the braking system should be replaced as complete assemblies, for example, instead of trying to salvage them by fitting new rubber parts from an overhaul kit. New rubbers in scored or corroded bores can have very short lives! The same principle applies to steering gear parts.

Again, where the clutch is concerned, renew everything that can wear — in this case as a matter of sound economics. It is much too time-consuming to remove and strip the clutch later should a worn part fail.

Similarly, when you strip a worn gearbox you will probably end up by replacing most of the parts, so there may not be much difference between the cost of these and the price of a reconditioned exchange unit.

In subsequent chapters, and in the notes on engine overhaul which follow, we deal with this subject more fully, indicating those jobs which are likely to be beyond the skill or the resources of the beginners, and suggesting 'repair by replacement' where this is likely to be more economical or more satisfactory.

A final point to bear in mind is that if special service tools will be needed to carry out an overhaul properly, the expense of these — assuming that they cannot be borrowed or hired — will seldom be justified for a one-off job.

Practical aspects of engine overhauls

It is possible to tackle virtually any degree of engine wear in the home garage by dividing the work into three stages and taking advantage of the replacement or reconditioned parts or assemblies which are available from specialist firms. The practical aspects of the work are fully covered in Chapter 9, so we can confine ourselves here to a brief discussion of the pros and cons of the various stages of overhaul, which can be summarized as follows —

Stage 1. Fitting new piston rings, including special oil-control rings, to the existing pistons.

Stage 2. Partial overhaul, including new special pistons with rings and gudgeon pins, fitting new connecting-rod bearings, exhaust valves, valve springs and timing chain.

Stage 3. Full overhaul, including fitting a rebored or linered cylinder block, a reground crankshaft, new bearing shells, a reconditioned flywheel with new starter ring, plus other work as Stage 2. Alternatively, fitting a 'half-engine' or 'short-motor' or a 'pin-up' (these terms will be described later) or a fully-reconditioned power unit.

Even if you are a novice, you should be able to tackle Stages 1 and 2 with every prospect of success. If you have had some experience of working on engines, there is no reason why you should not carry out the more ambitious Stage 3 overhaul, provided that you are able to borrow or hire lifting tackle to remove and refit the engine (don't rely on the roof beam of a prefabricated garage to carry the weight of the engine) and can call on the assistance of a friend when an extra pair of hands is needed.

Bearing in mind these points, a brief run through the pros and cons of the different reconditioning methods may help you to come to the right decision.

Fitting new piston rings (Stage 1)

A set of special piston rings can deal successfully with bore wear up to a maximum of about 0.004 in. for each inch of cylinder diameter, but their effectiveness depends on correct fitting.

It is usually necessry to send the pistons to the firm that supplies the rings so that the worn grooves can be machined to match the new rings. If the grooves are badly worn — particularly the top compression ring grooves — it may be necessary to fit groove inserts.

Never be tempted to fit a set of oil-control rings to worn pistons without enlisting the help of a specialist supplier. At best, the result may be disappointing; at worst, ring breakage may occur, scoring the cylinder walls and rendering a rebore essential.

Oil consumption should remain within reasonable limits for about 10 000 miles after a Stage 1 overhaul. If it is proposed to sell or exchange the car within this mileage, therefore, the fitting of special rings alone may well be an economic proposition.

Stage 2 overhaul

If you intend to keep the car for a longer period, however, and it has not covered more than about 40 000-60 000 miles, serious consideration should be given to a Stage 2 overhaul.

Most of the work entailed will be the same as that required when fitting new rings alone but the replacement of the pistons and the connecting-rod bearings, combined with a top-overhaul and the fittng of new exhaust valves, and a set of valve springs, will give the engine a new lease of life.

'Intermediate engine overhaul' kits are available from specialst firms such as AE Edmunds Walker and can be ordered through your garage. They contain everything that is needed for a Stage 2 overhaul — pistons and rings, bearing shells, exhaust valves, valve springs, gaskets, jointing compound and even an oil filter and a piston-ring clamp.

If the cylinder bore wear exceeds about 0.004 in. per inch of cylinder diameter, however — say, ten thousandths in a 2½ inch cylinder bore, which is a considerable amount of wear by modern standards — fitting special pistons and rings is unlikely to be effective. This calls for a Stage 3 overhaul.

Stage 3 overhaul

The simplest solution is to lift the engine out and install a reconditioned unit; or you can go to the other extreme and strip it right down, fit new or reconditioned parts as necessary and rebuild it.

If you decide to fit a 'recon' engine, you again have the choice of ordering a factory-rebuilt unit from your local dealer, or shopping around for a rebuilt engine at a lower price, among the smaller engineering firms which specialize in this work. The advertisements in the practical motoring papers will provide a list of prospects.

The fact that the prices charged by these firms are generally lower than the cost of an engine which has been rebuilt by the car manufacturer does not necessarily mean that the units are of lower quality. A specialist rebuilder does not have to carry the heavy overheads of a car manufacturer, nor does he have to allow a sizeable commission to a local dealer who supplies the engine.

Reputable engine rebuilding firms usually offer a worthwhile guarantee, however. In such cases their units should be just as satisfactory as factory-rebuilt units.

Although these are known in the trade as 'full' engines, they are not in fact complete. You will have to remove the carburettor, manifolds, ignition distributor, starter, fuel pump and possibly the water pump from your engine and fit them to the new unit — after suitably reconditioning them, of course.

It will probably be necessary also to remove and keep the securing studs, bolts and nuts for these items, which will not be supplied with the new unit. In some cases you may have to fit your own flywheel and valve cover, so check carefully just what is offered.

A cheaper proposition is the 'half-engine' or 'short motor.' This consists of a rebored cylinder block, fitted with a reground crankshaft in new main bearings, complete with reconditioned connecting rods, new pistons and rings, a reground camshaft, new or refaced cam followers and new timing sprockets. To this you add your own reconditioned cylinder head, the auxiliaries already mentioned and the other bits and pieces that go to make up the complete engine.

A short engine obviously entails a good deal more work on your part, but with a corresponding saving in expense. Few, if any, special tools are required and all the skilled work has been done for you.

Finally, the cheapest proposition is that known in the trade as a 'pin-up' — which sounds interesting, but in fact means simply that the parts supplied are limited to a reconditioned cylinder block, pistons, crankshaft and connecting rods, ready-assembled for you to build into a complete engine, using your own new and reconditioned parts for the remaining items.

The time factor

If this is to be your first attempt at carrying out, say, a partial engine overhaul, make sure that you allow plenty of time, plus a safety margin for unexpected delays. If you begin work on a Friday evening, it should be possible to complete the preliminary dismantling of the cylinder head that night, so that any replacements that are found to be necessary and are not included in the intermediate engine overhaul kit referred to earlier can be obtained on Saturday morning, when most garages and spares counters are open.

By making an early start on Saturday it should be possible to lift the engine out, withdraw the connecting rods and pistons, remove the old pistons and fit the replacements, reassemble the pistons and connecting rods (fitted with new bearing shells) in the cylinders and finally turn your attention to decarbonizing the cylinder head and grinding-in the valves.

The whole of Sunday will probably be occupied in finishing off the bottom half of the engine, fitting a new filter, refitting the cylinder head, manifolds and carburettor, reinstalling the engine and making adjustments, followed by a short test run.

9 The engine

In Chapter 8 we have explained how a do-it-yourself enthusiast can successfully tackle quite an ambitious engine overhaul without the need for special skills or an impressive array of workshop equipment.

The secret, of course is to confine oneself as far as possible to straightforward stripping and assembly, leaving the trickier jobs to the experts.

The engine repairs and adjustments that can be tackled without the use of special tools and equipment are mainly influenced by the design of the cylinder head, valve-operating gear and, in the case of major overhauls, by the 'bottom half' components, the most important of which are the crankshaft, pistons and connecting rods. A brief description of the main features of the engines will therefore be of interest to the practical owner who wishes to do as much of the work as possible.

The 1256 cc push-rod engines are well-tried designs, developed from the Viva power unit. The overhead valves are operated by rockers and push-rods from a camshaft which is carried in the cylinder block. The rockers are unusual in being in the form of cupped steel pressings, each mounted on a hollow stud which is pressed in to the cylinder head and retained by an adjustable nut which has a hemispherical seating. To adjust the valve clearance it is necessary only to turn the self-locking nut.

If a rocker retaining nut becomes slack, allowing the adjustment to alter in service, either the nut or the stud can be replaced, the latter normally being a job for a Vauxhall dealer. The valve springs are retained by conventional cups and split-cone cotters.

The pistons have solid skirts and the offset piston pins or gudgeon pins are an interference fit in the upper ends of the connecting rods. When installing the pins, the eye of the connecting rod *only* must be heated evenly to 230-260°C, so that the eye will shrink on to the pin as it cools, and special tools are used to align the pin with the rod. Obviously a job for a Vauxhall dealer!

The crankshaft is carried in three main bearings, the centre bearing being flanged to control the end-float of the shaft. The connecting-rod and main bearings are of the modern thin-shell, steel-backed type, which can be replaced without the need for special fitting or scraping.

The practical aspects of all these jobs are dealt with fully in the later sections of this chapter.

Routine engine maintenance

The jobs described in this chapter are those listed in the maintenance schedule. Engine maintenance, of course, also includes a certain amount of work on the cooling system, ignition system and the carburettor and petrol pump. These jobs are dealt with in Chapter 10, 11 and 12.

9.1 Engine lubrication

The engine oil has been aptly described as the life-blood of the engine. It therefore pays to use a first-class multigrade oil. The correct grades are given in Chapter 17.

Here are some important practical tips—

1 The intervals between oil changes recommended in the maintenance schedule *apply only when a multigrade oil is used, under favourable conditions.* Change the oil more frequently when most of the driving is done in cold weather, or when the car is used for short runs and frequent starts are made from cold, or in hot, dusty conditions. In such cases it is best to change the oil after 3000 miles, or, in extreme cases, as frequently as every 1000 miles.

2 The correct oil pressure is given in Chapter 17. If the pressure is appreciably below this figure at normal speeds in top gear, with the engine thoroughly warmed-up, investigation is called for. Running the engine with too low a pressure can result in expensive damage to the crankshaft, main and connecting-rod bearings and other components.

3 When an oil-pressure gauge is not provided, the oil-pressure warning lamp in the instrument panel will glow if the oil pressure should fall below a safe minimum figure. If the lamp does not light-up when the ignition is switched on or does not go out when the engine is running, check the switch on the cylinder block, which is operated by the oil pressure. Either fit a replacement switch, or ask a garage to check the oil pressure by temporarily connecting a gauge to the switch union.

9.2 Engine oil change

The sump should be drained when the car has just come in from a run, when the oil is hot and fluid.

Materials: Engine oil — 5 pints (2.8 litres).
Tools: 1 in. AF spanner. Wheel ramps or axle stands for front and rear (not essential). Funnel if refilling with oil from container without a spout.

1 Remove the large, 1 in. drain plug at the rear of the sump. It is just possible to reach this without raising the car, but it is easier, of course, if the front and rear wheels are raised on ramps or axle stands are used.

2 Place a container which will hold about two gallons (to provide a safety margin) beneath the drain plug and unscew the plug. Allow the oil to drain until the drips have ceased.

3 Clean the drain plug, check that the copper washer is in good condition and replace the plug. Refill the sump and warm-up the engine.

4 Check for leakage at the drain plug. Recheck the oil level with the car on level ground.

9.3 Changing the oil filter element

A full-flow, throw-away type of oil filter is provided, and this must be renewed after it has been in use for 6000 miles (10 000 km). Carbon, sludge and grit accumulate in the filter, and if the element becomes clogged, a safety valve opens in order to maintain adequate oil circulation to the engine — *but this oil will not be filtered.*

The renewable filter cartridge is enclosed in a metal casing which is retained by a single bolt. To renew the filter —

Materials: New filter element.
Tools: $\frac{9}{16}$ in. AF spanner.

1 Drain the oil (Section 9.2.).

2 Place a container beneath the filter to catch the oil which will run out when the filter casing is removed.

3 Unscrew the centre bolt and remove the casing, if

1 push-rod
2 rocker stud
3 adjusting screw for rocker
4 valve
5 valve spring
6 water pump impeller
7 fan belt pulley
8 viscous drive for fan
9 timing chain
10 crankshaft pulley
11 crankshaft front oil seal
12 front main bearing
13 connecting-rod bearing
14 crankshaft
15 piston
16 connecting rod
17 centre main bearing
18 oil-pump suction filter
19 rear main bearing
20 clutch assembly
21 crankshaft spigot bearing
22 flywheel
23 starter ring-gear
24 cam follower (tappet)

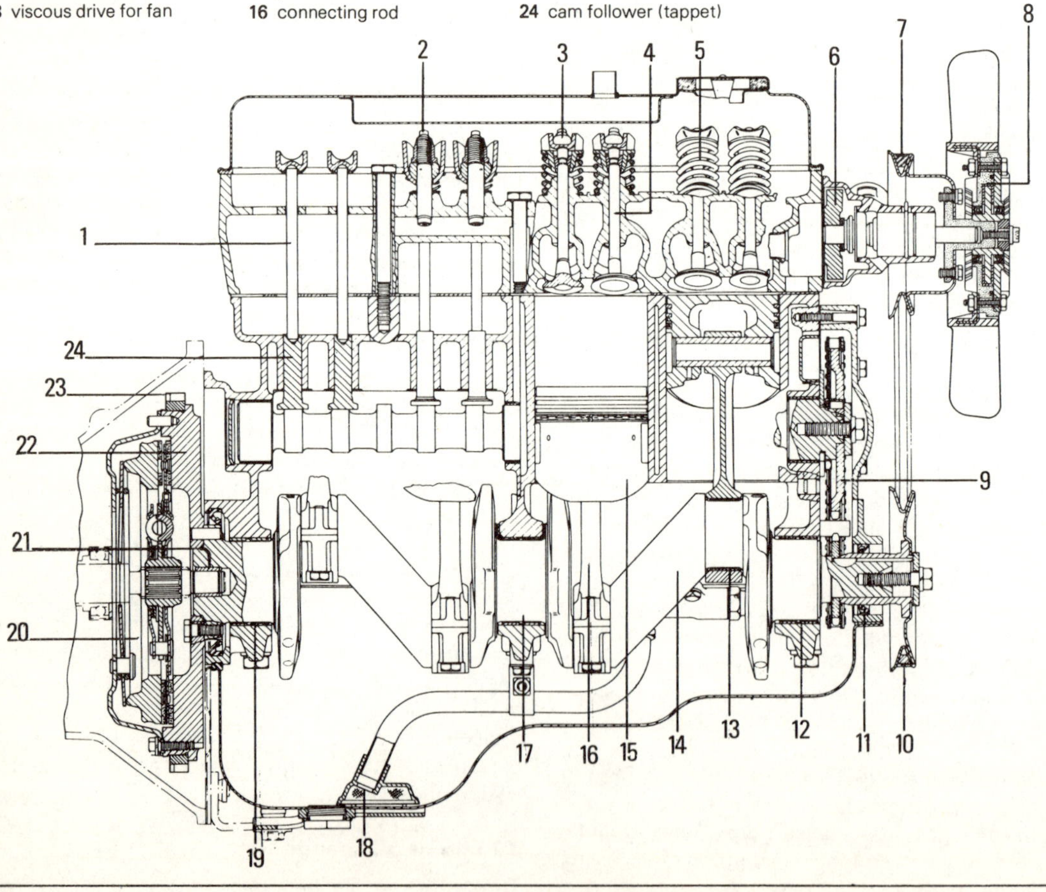

Fig. 9.1 A horizontal section through the engine, showing most of the parts referred to in this chapter

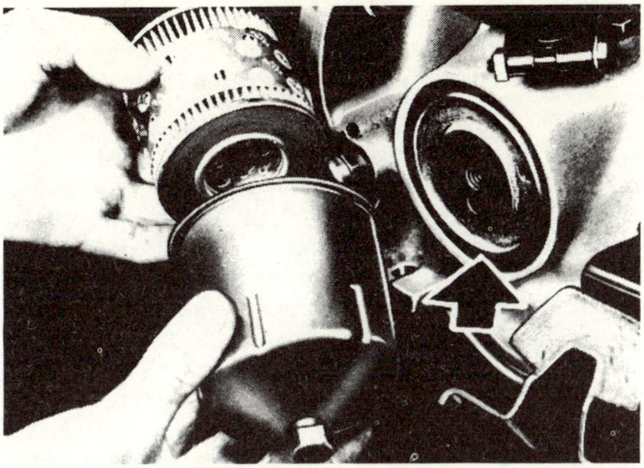

Fig. 9.2 Changing an oil filter element. The sealing ring indicated by the arrow should also be changed to prevent any risk of oil leakage. Do not remove the protective sleeve from the element

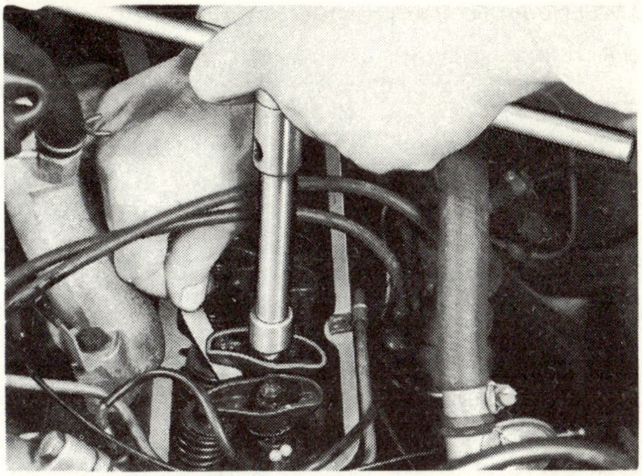

Fig. 9.3 Adjusting the valve clearances, using a strip of feeler gauge material and a socket spanner

necessary giving it a blow with the hand to break the joint at the crankcase seal.

4 Remove and discard the element. Do not attempt to remove the spring which fits over the centre bolt.

5 Wash the casing with paraffin, being particularly careful to remove any sludge deposits from the base of the casing, around and beneath the element seating plate and spring.

6 Remove the sealing washer from the crankcase housing and fit the new washer supplied with the replacement element. Install the element in the casing, refit the casing, being sure that it enters the groove in the crankcase, and tighten the bolt securely.

7 After refilling the engine sump, run the engine and check for oil leakage at the filter seal. Finally, recheck the oil level and top-up, if necessary, to compensate for the oil taken up by the filter.

9.4 Checking the valve tappet clearances

In order to maintain any engine in good tune, it is essential to check the valve tappet clearances at regular intervals.

The correct clearances between the ends of the rockers and the tops of the valve stems are given in Chapter 17.

The clearances must be adjusted while the engine is running. The pressed steel rockers operate on individual hollow studs pressed into the cylinder head. Each rocker is retained by a hemispherical ball seating and a self-locking nut. Screwing the nut down the stud will thus decrease the clearance between the tip of the rocker and the end of the valve stem, while unscrewing it will increase the clearance.

Before tackling the job for the first time, ask your local Vauxhall dealer to supply a suitable thin tubular spanner. At the same time buy strips of feeler gauge of the correct thicknesses for the engine, as given in Chapter 17. Checking the valve clearances while the engine is running can sometimes damage the blades of an ordinary set of feeler gauges; it is cheaper, therefore, simply to use a fresh section of the feeler strip.

The valve clearances should be checked *only when the engine is at its normal running temperature.* Four or five miles on the road should be sufficient to ensure that the temperatures of the cylinder block, cylinder head, valves, push-rods and rocker gear have become stabilized. It is not sufficient just to run the engine for a few minutes in the garage before checking the clearances.

To check the clearances –

Materials: Valve rocker cover gasket.
Tools: Feeler gauge strips. Tubular spanner, either $\frac{9}{16}$ AF or 15 mm (a $\frac{19}{32}$ AF spanner will fit the 15 mm nut). Consult your Vauxhall dealer about feeler gauges and spanner.

1 Switch off, disconnect the breather hose from the valve cover, temporarily remove the sparking plug leads from the plugs and from the rocker cover retaining points, unscrew the valve cover retaining screws. and lift off the cover.

2 Refit the sparking plug leads to their respective plugs and start the engine. Unscrew the carburettor throttle-stop screw (*not* the idling mixture adjustment) to obtain as low an idling speed as possible.

3 Check the valve clearances with the correct feeler strip. Counting from the front of the engine, the inlet valves are Nos. 2, 3, 6 and 7. The exhaust valves are Nos. 1, 4, 5 and 8. It should just be possible to slide the feeler strip between the valve stem and the tip of the rocker as it rises; you should feel a slight drag. The strip will, of course, be nipped when the rocker compresses the valve spring.

4 If the gauge feels too slack or too tight, adjust the rocker nut until the correct clearance is obtained.

9.5 Servicing the crankcase ventilation system

The crankcase fumes are drawn off through a hose which is connected between the rocker cover and the carburettor air cleaner, when the carburettor throttle is opened, and also through a branch hose, connected to a restricted pipe in the inlet manifold, when the engine is idling.

It is important to keep these hoses free from sludge and also prevent any air leakage at the manifold hose union as this will affect the engine idling.

The hoses should be checked at the 6000-mile service and flushed with paraffin. Choked hoses will cause a build-up of sludge in the engine and deposits of 'mayonnaise' in the valve cover.

The time factor

It is not always easy to estimate the time required for engine overhaul jobs, since so much depends on the facilities available. The following times, however, are suggested for typical jobs: Partial engine overhaul (see Chapter 8), 2-3 days; top-overhaul and decarbonizing, allow at least one full day – preferably a week-end; remove and refit new timing cover oil seal, including removing and refitting engine, 10½ hr; changing engine mountings, 2 hr; fitting new exhaust system, 1 hr; changing oil filter, 15 min.

Decarbonizing and top-overhaul

Removal of the cylinder head, cleaning off deposits of carbon and reseating the valves is usually termed 'decarbonizing', although a more correct term, in view of the work involved, is a 'top-overhaul'.

If the job is confined solely to removing and refitting the head – to replace a faulty gasket, for example – only Sections 9.6 and 9.13 apply. A full top-overhaul involves the work covered by all the Sections from 9.6 to 9.13.

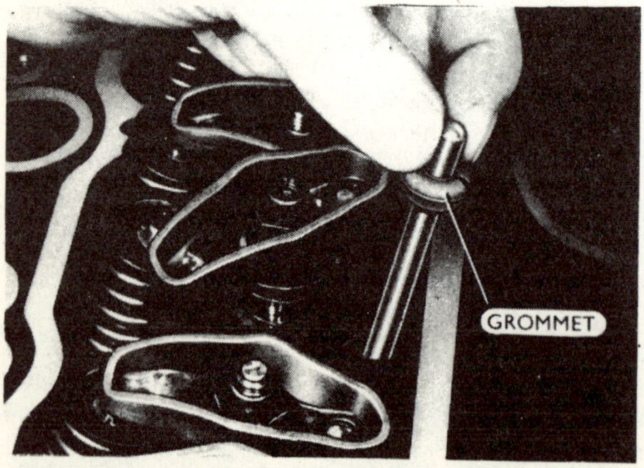

Fig. 9.4 A grommet fitted to a push-rod to prevent the rod falling into the crankcase during removal or replacement

The lists of materials and tools required which follow cover a complete top-overhaul, but can, of course, be modified to suit the actual stages carried out.

Materials: Gasket set. Water hoses. Set of valve springs. Spare exhaust valves (have at least two in reserve as a safety margin). Valve stem oil seals. Valve-grinding paste. Emery paper. Rags. Paraffin. Tins, jars, boxes for parts. Old piston ring.

Tools: Set spanners. Socket spanners. Screwdrivers. Pliers. Blunt scraper for carbon. Wire brush. Valve-spring compressor. Torque wrench. Electric drill with wire brushes – desirable but not essential. Eight small rubber grommets or spring clothes pegs (see text).

Practical pointers

Here are some practical tips which will help to ensure the success of the job.

If the water hoses are difficult to remove, they can be cut through with a knife. It is best to fit new hoses on reassembly.

The cylinder-head nuts *must* be slackened progressively, working diagonally from the centre of the head outwards. *This is most important to avoid distorting the head.*

Discard the valve springs and fit a new set.

As each valve is withdrawn from its guide, place it in the correct order on the bench. *The valves must not be interchanged.* Punch holes in a strip of cardboard to take the stems and number these to correspond with the positions of the valves in the head.

If the cylinder head does not come away easily, don't attempt to prise it up by inserting a screwdriver or similar tool between the head and the block, as this may damage the machined surfaces. A sharp tap with a wooden mallet, or a hammer on a block of wood held against the side of the head, should free the joint.

Do not use an abrasive, such as metal polish, on the pistons, owing to the risk of particles being trapped in the piston-ring grooves or between the rings and the cylinder walls.

Most authorities recommend that a narrow ring of carbon should be left around the edge of each piston crown and around the top edge of each cylinder bore, the theory being that these form useful oil seals if the piston rings and bores are no longer in perfect condition. There are conflicting views on this but it does no harm to play safe. This is where an old piston ring comes into the picture: placed on top of the piston, it protects the carbon seals from the scraper and the wire brush.

9.6 Removing the cylinder head

Materials and tools: see above.

1 Drain the cooling system and disconnect the radiator hoses and heater hoses. If any of the hoses are perished, it would be wise to renew the complete set.

2 Disconnect the battery in order to prevent the possibility of any accidental 'shorts.'

3 Disconnect the sparking-plug leads and number each cable to avoid confusion on reassembly. Remove the sparking plugs, putting them aside for cleaning and resetting of the gaps.

4 In order to remove the inlet and exhaust manifolds first take off the carburettor, after removing the air cleaner and disconnecting the petrol feed and vacuum ignition timing control pipes and the choke control. The carburettor, gaskets, and heat-insulating block can then be taken off.

5 Undo the setscrew that is fitted inside the inlet manifold by passing a socket spanner or a long box spanner through the opening over which the carburettor is fitted. The other setscrews that retain the inlet and exhaust manifolds are more easily accessible. Disconnect the exhaust pipe at its junction with the manifold.

6 Slacken the generator attachment bolts and the bolt on the adjusting strut and remove the fan belt.

7 Take off the ignition coil.

8 If a water temperature gauge is fitted, disconnect the wire from the transmitter on the cylinder head.

9 Slacken each rocker nut sufficiently to allow the rocker to be swung clear of the push-rod, but before doing this clip a small rubber grommet or a clothes peg on the push-rod, to prevent any risk of the rod falling into the crankcase if it should be dislodged from the tappet. Lay the push-rods out in sequence as they are removed so that they can be reassembled in their original positions, and the same way up.

10 Slacken the cylinder head bolts progressively in the order shown in Fig.9.11 (to avoid distorting the head); remove the bolts and lift off the cylinder head.

9.7 Dismantling the cylinder head

Materials and tools: see page 40.

If you do not intend to carry out a top-overhaul—for example, if the only reason for removing the cylinder head is to renew a faulty cylinder-head gasket—the combustion chambers can be decarbonized without further dismantling, although it is better to remove the manifolds if this has not already been done to allow the inlet and exhaust ports to be cleaned out. In any event, it is best to decarbonize the combustion chambers before removing the valves, to avoid the risk of damaging the valve seatings in the cylinder head.

During a top-overhaul, of course, it will be necessary to remove the valves for inspection and refacing of the valves and seatings, or renewal of any valves which are in too poor a condition to justify refacing and refitting them.

9.8 Removing the valve rockers

Materials and tools: see page 40. Also hypoid gear oil, SAE 90EP.

1 Remove the rocker nut and withdraw the rocker ball, the rocker and the push-rod, keeping each set of parts together, with its push-rod. Lay out the sets in the order in which they are removed from the engine so that they will be refitted in their original positions.

2 Remove the rocker retaining spring and shim and examine the threads of the rocker stud for signs of damage. Damaged studs can be trued-up by your Vauxhall dealer, using a special die nut.

3 Check the fit of each nut on its stud. To maintain the self-locking properties, the nut, when lubricated with *hypoid* gear oil, should require a force of 3 lb ft to turn it. If a torque wrench is not available, it should be possible to test with a spring balance, hooked over the jaws of spanner. Remember that the pull required will be proportionate to the length of the spanner. For example, a spanner 6 in. long would require a pull of 6 lb at its outer end. If the nuts are slack on the studs, the fitting of new studs is again a job for a Vauxhall dealer, since the bores for the studs must be accurately reamed to provide the correct interference fit for the new studs, which are supplied in 0.006 and 0.012 in. oversizes and a press should be used to fit the studs.

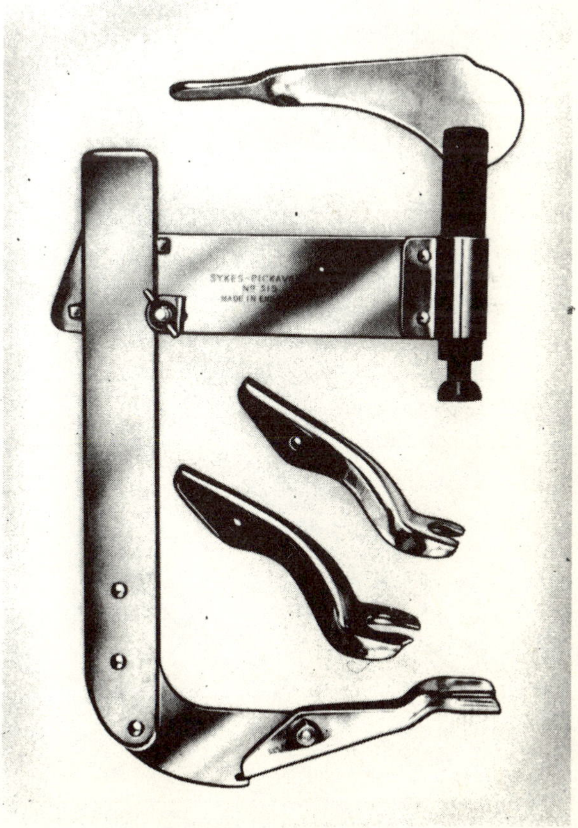

Fig. 9.5 A general-purpose Sykes-Pickavant valve spring compressor, adjustable to cover a wide range of engines

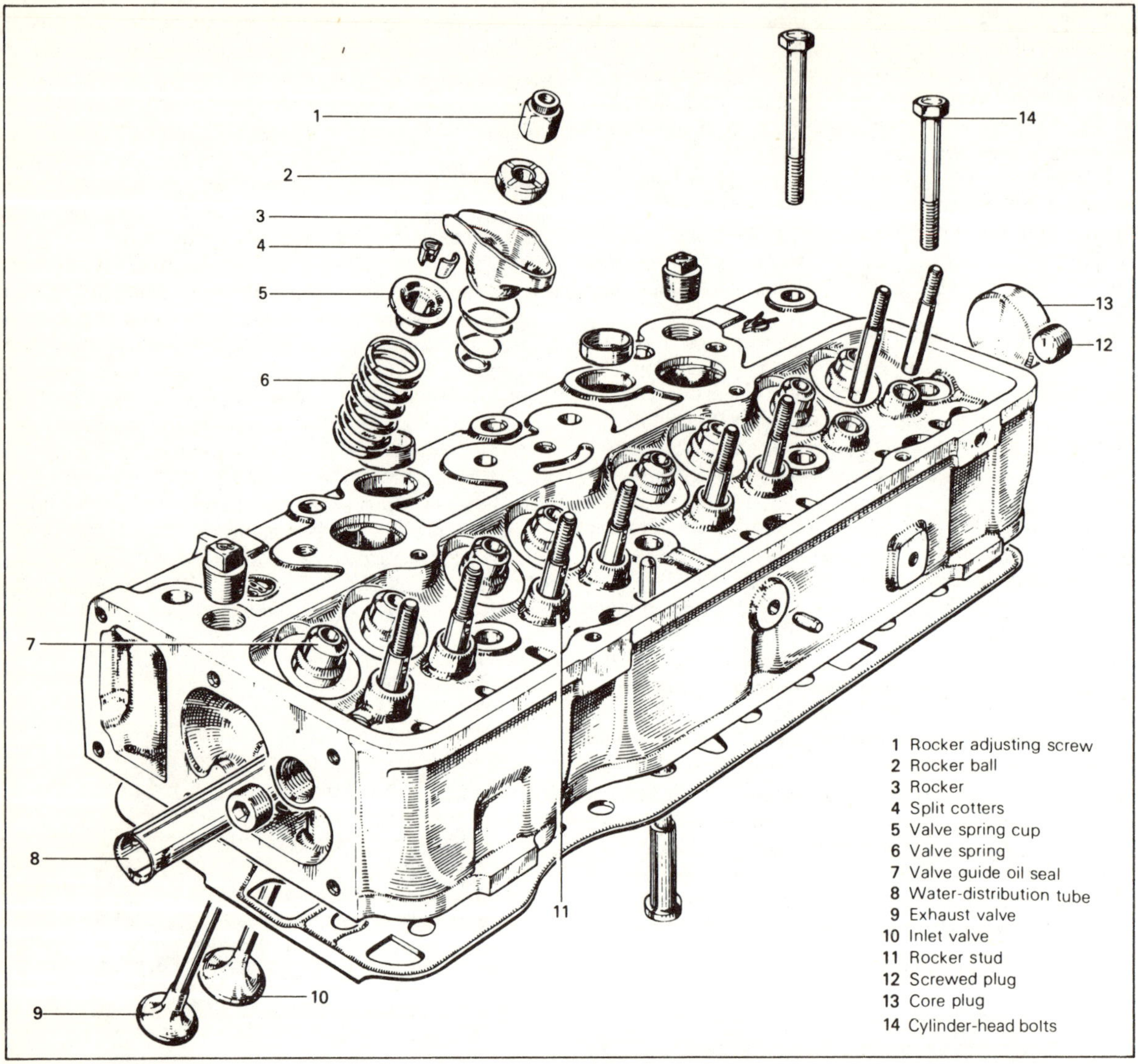

Fig. 9.6 The cylinder-head components

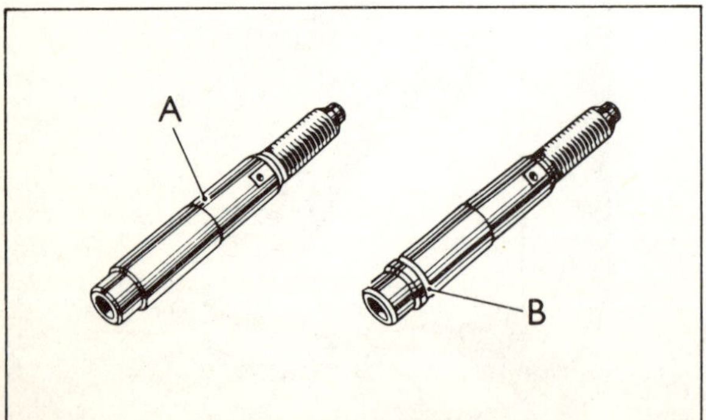

Fig. 9.7 A 0.006 in. oversize rocker stud is identified by a stepped shank A, and a 0.012 in. oversize by a groove B, in addition to the stepped shank

9.9 Decarbonizing the cylinder head

Materials and tools: see page 40.

1 Decarbonize the combustion-chamber faces before removing the valves, to avoid any risk of damaging the valve seatings. Scrape off every trace of carbon and burnish the underside of the head with a wire brush.

2 Thoroughly clean the cylinder-block and manifold mating faces of the head, taking particular care not to score them.

9.10 Removing and cleaning the valves

Materials and tools: see page 40.

The valve-spring caps are retained by split-cone collets and a valve-spring compressor is needed to remove them.

1 Compress each valve spring with the spring-compressor until the spring cap is clear of the split collets. Remove these and release the spring.

2 Take off the valve-spring retainer, sleeve, spring and the oil seal fitted to an inlet valve. Draw the valve out of its guide.

3 Clean the undersides of the valve heads, the stems and also the ports in the heads which could not be reached when the valves were in position. Be careful not to score the faces of the valves and their seats in the combustion chambers. Wire-wool soap-pads quickly remove carbon.

4 Scrape the valve stems clean. Don't use emery cloth on the sections that work in the guides. Clean out the guides themselves by drawing a paraffin-soaked rag through them.

5 Check each valve for fit in its own guide. If there is any noticeable degree of sideways shake, take the head to your dealer for advice. If he confirms that the valves and guides are worn, allow him to ream the guides, to recut the seats in the head and to fit new oversize valves.

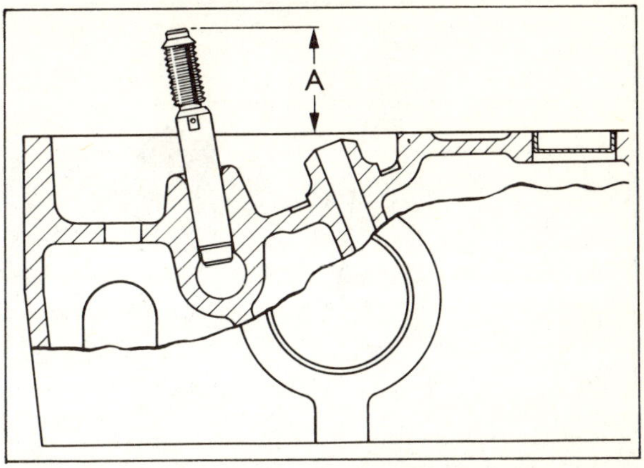

Fig. 9.8 A rocker stud must be pressed into a height of 1.1 in. (28 mm) measured vertically from the top face of the head as at A. The position of the oil discharge hole is not important

9.11 Reseating the valves

Materials and tools: see page 40.

If the seating faces on the valves are badly pitted, they can be trued-up by using a valve refacing tool (your garage should be able to do this for you).

Badly-pitted valve seatings in the cylinder head can be refaced with a special tool—normally this is also a job for your garage. If the pitting is only slight, however, the valves can be ground-in in the conventional manner, as described below.

The object of grinding-in the valves (or more correctly, lapping-in) is to obtain a gastight seal between each valve and its seating. The importance of making a really good job of valve-lapping cannot be over-emphasized, since not only the cylinder compressions but the service life of the valves depend on a first-class seal between the valves and their seatings.

Valve-grinding paste usually comes in a tin which contains two grades, fine and coarse. The coarse paste should be used only in an emergency, to remove pitting when proper reconditioning cannot be carried out, but light pitting may be removed with the fine paste, grinding being continued until a good matt finish has been obtained on the valve and seat.

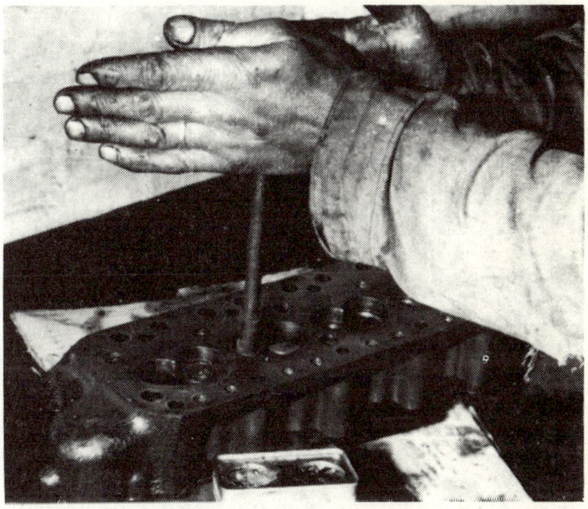

Fig. 9.9 Grinding-in a valve. The handle of the suction-cup tool should be spun between the palms of the hand while light pressure is applied to the head of the valve

1 Smear a little grinding-paste on the face of the valve and rotate the valve quickly and lightly on its seat with the suction-cup grinding tool, first in one direction and then in the other, by spinning the handle of the tool between the palms of the hands. From time to time, raise the valve from its seat and turn it through a quarter of a turn, before continuing the grinding. This will ensure that an even, concentric surface is obtained. A light coil spring, placed beneath the head of the valve, will make the job easier, as it will lift the valve whenever pressure on it is relaxed.

2 Check the progress of the grinding-in frequently. When correctly ground, both the valve seat in the cylinder head and the face of the valve should have an even, clean, grey matt finish with no signs of bright rings or any evidence of pitting. Bright rings are caused by grinding with insufficient grinding paste, while 'tramlines' are usually the result of continuously grinding the valve on its seat without taking up a different position.

3 Check the effectiveness of the seal by making a series of pencil marks across the face of the valve with a soft lead pencil. Replace the valve and rotate it once through a quarter of a turn on its seat. Each pencil mark should be erased at the line of contact. If any of the lines are unbroken, either the valve or its seat is not

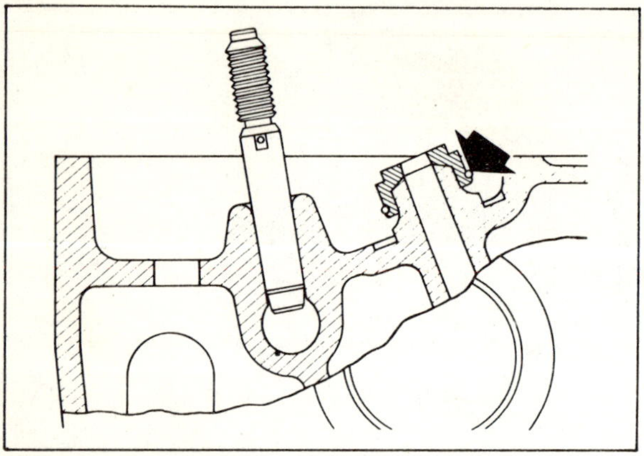

Fig. 9.10 A new inlet valve stem seal, secured by the circlip indicated by the arrow, should be fitted to each valve guide

truly circular and renewal or refacing of the valve or seat (or both) is required.

4 When grinding-in has been completed, wash the valves and seats with petrol or paraffin, making sure that all traces of grinding paste have been removed. Lubricate the valve stems with a little clean engine oil before refitting them and reassembling the new oil seals, springs and retainers. The oil seals must be fitted to the inlet valve guides before assembling the springs. The valve springs may be fitted either way up.

9.12 Decarbonizing the pistons

Materials and tools: see page 40.

1 Rotate the crankshaft until two of the pistons are at the top of the cylinders.

2 Stuff clean rags into the bores of the remaining cylinders and in the water-ways and other openings in the cylinder block.

3 Remove the carbon from the piston crowns with a suitable blunt scraper, taking care not to score the surfaces. Then burnish the crowns with a wire brush.

9.13 Replacing the cylinder head

Materials and tools: see page 40.

Before refitting the cylinder head, make sure that the piston crowns, cylinder walls and the top of the block are scrupulously clean. Pour a small quantity of engine oil around each bore so that it will be distributed over the cylinder walls and down the sides of the pistons when the engine is first rotated.

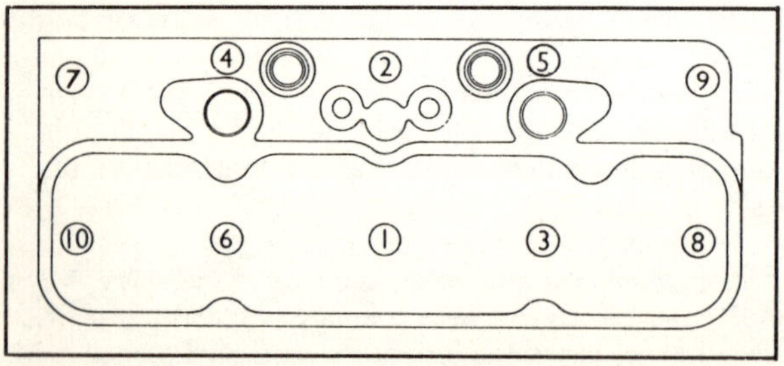

Fig. 9.11 The cylinder-head nuts should be slackened and tightened in the order shown

Do not use gasket cement on the cylinder-head gasket, as this is likely to cause subsequent leakage. A jointing compound such as Wellseal or Hermetite should, however, be used on all other gaskets and sealing washers.

1 Do not smear the new cylinder-head gasket with a jointing compound. It is of reinforced asbestos-based material which needs no sealant. It must be scrupulously clean.

2 Tighten the cylinder-head retaining bolts progressively in the order shown in Fig. 9.11 in order to pull the head down evenly.

3 Before replacing the push-rods, fit the clothes pegs to their upper ends to prevent a rod dropping if it does not engage with the tappet.

4 Assemble the light rocker springs with their smaller coils in contact with the cylinder head.

5 Lubricate the ball seatings and the rocker studs with hypoid gear oil before screwing on the nuts.

6 Adjust the valve clearances with both valves in each cylinder fully closed.

7 Complete the remainder of the reassembly, which is quite straightforward, but before attaching the front exhaust pipe to the exhaust manifold, insert the bolts 1 and 2 in Fig. 9.12 through the gasket and partially screw them into the flange of the manifold. Hook the slotted side of the pipe flange over these bolts to locate the pipes while the remaining bolts are being fitted. Tighten the centre bolts first and then the four outer bolts. Finally, check the tightness of the centre bolts.

8 Adjust the carburettor controls.

9 After a final check all round, refill the cooling system, start the engine and warm it up. Check the level of the water in the radiator after the engine has been running for a few minutes.

10 When the engine is at its normal running temperature, readjust the valve clearances as described in Section 9.4, adjust the carburettor idling speed and mixture strength as described in Chapter 11.

10 Switch off the engine and check the tightness of the cylinder-head and manifold nuts. These should be checked again after about 300 miles of running. Remember to readjust the valve clearances on each occasion, as they will be reduced when the cylinder head is tightened down.

Major engine overhauls

All the jobs described so far can be done without removing the engine from the car. A partial or complete overhaul – which will, of course, include these jobs in addition to attention to the pistons, connecting rod and crankshaft bearings, camshaft and followers, timing chain and tensioner, the oil pump and other components, depending on the amount of wear — calls for the removal of the engine.

At a pinch, the sump *can* be removed as described in Section 9.22, which would allow the oil pump and suction filter to be dealt with, and also the pistons, connecting rods and big ends to be removed after the cylinder head has been taken off. It is much more convenient and satisfactory, however, to do this sort of work with the engine on the bench.

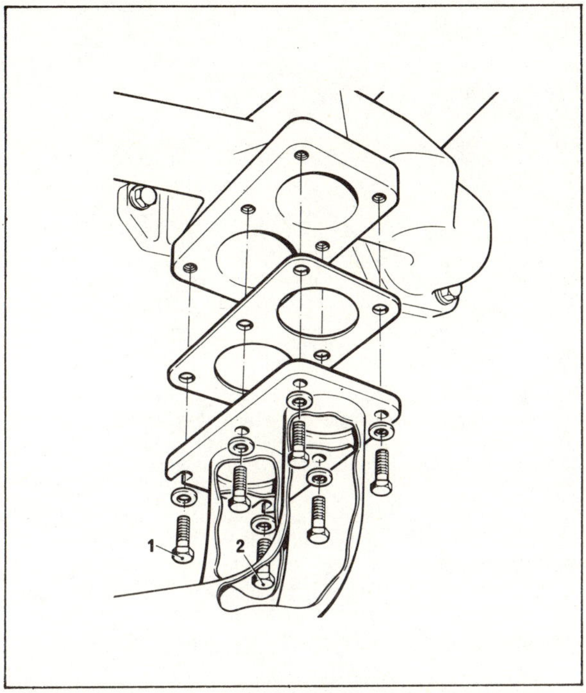

Fig. 9.12 Before attaching the front pipes to the exhaust manifold, screw the bolts **1** and **2** partly into the manifold flange and hook the slotted side of the pipe flange over these to support the pipe while inserting the remaining bolts. Tighten the centre bolts progressively before the remainder and then recheck the tightness

9.14 Removing the engine

The engine can be removed complete with the synchromesh gearbox, or it may be parted from the gearbox and removed alone.

If an improvised rope or wire sling must be used, make sure that this is sufficiently strong and check that it cannot damage any auxiliaries.

Nylon-cord multiple-pulley hoists can be purchased from most accessory dealers and can handle the weight safely, but be sure that the beam to which the hoist is attached is strong enough. To provide a safety factor, it should be able to support the weight of at least three men at the centre. If a suitable beam is not available or if you are working in the open it will be necessary to buy or hire an engine-lifting tripod or gantry.

To lift out the engine alone, see Chapter 13 for the method of disconnecting the engine from the gearbox.

Materials: New self-locking nuts for universal joint. Other spares as found to be necessary. Paraffin. Rags. Boxes and jars for parts.
Tools: Spanners. Sockets. Pliers. Screwdrivers. Lifting sling. Jack. Axle-stands or blocks for front wheels. Engine lifting hoist. Tripod or gantry.

1 Clear the decks by removing the bonnet (pencil around the hinges to ensure that they will be refitted in exactly the same positions). Disconnect the battery and remove the radiator (Section 10.8).

2 Remove the air cleaner.

3 Disconnect the vacuum servo pipe from the inlet manifold.

4 Disconnect the flange for the exhaust pipes from the manifold.

5 Disconnect the petrol feed pipe from the pump and plug the end to prevent loss of petrol.

6 Disconnect the following wiring at the engine end: ignition coil, distributor, oil-pressure switch, engine temperature gauge sender, dynamo, starter motor.

7 Disconnect the heater hoses from the engine.

8 Raise the car and support it on axle stands or rest the wheels on blocks, to give sufficient room to work beneath.

9 Place slings under the engine, behind the sump and at the front under the water pump, and take the weight of the unit.

10 Disconnect the engine earthing strap from the bodywork.

11 If the gearbox is to be removed with the engine, mark the flanges of the rear universal joint (to ensure correct reassembly, which is important to prevent vibration), and uncouple the flanges. Lower the shaft, pull it rearwards and remove it.

12 Disconnect the speedometer cable from the gearbox.

13 Remove the nuts that secure the front engine mounting rubbers to the brackets on the crankcase. Remove the short cross-member that carries the gearbox mounting.

14 If the engine is to be removed without the gearbox, separate the clutch housing from the engine by removing the flange bolts. To make it easier to remove the clutch housing front cover, slacken the gearbox brace bolts at the engine sump bracket. Carefully ease the engine forward to disconnect the gearbox primary shaft from the clutch hub and lift the engine out. Care must be taken at this stage, since if the gearbox primary shaft is allowed to carry any weight, the shaft may be bent or the clutch driven plate may be damaged.

15 Refitting the engine is simply a reversal of the removal sequence. If the mountings have been dismantled, assemble them as shown in Fig. 9.13. The special wrench VR2217 illustrated makes it easier to remove and refit the mounting rubber. If the mounting brackets have been removed from the crankcase, the

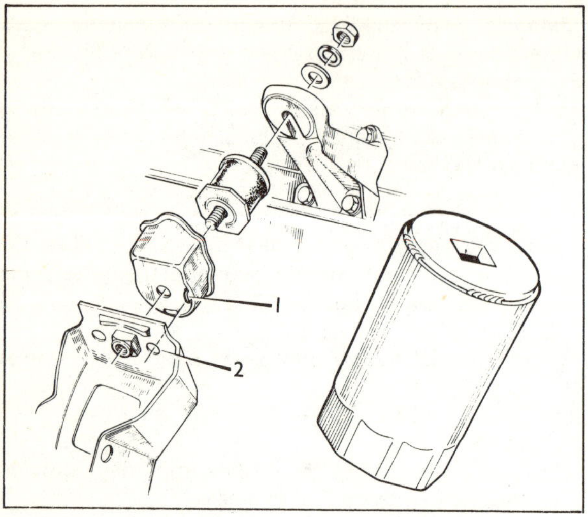

Fig. 9.13 A front engine mounting. The tang **1** in the impact cup must be inserted in the hole **2** in the axle bracket platform

threads of the bolts must be thoroughly cleaned and smeared with Loctite 270 (AVV) to prevent them working loose.
must be thoroughly cleaned and smeared with Loctite 270 (AVV) to prevent them working loose.

16 The rear mounting (Fig. 9.14) is attached to the gearbox by the single bolt 3 which incorporates a retaining clip 1. The large, straight washers fitted above and below the mounting must be installed as shown. The lower washer restricts upward movement of the gearbox on rebound. The platform for the lower mounting on the cross-member is inclined downwards at the rear to the extent of 3° to ensure correct alignment of the propellor shaft and it is therefore important to install the cross-member the correct way round, as shown in the illustration. In some cases an arrow indicates the front but when this is not provided the hole 2 (which is used only for manufacturing purposes) must be on the right-hand side of the car.

17 The arrangement illustrated is that used on later models (from chassis No. FY107261 onwards), which have two spacers, indicated by the arrows, between the mounting cross-member and the underbody in order to lower the rear of the gearbox slightly to improve the flow of oil to the bush in the rear cover. There had been cases of this bush failing on earlier cars, due to insufficient lubrication. If this modification has not been incorporated fit the two spacers, part No. 91040698, and the two longer mounting bolts, part No. 11499458.

18 After installing the gearbox, adjust the clutch cable as described in Chapter 13.

9.15 Dismantling the engine

Materials: Paraffin. Rags. Cleaning brushes. Boxes and tins to hold parts. Marking paint.
Tools: Spanners. Sockets, including a $\frac{7}{16}$ in. AF 'flank-drive' or 'surface' socket. Pliers. Screwdrivers. Soft-faced hammer. Scriber, if marking paint is not used.

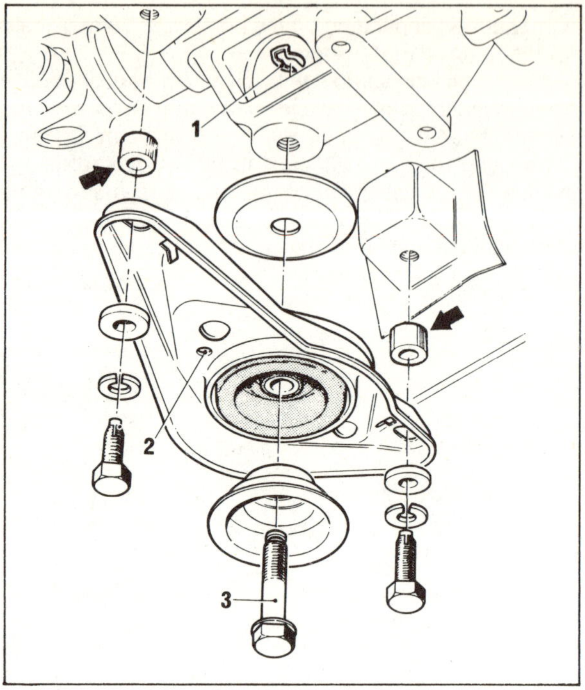

Fig. 9.14 The rear mounting for the engine and gearbox. The clip **1** secures the centre bolt **3.** The hole **2** must be on the right-hand side of the car. The arrows indicate the modified spacing washers mentioned in the text

1 Remove the gearbox, if this has been lifted out with the engine.

2 Drain the engine oil if this has not already been done.

3 Remove the fuel pump and distributor, if this has not been done previously.

4 Take off the cylinder head (Section 9.6).

5 Invert the engine and take off the sump and the oil pump.

6 Remove the clutch assembly (Chapter 13) and take off the flywheel.

7 Mark each piston and connecting-rod assembly on the side nearest the camshaft with the cylinder number, before taking off the connecting-rod caps. Do not use a centre-punch or a file, owing to the risk of creating stress points which could lead to subsequent failure. Any existing marks which are found on the rod and cap do not represent any cylinder number sequence.

8 Remove the piston and connecting-rod assemblies, using a special $\frac{7}{16}$ AF 'flank-drive' or 'surface' socket to avoid rounding off the corners of the bolt heads.

9 If it is necessary to separate the pistons from the connecting rods, take them to a Vauxhall dealer. Special equipment is needed to remove and refit the piston pins, which are an interference fit in the connecting rods.

10 Remove the timing case, chain and sprockets (Section 9.17).

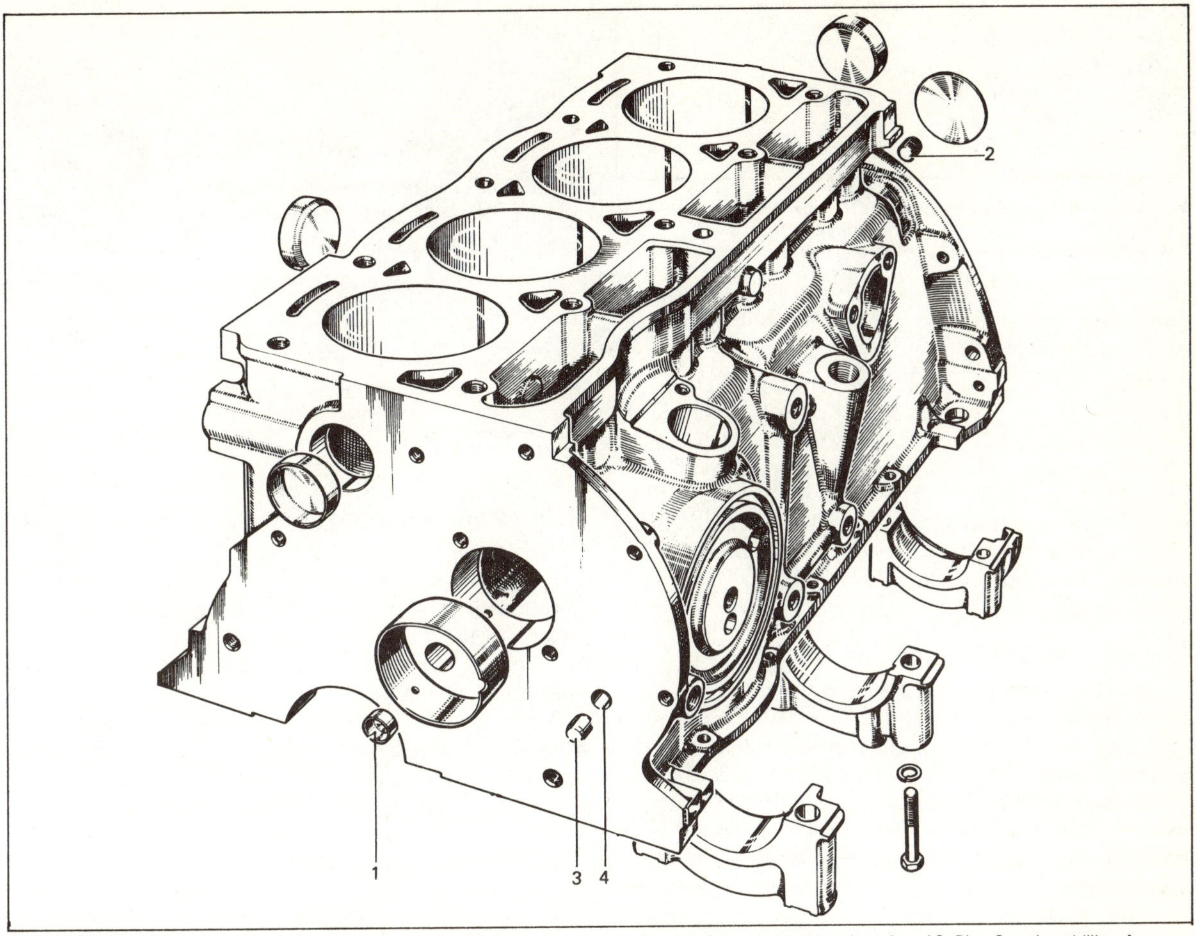

Fig. 9.15 The cylinder block. An oil gallery extends from front to rear of the block and is sealed by the plugs **1** and **2.** Plug **3** seals a drilling **4,** which connects the oilways to the oil warning light switch

11 Rest the engine on its right-hand side and remove the camshaft thrust plate.

12 Remove the camshaft and tappets, keeping the tappets in the correct order. If serviceable, they must be reinstalled in their original bores. Carefully examine the camshaft for signs of wear or scoring on the cams and on the journals, which run in the three bearings in the cylinder block. Also check the skew gear on the camshaft for wear or damage. If any of these faults exist, a new camshaft must be fitted and if the skew gear is worn it is also advisable to fit a new oil-pump driving gear. For further notes regarding the camshaft and its bearings see Section 9.19.

13 Take the suction pipe support off the centre main bearing cap, remove the two larger bolts from the oil pump and take off the pump. For further notes on the pump, see Section 9.20.

14 Remove the main-bearing caps.

15 Check the crankshaft end-play to determine whether it will be necessary to fit new thrust washers, before removing the main bearing caps and shells. Keep the caps (and shells, if new bearings are not to be fitted) in the correct order and mark each cap and its location on the crankcase to ensure correct reassembly.

16 Lift out the crankshaft and remove the remaining halves of the bearing shells and thrust washers. Inspect the main journals and crankpins on the crankshaft for wear, scores and scratches. If a micrometer is not available, have the degree of wear and ovality checked by a specialist. For notes on reconditioning see Chapter 8.

17 Tap the flywheel off its flange evenly, using a copper or lead hammer. Discard the crankshaft oil seal.

18 Thoroughly clean the crankcase, bearing shells, caps and housings and examine all the parts carefully for cracks or other damage. Normally the bearing shells should be renewed as a matter of course.

9.16 Renewing the timing case oil seal

A spring-loaded, lip-type oil seal runs in contact with the boss of the crankshaft pulley. The seal can be renewed without disturbing the timing case.

Materials: New oil seal. Special anti-scuffing paste (obtainable from a Vauxhall dealer).

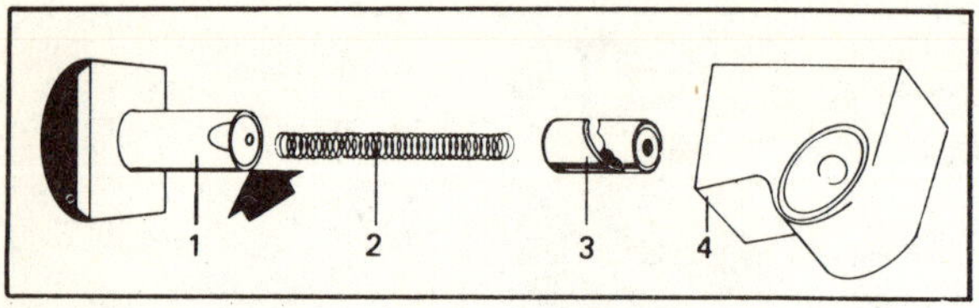

Fig. 9.16 The chain tensioner consists of a sleeve and pad assembly **1**, a spring **2**, the piston **3**, and the body **4**. The pip in the sleeve indicated by the arrow engages with the stepped groove in the piston

Tools: Seal installing tool VR 2092. Spanners. Hooked wire. Punch. Hammer.

1 Remove the anti-roll bar and crankshaft pulley.

2 Drive in one side of the seal to tilt it in the cover and then extract it with a hooked wire.

3 Drive in the replacement seal, open side first, until the front face is 0.24 in. (6mm) below the face of the timing cover, preferably using the special tool VR 2092.

4 Smear the lip of the seal with the special anti-scuffing paste and refit the pulley.

9.17 Servicing the timing chain and tensioner

An automatic tensioner is provided. In order to service the tensioner and to renew the chain it is necessary to take off the timing cover, which entails removal of the engine and the oil sump.

Although this involves a fair amount of work, it is unwise to ignore a noisy chain, since there have been cases of fairly rapid wear on the tensioner in which slackness in the chain has increased to such a degree that the chain can jump one or more teeth on the sprockets, which could lead to expensive damage to the engine.

To service the tensioner –

1 Remove the engine and take off the sump and timing cover.

2 Remove the timing chain and sprockets (Section 9.18). The tensioner can then be dismantled by pulling out the pad assembly, spring and piston from the body.

3 When reassembling the tensioner, insert the spring and the piston in the sleeve of the pad assembly, engaging the pip with the groove in the piston.

4 Press the piston and pad assembly together, turning the piston clockwise until the pip engages in the end of the groove in the piston, holding the piston in the retracted position and allowing the assembly to be installed in the tensioner body.

9.18 Renewing the timing chain

If the timing chain is badly worn and has been running slack for some time it will probably have worn the teeth of the sprockets, which should also be renewed when the new chain is fitted.

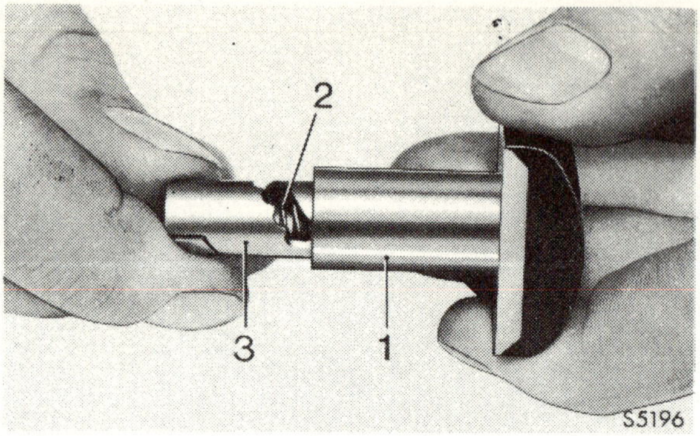

Fig. 9.17 When assembling the chain tensioner insert the spring **2** and the piston **3** into sleeve **1** and engage the pip inside the sleeve with the groove in the piston

Materials and tools: As for Sections 9.16 and 9.17 plus special tool Z8556.

1 Remove the timing cover and the chain tensioner (Sections 9.16 and 9.17). Remove the bolt, washer and locking washer that retain the camshaft sprocket and pull off the crankshaft and camshaft sprockets, complete with the chain.

2 If the chain or the timing sprockets show signs of premature wear, the oil hole in the nozzle in the crankcase is probably obstructed, and the nozzle should be renewed. It is a tight push-fit in the crankcase. The positioning of the discharge hole is not important.

3 When refitting the chain and sprockets, make sure that the dowel 1 in Fig. 9.19 is in the position shown and that the timing marks 2 are lined-up opposite each other.

4 The pad of the tensioner must be held as far as possible into the tensioner body until the chain and camshaft wheels are in position.

5 Refit the timing cover, with the sump and cover bolts finger-tight and insert the special aligning tool Z8556 into the bore of the cover to centralize the oil seal with the crankshaft. If this is not done the seal may have a short life.

9.19 The camshaft and bearings

The camshaft is carried in three renewable bearings in the cylinder block and is located by a thrust plate which engages with a groove in the front journal. If the bearings are worn it is better to allow a Vauxhall dealer to renew them, using suitable tools to avoid damage to the replacement bearings, which are pre-finished to the correct size.

If you decide to do the job for yourself, bear the following points in mind –

1 The rear bearing housing is sealed by an expansion plug. Before driving out the bearing and the plug, the flywheel must be removed.

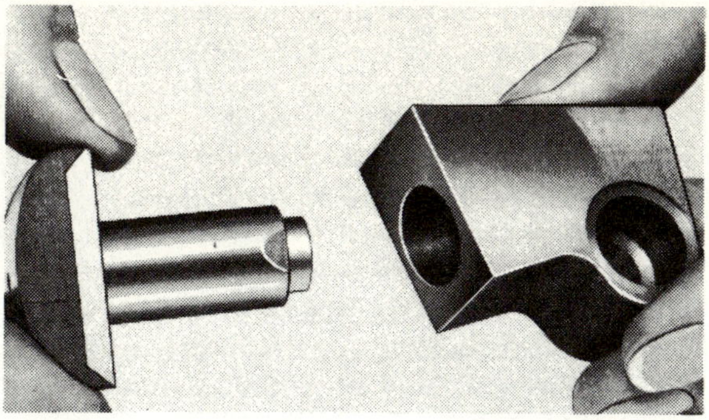

Fig. 9.18 The loaded pad assembly (see Fig. 9.17) can now be installed in the tensioner body

2 When installing the new bearing, check that the oil holes coincide with the oilways in the cylinder block. The notch in each bearing must be towards the front of the block.

3 Fit a new expansion plug in the counterbore of the rear bearing housing, applying jointing compound around the edge of the plug to obtain an oil-tight joint. Tap the plug gently at the centre to expand it into the groove.

4 The centre bearing has two oil holes. The smaller hole must coincide with the oil-feed drilling to the rocker oil galleries in the cylinder head, as shown in Fig. 9.21.

5 When installing the camshaft and tappets, smear them with graphited oil and make sure that the legs of the thrust plate are positioned as shown in Fig. 9.22, to ensure the correct radial location of the timing chain tensioner.

Fig. 9.19 Before fitting the timing chain, check that the dowel **1** is in the position shown and that the timing marks **2** are in line and adjacent to each other

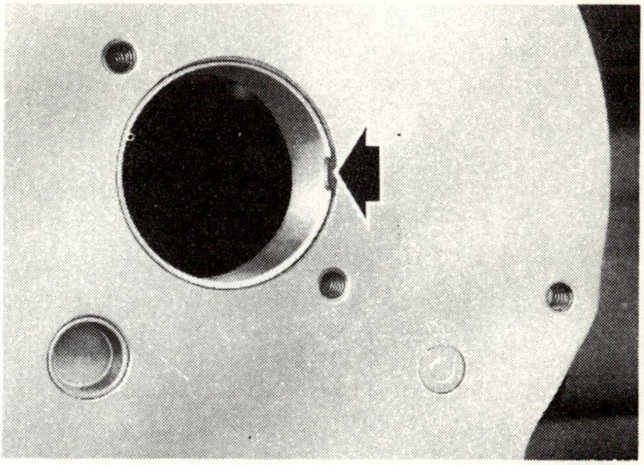

Fig. 9.20 The notch in each camshaft bearing indicated by the arrow should be towards the front of the cylinder block

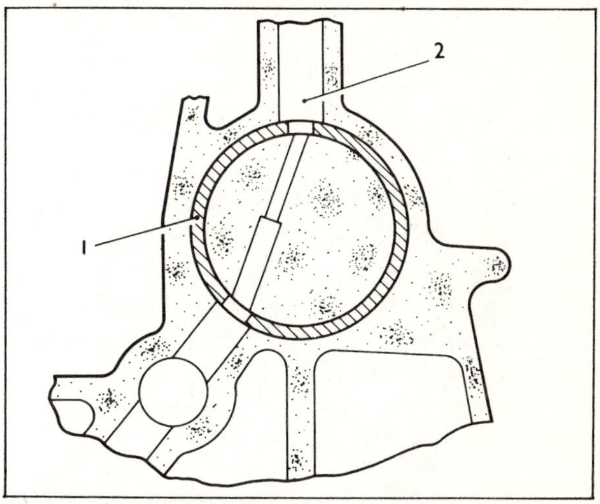

Fig. 9.21 The camshaft centre bearing **1** is identified by two oil holes, the smaller of which must coincide with the oil feed drilling **2** to the rocker oil gallery in the cylinder head

Fig. 9.22 The camshaft thrust plate **1** must be fitted as shown. The position of the oil discharge hole in the oil nozzle **2** is not important

Fig. 9.23 Stages in installing the oil-pump driving shaft. *Top,* align the pointer 2, on the camshaft pulley with the tdc pointer 1, on the crankcase. *Centre,* turn the drive gear until the offset slot in the pump spindle is in the position shown. *Bottom,* after installing the pump, check that the slot has moved to the position A, or is within the range A to B

9.20 Removing and refitting the oil pump

The gear-type oil pump is bolted to the underside of the cylinder block and is driven by a skew gear from the camshaft. If the pump is so worn that the oil pressure is low, it is better to fit a replacement than to attempt to recondition the individual parts.

To remove and refit the pump (with engine sump removed) –

Materials: New pump, if required.
Tools: Spanner.

1 Disconnect the support for the suction pipe from the main bearing cap.

2 Remove the two larger bolts which retain the pump.

3 Before refitting the pump, turn the crankshaft pulley to align the pointer on the pulley with the top-dead-centre indicator on the crankcase (Fig. 9.23) with No. 1 piston on the compression stroke – i.e., with both valves closed.

4 To ensure that the offset in the pump spindle which drives the distributor will be in the correct position when the pump has been installed, turn the driving spindle until the slot is positioned as shown in Fig. 9.23. As the pump driving gear engages with the camshaft gear, the spindle will turn to the position shown in the lower drawing. The offset slot should then be within the range between A and B.

9.21 Reassembling the engine

Materials: Gaskets and replacement parts as specified for a top-overhaul. Oil and air-filter elements. Replacement pistons, rings, bearing shells, thrust washers and other components as required for the stage of overhaul which is to be undertaken – see Chapter 8. Graphite assembly compound. Gasket cement, sealing compounds and anti-scuffing paste – see text.
Tools: Spanners. Pliers. Screwdrivers. Piston-ring clamp. Torque wrench.

Rebuilding the engine is simply a question of reversing the dismantling instructions, observing scrupulous cleanliness at each stage. The following notes will help to ensure a first-class job.

1 If you are fitting an intermediate engine overhaul kit, as described in Chapter 8, you will find that standard-size pistons and bearings are supplied (thus allowing the kits themselves to be standardized). The majority of engines requiring an intermediate overhaul do in fact have standard-size cylinder bores and crankshaft journals, but if your engine has oversize bores or undersize journals, the standard parts will have to be exchanged for the appropriate sizes, so do not unpack the new parts until the engine has been stripped and the sizes of the existing components have been checked.

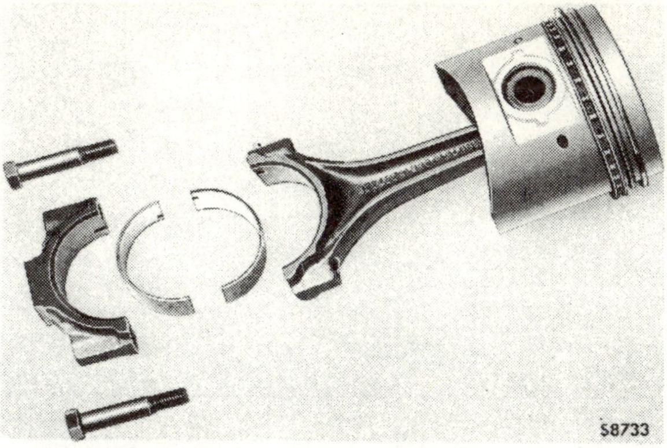

Fig. 9.24 A piston, connecting rod and bearing assembly. The piston pin is an interference fit in the connecting rod, without circlips or a clamping bolt

2 It is possible that oversize pistons may have been fitted when the engine was new, in order to salvage parts which were slightly outside the manufacturing tolerances. So although you may know that the engine has not been rebored, or the crankshaft has not been reground, don't take the sizes for granted.

3 Oversize pistons for use in rebored cylinders are marked on the crown with the appropriate oversize, representing the bore dimension. The correct running clearance has been allowed for and the piston-ring gaps are usually correct.

4 Always use a piston-ring clamp when fitting the pistons. Lubricate the rings, tighten the clamp just sufficiently to compress the rings in the grooves and gently press or tap each piston through the clamp into the *bore, using the handle* of a hammer.

Vauxhall pistons have a notch on the crown which must face the front of the engine.

5 Lubricate all parts with clean engine oil before assembly, or smear the working surfaces with graphite assembly compound, a tube of which is usually included in intermediate engine overhaul kits.

6 The crankshaft end-float is controlled by the flanges on the halves of the centre bearing which are fitted to the crankcase – *not* to the bearing cap. A crankshaft which is 0.010 in. undersize on the main journals or the crankpins – or on both – may have been fitted during production. Replacement shafts, however, are to standard dimensions and the bearings should be ordered against the numbers listed in the parts catalogue, ignoring any discrepancies between the markings on the original bearings and on the replacements. A worn shaft may be reground to not more than 0.040 in. undersize – a job, of course, for a Vauxhall dealer or an engine-reconditioning specialist.

7 Before refitting the crankshaft, smear the lip of the new oil seal and the crankshaft flange with a special anti-scuffing paste (obtainable from your Vauxhall dealer). Do not use engine oil. The outer circumference of the seal should be smeared with Hylomar SQ32/M

Fig. 9.25 The pistons and connecting rods must be withdrawn and refitted through the top of the cylinder block

Fig. 9.26 When lowering the crankshaft into position, push the seal firmly into the groove in the crankcase. Do not allow the weight of the shaft to rest on the lip of the seal

compound. Install the cap within five minutes, as the sealant hardens quickly.

8 Press the seal firmly into its groove while lowering the crankshaft, being careful not to allow the weight of the shaft to rest on the lip of the seal. The centre main bearing cap must be installed with the tapped hole for the oil-pump pipe support towards the camshaft.

9 Before installing the rear main bearing cap, apply a continuous bead of Silastic 732 RTV to the cap register, but leave a gap between the sealant and the vertical face of the cap as shown in Fig. 9.27. Sealant should not be applied to the bearing cap face.

10 When assembling the flywheel Bostik 771 sealer must be smeared around the centre part of the thread

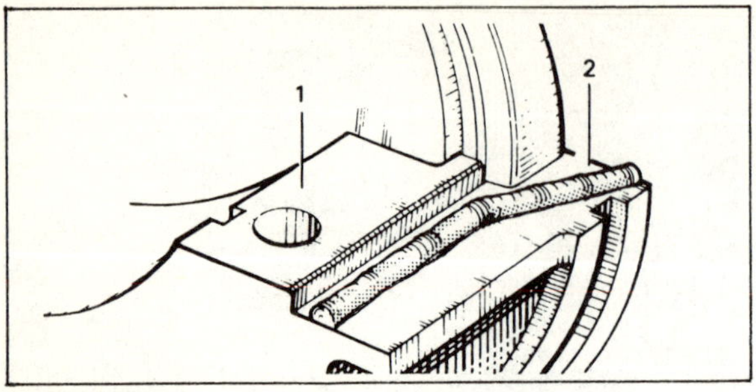

Fig. 9.27 In order to seal the rear main bearing apply an $\frac{1}{8}$ in. bead of Silastic 732 RTV to the cap register **2,** leaving a gap between the sealant and the vertical face. Sealant should not be applied to the upper surface **1**

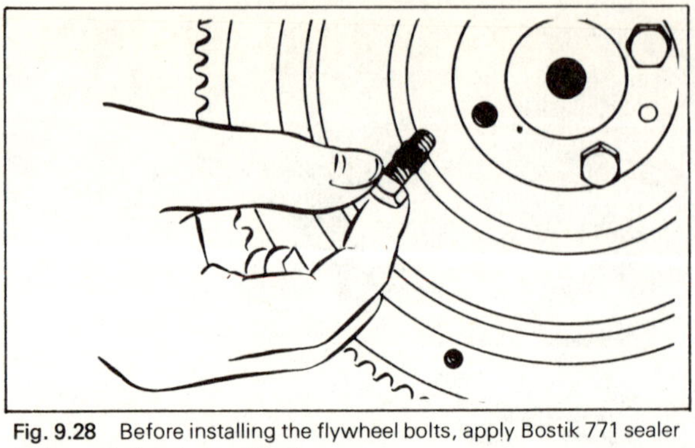

Fig. 9.28 Before installing the flywheel bolts, apply Bostik 771 sealer to the central part of each bolt

of each bolt. Do not apply too much sealer, or use anything but the recommended type, as this may result in the sealer being squeezed out of the forward end of the bolt holes and contaminating the crankshaft oil seal.

11 When refitting the camshaft thrust plate the projections on the plate must be in the position shown in Fig. 9.22, in order to locate the chain tensioner correctly.

12 Before refitting the sump, smear jointing compound on the area of the crankcase and the timing case which contacts the gasket. Seal the ends of the gasket and the crescent-shaped rear seal with Silastic 732 RTV sealer (which hardens quickly, so complete the assembly within five minutes). The ends of the gasket must be fully engaged in the groove in the bearing cap.

13 The crescent-shaped seal should be warmed and shaped to the contour of the bearing cap, with the chamfers facing inwards. The ends of the seal must overlap the gasket by an equal amount on each side and the juction must be sealed with the Silastic sealer.

14 To ensure the correct friction-grip between the transmission brace and the bracket on the sump, an internally toothed locking washer must be fitted between the brace and the bracket.

15 If any of the bolts which attach the engine mountings to the crankcase are disturbed, Loctite grade 270 AVV must be applied to the threads of the front engine mounting bolts to prevent them working loose. Clean the threads on the bolts and in the crankcase thoroughly before applying the Loctite.

16 Always use new locking washers, split-pins and tab washers. As a precaution it is advisable to fit new big-end bolts. Tighten all nuts and bolts to the recommended torque figures (Chapter 17).

9.22 Removing and refitting the sump

Normally, the sump is only likely to be removed when attention to the crankshaft, main and connecting-rod bearings or the pistons is necessary and these jobs should be done with the engine out of the car.

It is possible to remove the sump, however, by raising the engine to give sufficient clearance. This entails disconnecting the radiator hoses and the steering-gear coupling, removing the four bolts which secure the steering gear to the axle cross-member and removing the engine mountings. When refitting the sump, pay particular attention to obtaining an oil-tight seal as described in items 12 and 13 in Section 9.21.

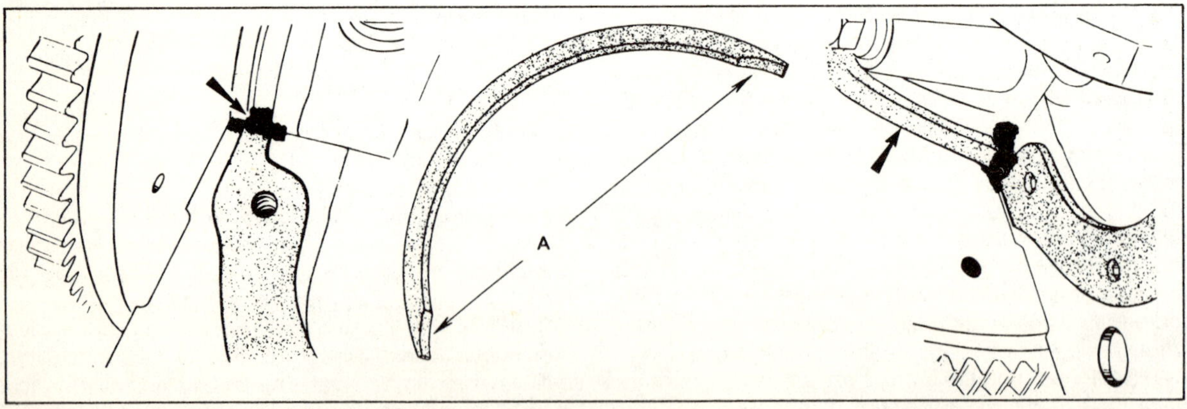

Fig. 9.29. Correct sealing of the sump gaskets is important. *Left,* apply Silastic 732 RTV sealer to the corners of the rear main bearing cap seal groove and the crankcase. *Centre,* warm the sump rear seal and shape it to the contour of the bearing cap, with the chamfers A, facing inwards. *Right,* the ends of the seal indicated by the arrow must overlap the gasket by an equal amount on each side and the junctions must be sealed with Silastic 732 RTV.

10 The cooling system

A pressurized water cooling system is used on all Chevettes. The radiator filler cap incorporates a spring-loaded valve which opens when the pressure in the system reaches about 15 lb/sq in. (1.1 kg/cm²), maintaining the coolant at well above atmospheric pressure and thus raising the boiling point to about 125°C (257°F) and reducing the risk of 'brew-ups' on steep hills and in traffic jams.

A second spring-loaded valve in the expansion tank cap works in the opposite direction to the main valve, preventing the development of a vacuum in the cooling system when the engine cools down. If this valve were not provided, the hoses would collapse and the radiator might be damaged.

The coolant (normally a mixture of water and anti-freeze solution) is circulated by a pump which is mounted at the front of the cylinder head. It is drawn from the base of the radiator, forced through the cylinder head and cylinder block and returned to the header tank at the top of the radiator. A current of air is blown through the radiator by a fan which is driven by a vee-belt from the crankshaft pulley.

The fan is driven by a viscous coupling which is filled with oil, allowing a direct drive up to an engine speed of about 1000 rpm but 'slipping' progressively at higher speeds, thus reducing fan noise and the amount of power required to drive the fan.

A thermostat (Fig. 10.2) is provided to restrict the flow of water to the radiator until the engine reaches its normal running temperature.

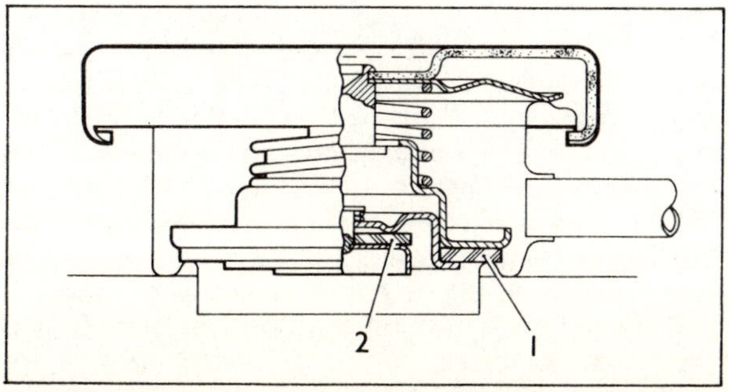

Fig. 10.1 The radiator filler cap incorporates a pressure valve **1** and a vacuum valve **2**, maintaining a pressure of 15 lb/sq in. (approximately 1 bar) in the cooling system when the engine is hot

The time factor

Routine jobs such as topping-up or flushing the system, checking for leaks and so on, do not call for pre-planning. Suggested times for other jobs are: Removing and refitting thermostat, 40 min; removing and refitting radiator, 1 hr; fitting a new fan belt, 30 min; adjusting fan belt tension, 15 min; fitting a new water pump, including removing the radiator, 1½ hr.

10.1 Topping up the system

The water level should normally be checked when the system is cold. If the engine is hot, place a cloth over the filler cap and turn it *slowly* until the safety stop is reached. *Allow all steam or air pressure to escape*.

If frequent topping-up is needed, check the system for leaks (see following section). Always use a water/anti-freeze solution in the correct proportions (see Section 10.3) for topping-up. If plain water is used the concentration of anti-freeze and the special corrosion inhibitors which it contains will be progressively weakened.

10.2 Checking for leaks

It is often difficult to trace the source of a small leak which necessitates frequent topping-up of the expansion tank. Perished water hoses are likely culprits. Get the engine really hot and rev it up while carefully examining each hose. It is a good plan to renew the hoses and the pressure cap every two years.

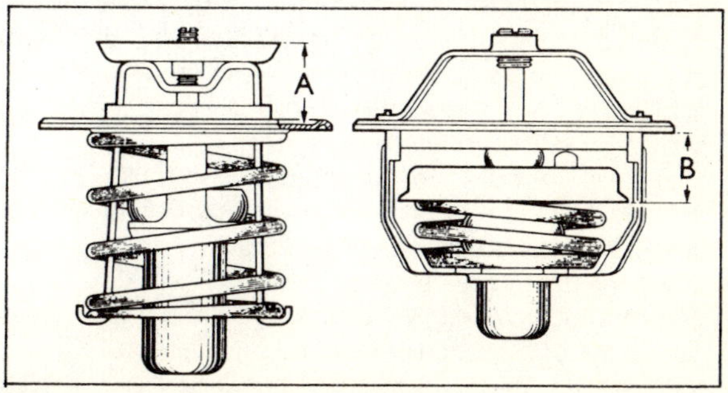

Fig. 10.2 Alternative types of thermostat: left, Western Thomson; right, AC. A and B show the fully-open position when the thermostat is immersed in water heated to the temperature given in Chapter 17

Sometimes internal seepage occurs past the cylinder-head gasket. Tighten the cylinder-head nuts progressively, *using a torque wrench, to the torque quoted in Chapter 17.* If necessary, ask a garage to do this for you.

A preparation known as Bars Leaks, obtainable from garages and accessory shops, will usually cure internal seepages and external leaks very effectively. It is an inexpensive precaution to add it to the cooling water whenever the system is flushed-out and refilled.

10.3 Using anti-freeze

A first-class, fully-inhibited anti-freeze can be left in the system for two years, but it is better to drain it off each spring, flush-out the system and refill with new anti-freeze (Section 10.4), since the anti-corrosion inhibitors which are incorporated in the ethylene-glycol mixture slowly lose their effectiveness.

There will be no risk of a cracked cylinder block or a damaged radiator if an anti-freeze mixture is used in the proportions recommended in the accompanying table, but the solution will form ice crystals at low temperatures which will prevent an adequate flow through the water pump and may cause severe overheating.

In these conditions the engine must be run at a brisk idle for at least five minutes after being started from cold, to allow the system to warm-up. To obtain complete protection at very low temperatures, equal volumes of anti-freeze and water are required. Except in arctic conditions, it will then be safe to drive the car away immediately after a cold start.

Protection give by anti-freeze mixtures

Anti-freeze (per cent in water)	Crystals begin to form		Solution is frozen solid	
	°C	°F	°C	°F
25	-13	9	-26	-15
33⅓	-19	-2	-36	-33
50	-36	-33	-48	-53

If the system has been topped-up with plain water during the summer months instead of with a solution of water and anti-freeze, the effectiveness of the remaining anti-freeze should be checked by using a special hydrometer (most garages should have this) or by drawing off a small quantity and placing it overnight in a plastic container in the freezing compartment of a refrigerator. If the coolant remains fluid after this test, it should be safe for normal use.

Ethylene-glycol anti-freeze is poisonous. In the unlikely event of it being swallowed it can cause serious illness or even death. Never take risks — for example, don't try to start a siphoning action by sucking at the end of a tube dipped in the coolant — and always keep the tin out of the reach of children.

10.4 Draining, flushing and refilling the system

A drain plug is provided in the right-hand side of the cylinder block and this must be removed if it is necessary to drain the system completely. When refitting the plug, apply a non-setting jointing compound, such as Hylomar SQ32/M, to the threads to prevent any seepage of coolant.

As is the case with the majority of cars nowadays, there is no drain plug or tap in the base of the radiator and it is therefore necessary to disconnect the bottom hose at the radiator stub-pipe in order to drain the system.

If the heater is inefficient after the system has been drained and refilled, there is probably an air-lock in the element. To clear this, set the heater control to 'Hot' and detach the hose from the heater control valve. With the radiator cap in place, hold the end of the hose higher than the heater and using a funnel, pour water into the hose until it overflows from the valve. Refit the hose to the valve, run the engine and check for leakage.

If straightforward flushing does not cure a persistent case of overheating ask a garage to remove the thermostat and reverse-flush the cylinder block and radiator separately, using a special flushing gun fed with water and air under pressure.

10.5 Checking the thermostat

As explained earlier, the thermostat regulates the cooling-water temperature. It therefore has a vital effect on the engine efficiency and the fuel consumption. Thermostats, of course, are not infallible and if overheating occurs, or if the engine is slow to warm-up, it is logical to check this item; but remember that overheating can be caused by a number of other faults (see the chart in Chapter 5).

Many authorities recommend that the thermostat should be changed every two years, as corrosion, deposits of sludge or hard scale, or a distorted valve, can all cause sluggish action.

To check the thermostat —

1 Drain the cooling system to below the level of the thermostat.

2 Remove the securing nuts and remove the thermostat cover (Fig. 10.6) to allow the thermostat to be extracted. The gasket should preferably be renewed.

3 If the thermostat valve is open, discard the unit and fit a replacement, which should be the correct type — see Chapter 17. If the valve is closed, place the thermostat in a pan of boiling water. If the valve does not open, the thermostat is faulty. If a kitchen thermometer is available, the opening temperature can be checked while heating up the water. Move the thermostat in the pan to ensure an accurate reading — and do not let it rest on the bottom. When a new thermostat is tested, the valve should open at the temperature given in Chapter 17. A used thermostat will give slightly less-precise control of the cooling-water temperature.

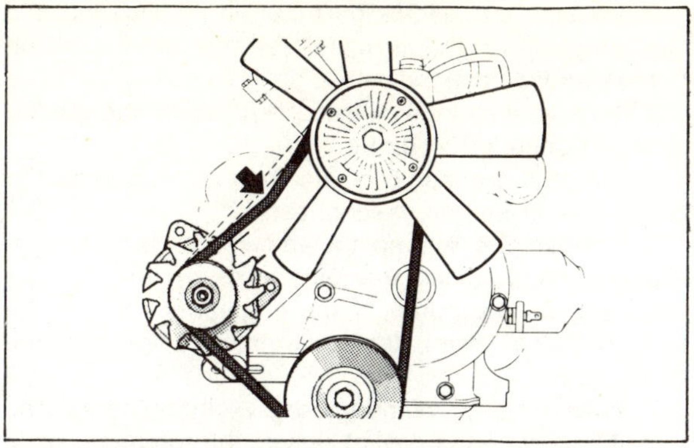

Fig. 10.3 When the tension of the fan belt is correct, it should be possible to depress the belt by thumb pressure at the point shown to the extent of ½ in. (13 mm)

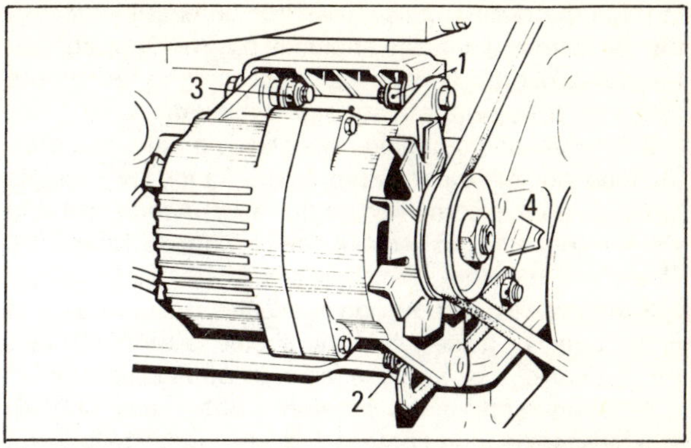

Fig. 10.4 The alternator mounting and strut bolts must be tightened in the correct order: front mounting bolt nut **1**; slotted brace to alternator bolt **2**; rear mounting bolt **3**; and finally the bolt securing the slotted brace to the engine **4**

4 When refitting the thermostat, clean the joint faces of the housing cover and use a new gasket if there is any doubt concering the original. If the flange of the cover or housing is badly corroded fit a new part. The word 'Top' stamped on the flange of the thermostat must be uppermost.

10.6 Adjusting the fan and generator driving belt

The fan belt, which also drives the alternator, must be kept correctly tensioned. It should be possible to deflect the centre of the belt between the generator and fan pulleys by about ½ in. (13 mm), using a very firm thumb pressure. If the belt is too slack, it will slip; if it is too tightly adjusted, an excessive load will be placed on the water pump and generator bearings.

Check and if necessary adjust the tension only when the engine is cold. It may be necessary to use careful leverage to move the dynamo, especially if the pivots and strut are binding, making it difficult to obtain sufficient tension on the belt by hand. *Be careful to lever only on the drive-end bracket.*

The belt must be kept free from grease or oil. If it develops a squeak or a whistle, dust it with French chalk or smear the edges with a little brake fluid or spray them lightly with silicone rubber lubricant from an Aerosol can.

To adjust the tension on the belt –

Tools: $\frac{9}{16}$ in. AF spanner.

1 Slacken the nuts on the two mounting bolts on the generator bracket and the bolt on the adjusting strut at the pulley end of the generator.

2 Swing the generator outwards to increase the tension on the belt, or inwards to decrease it.

3 A split, sliding bush is fitted to the rear mounting lug of the alternator, so that the alternator can be assembled to the mounting bracket without any risk of imposing side loads on the lugs and cracking them. *The nut on the front alternator mounting bolt must be tightened first, followed by the nut on the slotted strut, the rear alternator mounting bolt and finally the pivot bolt for the strut.*

4 If a new fan belt has been fitted, recheck the tension after the first 1000 miles in service. It will probably be found that the belt has stretched slightly.

10.7 Fitting and removing the fan belt

To remove and refit the belt –

1 Slacken the bolts in the alternator pivots and in the adjusting strut and push the generator towards the cylinder block.

2 Remove the belt by easing it over the pulleys.

3 Refit the belt in the same way and adjust the belt tension as described in Section 10.6.

10.8 Removing and refitting the radiator

Home repairs on a leaky radiator are seldom very effective. The header tank and matrix can be repaired by a specialist, but a service-exchange radiator is sometimes cheaper.

To remove the radiator –

1 Drain the cooling system (Section 10.4) and remove the top hose. Disconnect the bottom hose from the water pump, the heater hose and the expansion tank pipe.

2 Remove the screws that retain each radiator bracket at the side of the radiator, and lift the radiator out.

3 When refitting the radiator, take the opportunity to fit new hoses.

4 Fill the system as described in Section 10.4

10.9 Removing and refitting the fan

As mentioned at the beginning of this chapter the fan is driven by an oil-filled viscous coupling, which allows a direct drive up to an engine speed of approximately 1000 rpm, after which the coupling slips progressively.

To check and renew the fan and coupling assembly –

Tools: 6 mm Allen key.

1 As there is no mechanical connection between the

fan and the driving pulley, it should be possible to turn the fan blades when the engine is not running, against the resistance of the viscous coupling. The fan should rotate smoothly without any sign of binding.

2 The fan and coupling assembly is a balanced unit, retained on the water pump pulley flange by a single hexagon socket screw *which has a left-hand thread.* It will be necessary to remove the radiator to reach this screw.

3 As the viscous coupling is a sealed unit, any sign of oil leakage, or noise when the engine is running, calls for renewal of the complete fan and coupling assembly.

4 When refitting the assembly, the screw should, strictly speaking, be tightened to a torque of 14 lb ft but it is unlikely that you will have a suitable 6 mm hexagonal adaptor for a torque wrench. When using a conventional 6 mm Allen key, the specified torque represents a fairly firm pull. Again remember that the screw has a left-hand thread.

10.10 Removing and refitting the water pump

It is possible to dismantle and recondition the water pump, but this is not normally a job for the home garage, since the impeller must be pressed on to the shaft to give a critical clearance between the impeller and the housing.

Also, if the pump seal is worn, the face of the impeller against which it bears is also usually worn, while there will probably be a good deal of erosion of the impeller blades, which affects their efficiency. The most effective course, therefore, is to fit a new pump or a service-exchange unit.

To remove the pump –

Materials: New radiator hoses if the original hoses are more than two years old. Gasket. Jointing compound.
Tools: Spanners.

1 Drain the cooling system.

2 Disconnect the radiator hoses from the pump. To avoid straining the stub-pipe on the radiator header tank and causing a leak, it is best to remove the top hose completely.

3 Slacken the generator mounting bolts and the clamping bolt on the strut, release the tension on the fan belt and remove the belt.

4 Remove the fan, as this makes it easier to undo the bolts that secure the pump.

5 Unscrew the pump retaining bolts and ease the pump away from the cylinder head.

6 Remove the thermostat and check its operation (Section 10.5). Clean the joint faces on the cylinder head and on the pump, if the original pump is to be refitted. Also clean the mounting flange for the thermostat.

7 When refitting the pump, apply jointing compound to both sides of the gasket. Insert the mounting bolts and push the gasket on to them, offer-up the pump to the cylinder block and screw in two of the retaining screws finger-tight to position it while the other screws are started in their threads – a fiddling job, which sounds easier than it usually turns out to be in practice.

8 After refitting the thermostat and completing the reassembly, tension the fan belt (Section 10.6), refill the cooling system and bleed off any air as described in Secton 10.4.

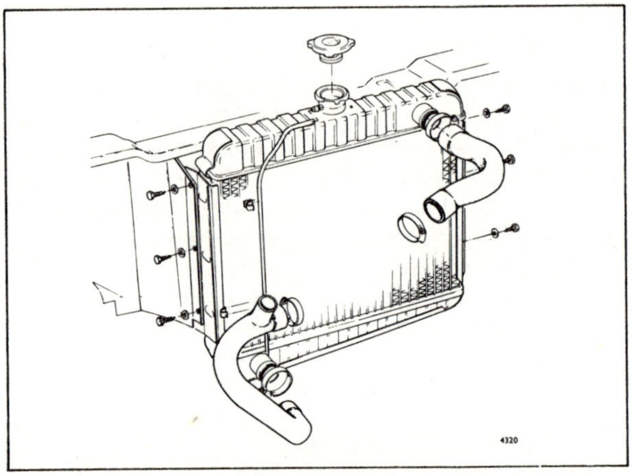

Fig. 10.5 The radiator, hoses and filler cap

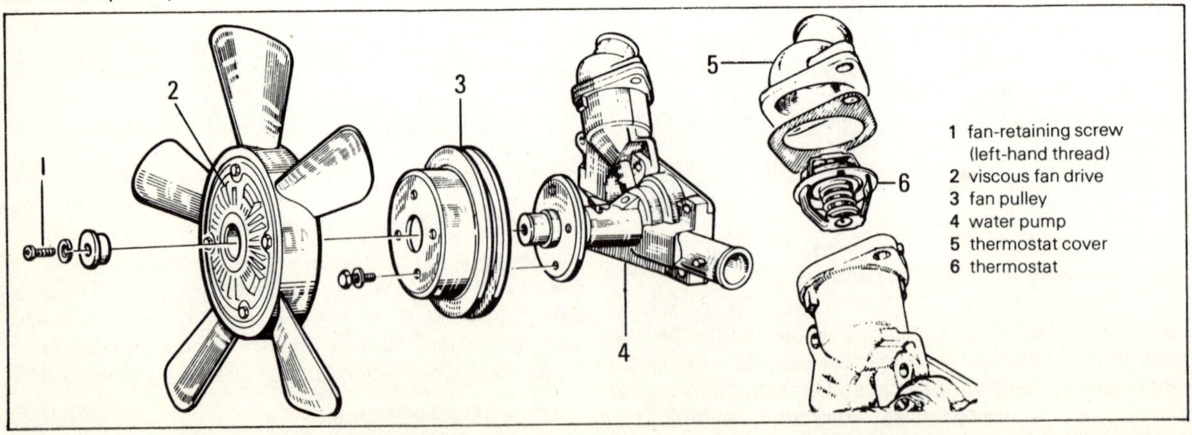

Fig. 10.6 The fan, water pump and thermostat assembly

11 The carburettor and petrol pump

The Zenith-Stromberg 150CD-SEV carburettors fitted to Chevette models are of the constant-depression type. A single jet is used, and the opening at the top of the jet is metered by a tapered needle which is clamped in the base of a piston or air valve which rises and falls as the airflow through the carburettor — which causes a depression and semi-vacuum in the carburettor throat — varies with changes in engine speed and throttle opening.

In this way the amount of petrol drawn from the jet is controlled to give the correct mixture under all running conditions, except for starting from cold, when an extra-rich mixture is needed.

This is provided by a disc-type cold-starting carburettor, rotated by the choke control, which admits fuel through a series of holes of different diameters. At the fully-rich position all the holes communicate with a mixing chamber in the starting carburettor but as the choke is released fewer holes admit fuel, thus weakening the mixture progressively until the starting carburettor is finally put out of action.

A temperature compensator is provided to cater for minor changes in the mixture strength which are caused by heat transferred from the engine to the carburettor body. This consists of a bi-metal thermostatic blade carrying a tapered plug which controls the amount of air entering the carburettor through bypass drillings. These create an air bleed which affects the depression which controls the rise and fall of the air valve piston and the jet needle, and therefore slightly alters the mixture strength. The compensator is preset and no attempt must be made to adjust it.

There is also an idle trimming screw which allows the mixture to be weakened slightly during the running-in period of a new engine, which can run on a leaner mixture. As running-in progresses the screw should be turned clockwise until finally it is on its seating — see Section 11.5.

The time factor

It is difficult to allot definite times for any carburettor jobs, especially when adjustment and tuning are involved. If you are a perfectionist, for example, it is quite possible to spend a morning or an afternoon on carburettor tuning. Some suggested times are: Remove and refit the carburettor, 1 hr; strip, service and rebuild the carburettor, 1 hr; tune the carburettor, 45 min; remove and refit the fuel pump, 30–40 min; change the air cleaner element, 15–30 min.

Materials and tools required

The only tools needed for the work described in this chapter are a screwdriver, a pair of pliers and the special wrench VR2156 mentioned in Section 11.5, which is needed to adjust Zenith-Stromberg 150CD-SEV carburettor only.

Gaskets and other spares can be obtained as required or a carburettor overhaul kit can be purchased. The only other materials needed will be some petrol and clean cloths.

Routine maintenance

Before dealing with carburettor servicing and adjustment, we can dispose of the simple routine maintenance jobs for the carburettor and petrol pump.

11.1 Topping-up the carburettor piston damper — Zenith-Stromberg carburettors

There is a small hydraulic damper, consisting of a piston, fitted with a one-way valve and working in an oil-filled recess, in the depression-chamber cover that forms the upper part of the carburettor. The damper prevents the carburettor piston from rising too quickly when the throttle is opened suddenly, which would cause an unduly weak mixture and a 'flat spot' during acceleration. The damper also prevents the piston 'fluttering' under certain running conditions.

To top-up the damper—

1 Remove the air-cleaner element.

2 Unscrew the plastic cap and withdraw the damper.

3 Insert a finger in the air intake and lift the air valve so that the level of the oil in the hollow guide rod can be checked. It should be within $\frac{1}{4}$ in. (6 mm) below the top of the hollow guide rod. If necessary, top-up with 10W/30 engine oil *only*.

4 When refitting the damper, the small collar surrounding the damper rod must be fitted into the guide rod. To do this, insert the damper in the guide rod, allow the air valve to drop, screw down the plastic cap and again lift the air valve in order to press the collar into the hollow guide rod. Check that it is properly seated by lifting the air valve and unscrewing and raising the plastic cap just sufficiently to allow the top of the guide rod to be seen.

11.2 Renewing the carburettor air-cleaner element

The air-filter element should be changed during the 12 000-mile service, or earlier if the car is operating in very dusty conditions or if the element has acquired a greasy coating, caused by condensed crankcase fumes. A clogged air filter will reduce engine performance and increase the petrol consumption.

To change the element without taking off the air cleaner –

1 The temperature-controlled air cleaner is attached to two studs in the carburettor intake flange by internally threaded bolts, but it is not necessary to remove the cleaner in order to change the element.

2 Take off the top cover, which is retained by six screws, lift out the old element and install the new one. The rubber sealing ring must be downwards, towards the air cleaner body. To prevent incorrect assembly the upper side of the element may be marked 'Up'.

11.3 Checking the warm-air control in the air cleaner

The temperature of the air entering the air cleaner is regulated by a flap valve in the air intake which is controlled by a vacuum-operated diaphragm. A temperature sensor in the air cleaner housing, connected by pipes to the inlet manifold and to the diaphragm unit, varies the strength of the vacuum which is applied to the diaphragm.

When the engine is started from cold and the temperature of the air in the air cleaner is below 33°C (91.4°F), the air-bleed valve in the sensor unit is closed and the full inlet manifold vacuum is applied, moving the flap so that it closes the cold-air inlet and opens the hot-air port, which is connected by an air hose to a shroud on the exhaust manifold.

As soon as the exhaust manifold begins to warm up, the sensor bleeds air into the vacuum pipe, allowing the valve to begin to uncover the cold-air port and mixing the warm and cold air to maintain the ideal air intake temperature of 40°C, plus or minus approximately 7°C (104°F, plus or minus 12.6°F). This is important, as the emission-controlled carburettor is specially calibrated for an air supply within this temperature range.

When the car is accelerating, however, the wider throttle opening used will reduce the vacuum in the inlet manifold and the diaphragm return spring will move the valve to open the cold-air port fully, thus allowing the maximum flow of cool air needed for full-power operation.

A fault in the sensor or in the diaphragm unit usually results in the cold-air port remaining open. This may not

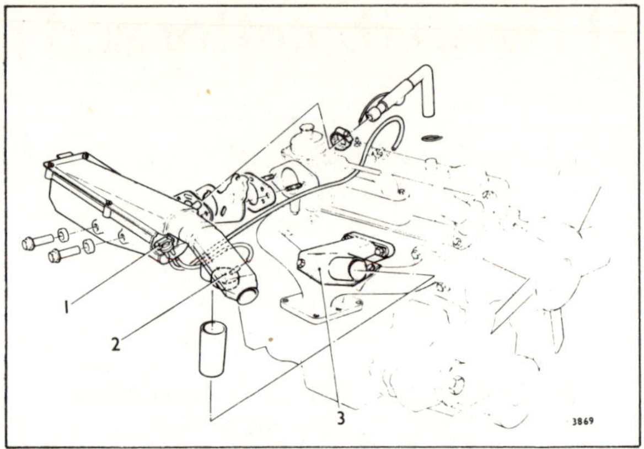

Fig. 11.1 The heated carburettor air intake incorporates a temperature sensor **1**, a vacuum motor **2** which controls a flap valve, and an exhaust-heated muff **3**

be noticed in warm weather but will cause hesitation or stalling in cold weather.

To check the operation of the valve –

1 Check that the air hoses and vacuum pipes are properly connected and undamaged. The vacuum pipes must not be kinked.

2 Using a mirror and a torch if necessary, and with the engine cold and not running, check the position of the flap valve. The cold-air port should be fully open, giving a free passage through the open intake.

3 Start the engine and allow it to idle. The cold-air port should immediately be closed. Open the throttle and check that the flap valve opens as the engine accelerates. When the engine has reached its normal running temperature the cold-air port should be partially or fully open, depending on the air temperature in the engine compartment.

4 If the valve does not seem to be operating correctly the vacuum motor can be tested by pulling the vacuum tube off the connection to the sensor in the air cleaner housing and sucking at the end of the tube. This should cause the flap valve to close the cold-air port and open the hot-air port. If it does not do so, check that there is no air leakage and that the linkage is not binding.

5 While still sucking at the end of the tube, kink the hose and pinch it to trap the vacuum in the motor assembly. The valve should remain with the cold-air port closed. If it does not, there is a vacuum leak in the diaphragm unit and as the motor assembly cannot be repaired, a new vacuum motor and intake tube must be fitted.

6 The operation of the sensor can be checked by removing the air-cleaner element and taping a small dial thermometer inside the air cleaner housing as close to the sensor as possible. Allow the engine to cool down for at least 30 minutes before fitting the thermometer. Then start the engine and check that the cold-air port is closed. When the valve opens this port – which should happen within a few minutes of starting the engine – remove the air cleaner cover or the intake elbow and

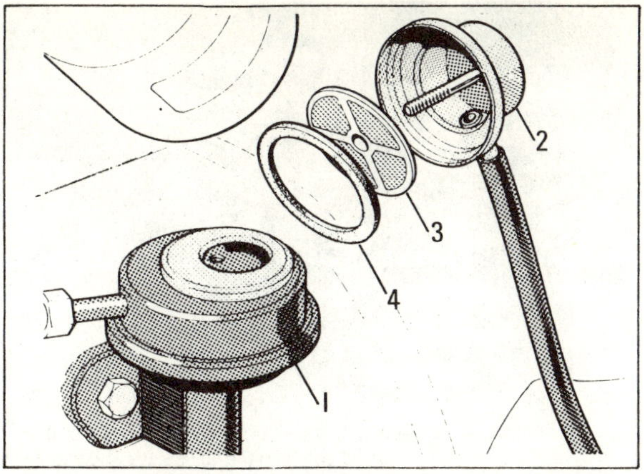

Fig. 11.2 The petrol pump **1** is a sealed unit, except for the filter cover **2**, the filter gauze **3** and the sealing ring **4**

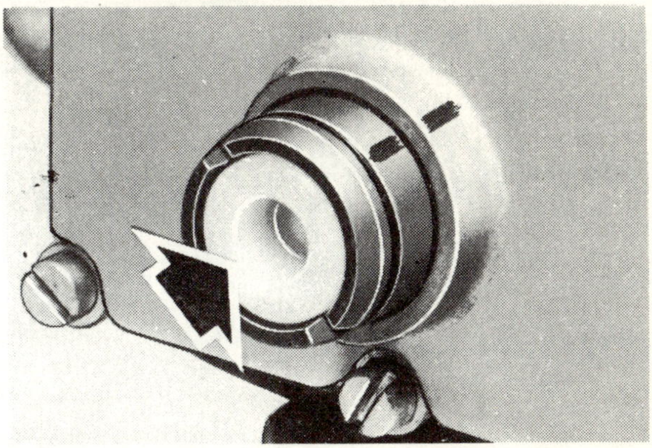

Fig. 11.3 The jet adjuster is sealed by the nylon plug indicated by the arrow, which should not be removed. The tool shown in Fig. 11.4 fits the notches in the adjuster

check the reading on the thermometer. It should be between 33-47°C (91-116.6°F).

7 If the sensor is faulty it can be removed by detaching the metal clip. It cannot be repaired, so a new unit must be fitted.

11.4 Cleaning the petrol-pump filter

The petrol pump is mounted accessibly on the left-hand side of the engine. The body of the fuel pump is sealed. Only the top cover can be removed to allow the filter gauze to be cleaned, so there is no option regarding renewal of the pump if it causes trouble.

To clean the filter –

1 Thoroughly clean the petrol pump externally and remove the setscrew that retains the filter cover.

2 Check the condition of the cork sealing washer. An air leak at the filter-cover flange is one of the most common causes of petrol starvation, due to insufficient output from the pump. Renew the gasket if there is the slightest doubt about its condition.

3 Lift the gauze filter out of its recess. Mop out any water or sediment which has accumulated in the base of the filter chamber. Swill the gauze filter in petrol but do not use a fluffy rag or a wire brush to clean it.

4 Check the soundness of the petrol-pipe connections and look for any signs of petrol leakage.

5 Refit the filter gauze, sealing-washer and cover, run the engine for a few minutes and re-check the filter for any signs of leakage. This test will show up a faulty sealing ring or a distorted cover, caused by over-tightening the retaining screw.

Slow-running adjustments

The increasingly stringent regulations concerning exhaust-gas pollution which have been introduced during recent years have resulted in the development of precisely-calibrated versions of Zenith-Stromberg carburettors.

There should be no need to alter the pre-set idling mixture adjustment during normal carburettor servicing, but adjustment of the mixture strength will, of course, be needed if the carburettor has been completely stripped.

It is for this reason only that we include notes on the adjustment of emission-controlled carburettors and it must be stressed that the final setting should, if possible, be left to a Vauxhall dealer, since the regulations affecting emission-controlled engines call for the use of a carbon monoxide (CO) meter, which is clipped to the exhaust pipe. The percentage of carbon monoxide in the exhaust gas, with the engine at its normal operating temperature, should be 2.5–3.5 per cent.

11.5 Slow-running adjustments on Zenith-Stromberg carburettors

The throttle-stop screw controls the idling speed and the jet-adjusting screw regulates the mixture strength. When turned clockwise it weakens the mixture.

These carburettors also have an idle trimming screw which regulates an air bleed. This may have to be slightly open during the running-in period but should subsequently be closed to restore smooth idling. On no account should it be overtightened.

The jet adjuster is sealed by a nylon plug, which should not be removed. The flange of the adjuster has two notches which allow it to be rotated, preferably using wrench No. VR2156, which has two pegs which engage with the notches in the adjuster.

Fig. 11.4 The special tool VR2156 can be used to rotate the jet adjuster, although this is not essential

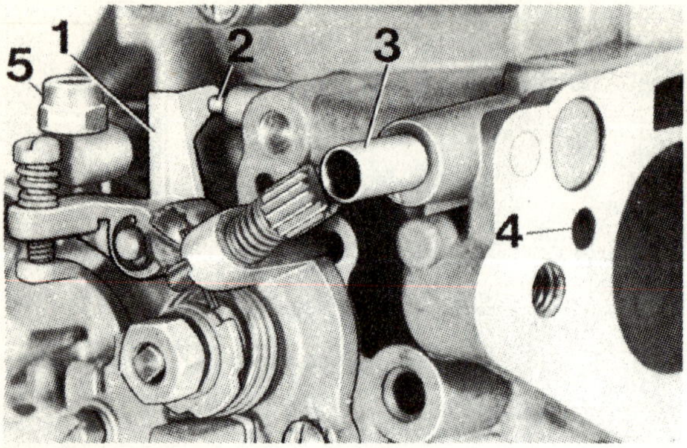

Fig. 11.5 The float chamber ventilation valve is controlled by the lever **1** which operates the valve **2**, allowing the petrol vapour to escape through the outlet **3**. When the valve is closed venting is by the passage **4**. The stop-screw **5** allows the valve to be adjusted

Fig. 11.6 To adjust the ventilation valve turn the stop-screw **1** until a 2 mm (No.46) drill can be inserted between the valve lever and the stop-screw post. It may be necessary to reset the throttle stop-screw **2** to restore the correct idling speed

The initial setting of the adjuster is about two turns down from the fully-in position. The idle-speed trimming screw (Fig. 11.8) should not be more than four turns from the fully-closed position to begin with and final adjustment should be made with the engine hot, and with the idle speed trimming screw two turns off its seat.

Never set the mixture strength when a carburettor is overheated – for example, after the car has been standing for some time with the engine hot and the bonnet closed. There is a risk that the mixture will be set too weak and this may damage the exhaust valves and pistons.

If satisfactory idling cannot be obtained when the adjusting screw is within half-a-turn up or down from the starting position (see 2 and 3 below), check that the shoulder on the needle is flush with the base of the air-valve piston and that the securing screw is tight. See Section 11.8.

1 It is best to begin the adjustment from a basic setting. Bring the engine up to its normal working temperature, remove the air cleaner, unscrew and remove the hydraulic dashpot plunger and insert a pencil in the bore so that the air valve can be held down on to its seating on the bridge in the throttle passage.

2 Screw the jet adjustment screw upwards until the jet just contacts the underside of the air valve, as indicated by increased resistance to screwing-up the jet. If the jet screw is stiff to turn, it is difficult to judge when it makes contact with the air valve. In this case, shine a torch beam into the carburettor intake, lift the air valve, and screw the jet until its edge is just flush with the bridge. Then screw it down by two turns.

3 Top-up the dash-pot, refit the hydraulic damper. Check that the air valve falls freely on to the bridge when lifted and released. If it does not, see Section 11.8.

4 Start the engine, run it until it has regained its normal temperature and then adjust the throttle-stop screw to give smooth idling at a speed of 800-850 rpm.

5 If the exhaust note is irregular, lift the air valve of the carburettor a very small amount – *not exceeding* $\frac{1}{32}$ in. – with the tip of a penknife blade or a thin screwdriver. If the engine speed rises appreciably, the mixture supplied is too rich. If the engine stops, the mixture is too weak.

11.6 Adjusting the cold-starting setting

The spring-loaded stop pin (shown in Fig. 11.7) is normally set fully 'in', with the pin vertical, for all temperatures down to −18°C. In very cold climates, a richer mixture can be obtained by turning the pin to the horizontal position so that it engages with the groove in the housing.

11.7 Adjusting the float chamber ventilation valve

At engine speeds above the fast-idle setting the petrol vapour in the float chamber is drawn through a drilling in the carburettor flange into the air cleaner. At lower speeds, however, the vapour escapes externally through the outlet shown in Fig. 11.5, when the ventilation valve is opened by a lever which is operated by the throttle linkage.

If necessary the ventilation valve can be adjusted by the stop-screw.

To obtain the correct setting –

1 Turn the stop-screw until the shank of a 2 mm (No. 46) drill can just be inserted between the valve lever and the stop-screw post (Fig. 11.6).

2 If necessary readjust the throttle-stop screw to restore the correct engine idling speed.

Carburettor servicing

It is not necessary to strip the carburettor completely during normal servicing, although the 'exploded' drawing shows the relationship of all the parts. It must

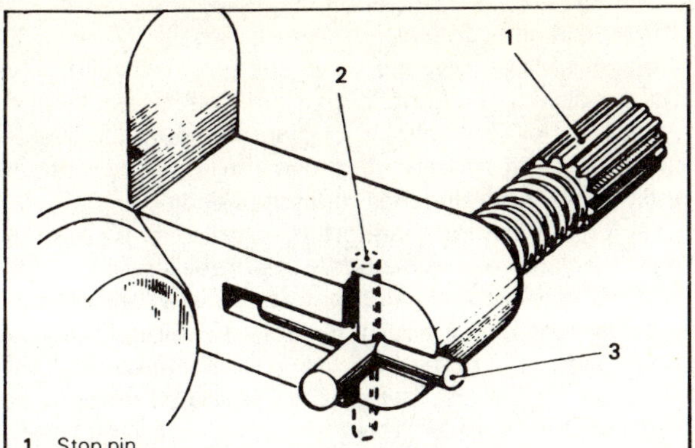

1 Stop pin
2 Normal position
3 Position for very cold weather

Fig. 11.7 Starting carburettor adjuster on a Zenith-Stromberg carburettor

be emphasized that we are dealing here only with normal cleaning and inspection.

Before describing the work an important word of warning must be given: *Never dismantle a carburettor when the engine is hot, owing to the risk of fire – and, of course, do not smoke while working on the carburettor.*

11.8 Servicing Zenith-Stromberg carburettors

The only routine maintenance required is occasional topping-up of the small oil-well in the upper part of the suction chamber and an occasional check on the adjustment of the slow-running mixture strength and the idling speed. At comparatively long intervals – say, once every 12 000 miles or yearly – the suction chamber and the piston should be cleaned and the diaphragm should be checked for cracks or pin-holes.

One of the most likely causes of carburation troubles with a Stromberg carburettor is a cracked or perforated diaphragm. It can be inspected, and renewed if necessary, without removing the carburettor from the engine. At the same time the piston and needle can be checked and cleaned.

To inspect the diaphragm, piston and needle—

1 Remove the depression cover from the top of the carburettor, after taking out the screws.

2 Lift out the piston and detach the diaphragm by removing the screws that clamp the retaining ring.

3 Fit a new diaphragm, if necessary, making sure that the locating tabs on its rim fit into the recesses in the carburettor body and in the upper end of the air-valve piston. The diaphragm retaining-ring must be

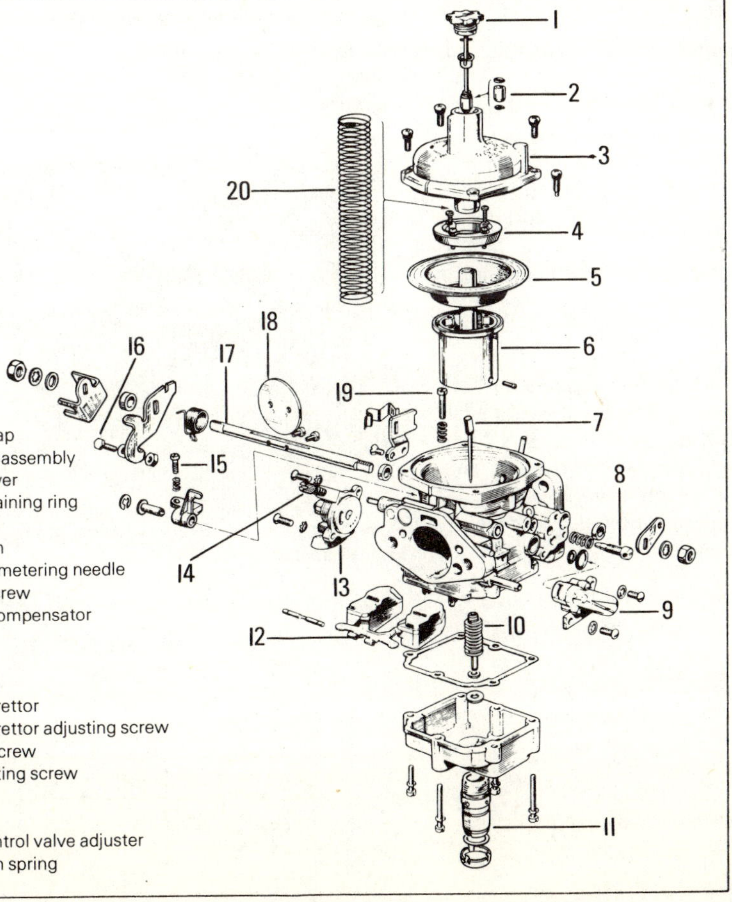

1 damper filler cap
2 damper piston assembly
3 depression cover
4 diaphragm retaining ring
5 diaphragm
6 air-valve piston
7 spring-loaded metering needle
8 idle trimmer screw
9 temperature compensator
10 jet
11 jet adjuster
12 float assembly
13 starting carburettor
14 starting carburettor adjusting screw
15 throttle-stop screw
16 fast-idle adjusting screw
17 throttle shaft
18 throttle disc
19 ventilation control valve adjuster
20 air valve piston spring

Fig. 11.8 The Zenith-Stromberg SEV carburettor dismantled

replaced very carefully. It is easy to displace the diaphragm from its correct position on the air-valve piston.

4 The metering needle should be installed so that the nylon washer is flush with the recessed base of the air-valve piston. The flat which is ground on the needle sleeve must be aligned with the securing screw so that the needle will lean *away* from the depression holes in the base of the valve. Be careful not to overtighten the securing screw, as this will distort the needle sleeve.

5 The piston-return spring must not be stretched or shortened. It has a critical effect on the mixture strength at all engine speeds.

To check the float-chamber level —
If it is not possible to obtain smooth idling after carrying out the adjustments described earlier, the trouble may be due to an incorrect petrol-level in the float chamber of the carburettor.
To check the level —

1 Remove the carburettor from the engine.

2 Take off the float chamber and invert the carburettor so that the highest point of the float above the face of the main body can be measured when the needle valve is resting on its seating. The correct height is 16-17 mm (0.63-0.67 in.).

3 If necessary, reset the level of the float by carefully bending the tag that makes contact with the end of the needle valve.

4 If correct setting of the float does not cure over-richness or flooding, the wisest plan is to renew the needle-valve assembly in the carburettor. These are not expensive items and do not have an unlimited life. It is often advised that they should be renewed after about 20 000 miles. The needle-valve assembly has a small thimble-shaped gauze filter which is not detachable.

To cure a sticking air-valve piston —
Difficult starting and other carburettor troubles can be caused by a sticking air valve. Check for this fault by lifting the valve and allowing it to fall. If it does not fall freely, with an audible click, remove it and clean the sliding portion and the bore in which it works. Use only petrol or paraffin. Do not lubricate the valve and don't be tempted to use emery cloth or metal polish to brighten it up, as the clearance between the valve and the bore is fairly critical.

If, on reassembly, the valve still does not fall freely, the needle may be bent. With a serviceable needle there is intentional light rubbing contact between the needle and the jet in order to improve the regulation of the mixture strength under all running conditions.

The identification mark on the needle can be seen by gently pulling the needle partly out of the sleeve.

If the jet assembly has been dismantled, screw the jet adjuster fully into the carburettor body before fitting the float chamber. Otherwise the chamber may foul the shoulder on the adjuster before it is seated properly on the carburettor body gasket.

To check the temperature compensator —
A temperature compensator is fitted to the side of an emission-controlled carburettor to cater for minor variations in mixture strength that are caused by the transfer of heat from the engine to the carburettor body. To check this —

1 With the engine and carburettor cold, remove the cover and check that the tapered plug is on its seat. Lift the valve carefully and make sure that it returns freely.

2 If the valve is faulty a new compensator must be fitted as a complete assembly. When installing it, check the condition of the rubber seal between the compensator and the carburettor body and the seal in the body.

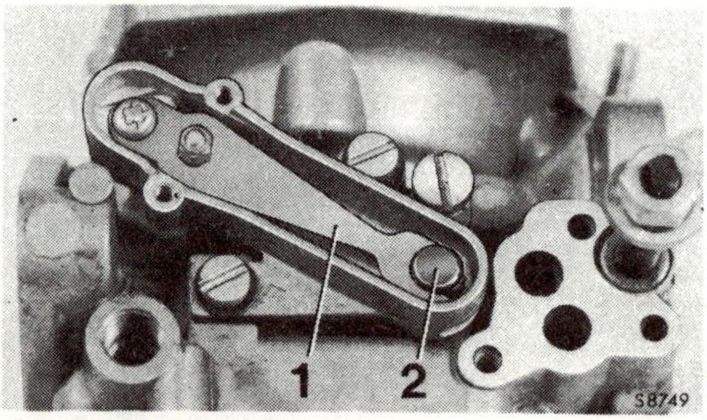

Fig. 11.9 The temperature compensator incorporates a bi-metal thermostatic blade **1**, and a tapered plug **2**, in a housing which is closed by a cover

12 The ignition system

The ignition system shares with the carburettor the doubtful distinction of being responsible for a large percentage of roadside breakdowns, difficult starting, loss of power and heavy fuel consumption. This may seem a depressing catalogue of faults – and the experience of the road patrols of the motoring associations bears it out – but it is equally true to say that given conscientious maintenance, there is no reason why the ignition system should not operate with entire reliability between routine services.

The system consists of a number of related components, all of which play their part in ensuring maximum efficiency. When the engine is running, current flows from the battery through a low-voltage winding in the *ignition coil* to a pair of *contacts* in the *contact-breaker* inside the *distributor,* before returning to the battery through the metal of the engine and body.

The contact-breaker contacts – termed *'points'* – are opened and closed by a *cam* on a shaft in the distributor which is driven by the engine, interrupting the flow of current in the low-voltage winding in the ignition coil and causing a surge of high-voltage current in a *high-tension winding* in the coil. This current is carried by a *high-tension cable* to the central terminal in the moulded plastic *distributor cap,* from which it passes through a spring-loaded carbon contact to a *rotor* mounted on the top of the distributor spindle.

As the rotor turns, its tip passes close to terminals inside the distributor cap, which are connected to the *sparking-plug leads.* At the moment that the contact-breaker points open the correct plug will receive the surge of current. A spark then jumps across the *sparking-plug electrodes,* which project into the combustion chamber, firing the compressed mixture of petrol and air in the cylinder.

12.1 Cleaning and adjusting the sparking plugs

The correct type of plug is given in Chapter 17. Plugs which have similar characteristics are also available from other sparking-plug manufacturers, *but it is essential to make sure that the correct 'heat' grade is used.* Fit new plugs after 10 000 miles (16 000 km) in service.

The use of a garage plug-cleaner is the only really effective method of removing carbon and deposits from the internal surfaces and insulator.

To check the sparking-plug gaps and re-set them if necessary –

1 Pull off the connectors and unscrew the plugs. Since the plugs are mounted at an angle and space is very restricted, it is not possible to use most types of plug spanner without the risk of breaking the insulation on a plug. Garages have devised various methods of coping with this difficulty, one scheme being to use a $\frac{9}{16}/\frac{5}{8}$ in. AF spanner on the plug, and to turn it with a $\frac{13}{16}/\frac{7}{8}$ in. AF ring spanner. If in doubt, ask your local Vauxhall dealer for his suggestions.

2 Clean the electrodes or 'points' with a wire brush. If the internal insulators are dirty, or the plugs have been in service for more than 5000 miles (8000 km) have them cleaned by a garage.

3 Set the gap between the points to 0.030 in. (30 thousandths of an inch, 0.75 mm), using an inexpensive gauge and setting tool such as the Champion gap-servicing tool sold by accessory shops, and bending the *side* electrode only.

4 Clean the threaded portion of each plug with a stiff brush and smear a trace of graphite grease on the threads.

5 Blow or wipe any dust or grit out of the plug recesses in the cylinder head. Make sure that the sealing washers are in place and screw the plugs home by turning the plug spanner *without using the tommy-bar.* Use the bar only for the final half-turn to ensure a

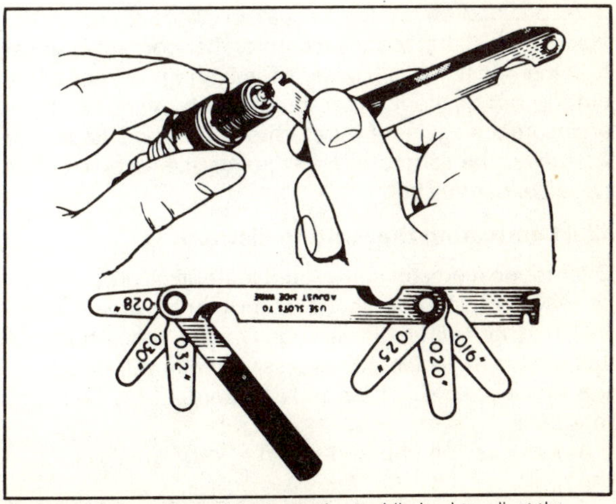

Fig. 12.1 Using a Champion gap-setting tool (below) to adjust the sparking-plug gap. The tool also contains an electrode file

gastight joint. Over-tightening is unnecessary and is likely to lead to trouble. If the plugs cannot be easily screwed in by hand, ask your garage to clean-up the threads in the cylinder head with a plug-thread tap.

12.2 Ingition coil and high-tension leads

Although the Chevette is fitted with a 12-volt electrical system, during normal running the ignition coil operates on a voltage of 5–6 volts. It is fed through a resistance wire which is incorporated in the wiring harness.

When the starter motor is operating, however, the current is fed directly to the coil from the starter-motor solenoid switch, by-passing the resistance. The coil thus receives at least 8 volts during starting, after allowing for the voltage drop caused by the heavy current which is drawn by the starter motor. This provides a much better spark, especially in cold weather. The white wire is the resistance wire for normal running.

A neoprene cap is fitted to the top of the ignition coil. Make sure that the high-tension wire is pushed fully down into the centre of the coil and that the cap is also pushed down snugly. Otherwise the cap tends to raise the wire slightly in its socket, leading to sparking which will quickly burn away the contact terminal.

Test the high-tension leads between the coil and the distributor and between the distributor cap and the sparking plugs for surface cracks by doubling the cable between the fingers. Renew the leads if necessary. If they are the modern resistance type — as they should be, to prevent electrical interference with radios and television sets — change them after two years.

12.3 The ignition capacitor

An inefficient capacitor will cause rapid burning of the contact-breaker points and a weak spark or — if it should short-circuit internally — failure of the plugs to fire at all.

Test by substituting a new capacitor for the doubtful one, but first check for a break or short-circuit in the flexible lead that connects it to the contact-breaker terminal post — a cause of misfiring or complete cutting-out of the ignition that is often overlooked. As an insurance against future trouble, fit a new capacitor whenever the contact-breaker points are renewed. It is not an expensive item.

12.4 Lubricating the ignition distributor

Over-lubrication can cause trouble. If oil or grease finds its way on to the contact-breaker points, it will cause misfiring and difficult starting. On the other hand, if lubrication is neglected, excessive wear will occur on the moving parts, or the moving contact-breaker arm may stick.

1 Remove the cap and pull the rotor off the end of the shaft.

2 Put two or three drops of oil on the felt pad in the hollow end of the rotor shaft.

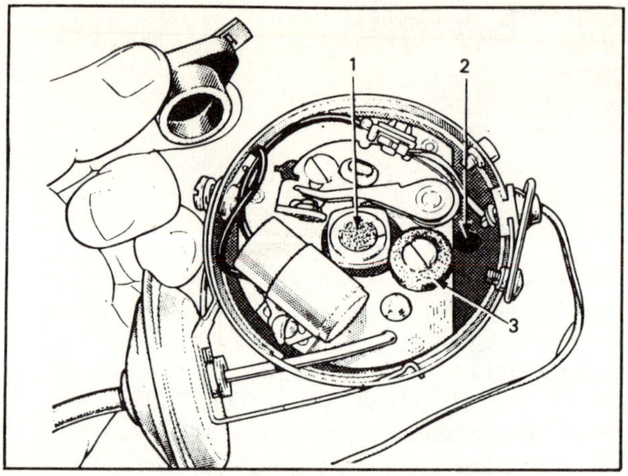

Fig. 12.2 Lubricating the ignition distributor. Apply a few drops of engine oil to the cam spindle lubricator **1**, and through the hole **2**, to lubricate the timing mechanism. Do not apply oil to the grease-impregnated pad **3** — see text

3 Drip about a teaspoon of engine oil through the hole marked 'Oil' in the contact-breaker baseplate.

4 Lubricate the cam. These models have a foamed-plastic lubricator which contacts the cam. Apply a little lithium-base grease to this and work it in with the fingers. *Do not use oil.* When the foam becomes dirty, remove the lubricator by pinching the legs of the clip together with pointed-nose pliers and fit a new one.

5 Place a drop of oil on the contact-breaker pivot pin.

6 Refit the distributor cap.

12.5 Cleaning the distributor cap and rotor

1 Lightly scrape the contact strip on the rotor and the terminals inside the cap to expose bright metal. *Do not file them or rub them down with emery paper.*

2 Wipe the interior of the cap with a cloth moistened with methylated spirits (denatured alcohol) to remove dust or oily deposits, which will provide a leakage path for the high-tension current. A cracked cap or condensed moisture on the inside or outside of the cap is a common cause of difficult starting and misfiring.

3 Examine the rotor for signs of 'tracking' in the form of dark tracks on the surface of the plastic. If the tip of the terminal is badly burnt, fit a new rotor. To ensure adequate pressure on the carbon contact in the cap, the top of the domed end of the spring contact should be 0.30–0.34 in. (7.5–8.6mm) above the metal strip to which the spring is riveted.

12.6 Testing the distributor cap and rotor

1 Detach two alternate sparking plug leads, and the distributor-end of the coil high-tension lead, from the cap. Insert the end of the coil lead into each of the empty sockets in turn. Leave the remaining leads in place and connected to sparking plugs.

2 Switch on the ignition, make sure that the contact-breaker points are closed, and with the tip of a

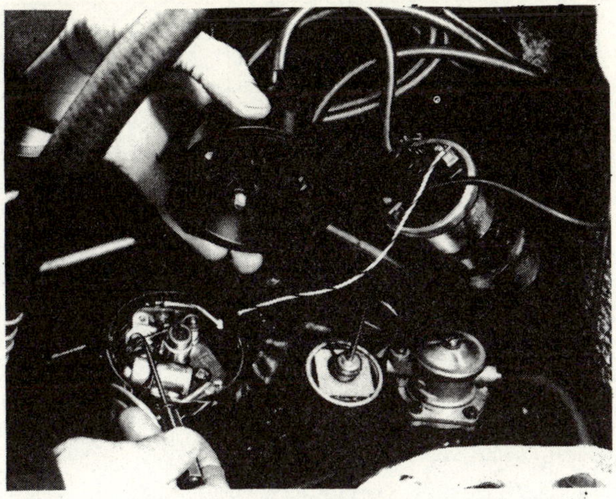

Fig. 12.3 Testing the distributor cap for electrical faults. The method of testing for 'tracking' is described in the text

screwdriver flick the points apart. If there has been any tracking, a spark will jump across the interior of the distributor cap.

The rotor can be checked for breakdown of the insulation as follows, without removing it from the cam spindle—

1 Remove the coil high-tension lead from the distributor cap.

2 Hold it almost in contact with the edge of the rotor blade and flick the contact-breaker points open. If the rotor is faulty a spark will jump the air gap between the high-tension lead and the rotor blade. Occasionally, internal leakage develops from the underside of the brass electrode of the rotor, through the plastic to the interior suface, allowing the high-tension current to jump to the cam spindle and so to earth. This can be a very elusive fault to spot but will be revealed by the above test. Fit a new rotor whenever you fit new sparking plugs and you should have no trouble.

12.7 Checking the vacuum timing control

When a vacuum-operated timing control is fitted (an example is shown in Fig. 12.4), check the following points—

1 Make sure that the suction chamber does not contain any condensed fuel. Test the action of the diaphragm by applying suction to the union. If the diaphragm appears to be faulty, fit a new unit.

2 Check the rubber connections at each end of the vacuum pipe and renew them if they have split or are a loose fit on the pipe. This is very important. Even a slight air-leak will affect the action of the control.

The time factor—servicing and overhauls

None of the jobs described in the following sections is very time-consuming. For example: removing the distributor contacts, refitting and adjusting the gap, 40–50 min; removing and refitting the distributor, 45-60 min; stripping and reassembling the distributor, about 40 min; checking and adjusting the ignition timing, 20 min but longer, of course, if a series of road tests is made as described in Section 12.13.

12.8 Checking the distributor contact points

Materials: Replacement contact-breaker set. Clean cloth. Petrol. Engine oil. Grease.

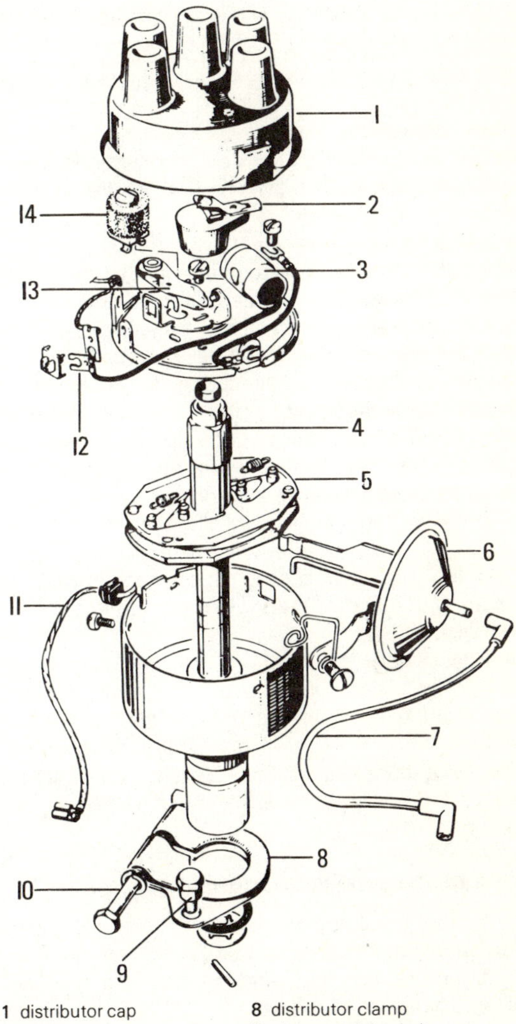

1 distributor cap
2 rotor
3 condenser or capacitor
4 cam
5 centrifugal advance-retard mechanism
6 vacuum timing control
7 vacuum control pipe
8 distributor clamp
9 clamp retaining bolt
10 pinch-bolt
11 low-tension wire
12 low-tension connection
13 contact-breaker assembly
14 cam lubricator

Fig. 12.4 The ignition distributor dismantled

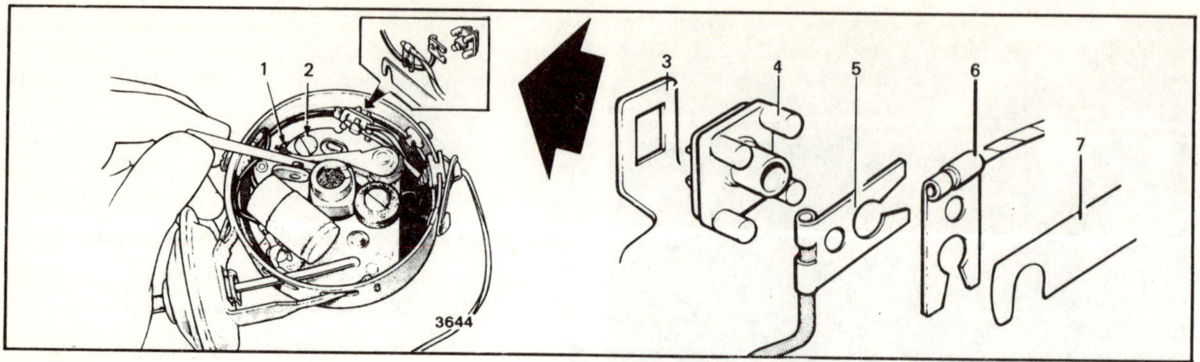

Fig. 12.5 Servicing the contact-breaker points. Measure the gap between the points with a feeler gauge as described in the text and if adjustment is needed, slacken the screw 2, and move the fixed contact plate by inserting a screwdriver blade in slot 1, and rotating it. The correct method of installing the terminal tags if the contacts have been removed is shown above. 3, contact-breaker plate; 4, insulator (do not lever the ears with a screwdriver); 5, capacitor lead terminal; 6, low-tension wire terminal; 7, contact spring

Tools: Screwdriver. Pointed-nose pliers.
The contact-breaker points can be examined after the rotor has been pulled off the end of the distributor shaft.
To service the contacts –

1 Lever the pivoted contact arm away from the fixed contact. The contact surfaces should have a clean, frosted appearance, apart from a small 'pip' and crater.

2 If the contacts are dirty or seem to be badly pitted, lever the slotted end of the spring on the moving arm clear of the retaining pips on the insulator and pull the moving arm off its pivot. Lift the two wires off the insulator, remove the single retaining screw which retains the fixed contact plate and remove the plate.

3 If the contacts are merely oily, they can be cleaned with petrol, but if they are burnt or badly pitted, it is better to fit a new set. Contacts which have been refaced with a carborundum stone or a file seldom last very long.

4 Reassemble the contacts, making sure that the fixed contact plate is pressed firmly down on to the collar at the base of the moving arm pivot pin, and that the terminals on the two wires are replaced in the correct sequence, as shown in Fig. 12.5. Lubricate the cam and the contact-breaker pivot as described in Section 12.4.

12.9 Adjusting the contact-breaker gap

The contact-breaker gap should not be measured with a feeler gauge unless the contact faces have been trued-up to remove the 'pip' and crater, or a new set of contacts has been installed.

When new contacts have been fitted, check the gap after they have run for about 500 miles, to allow for the initial bedding-down of the heel of the rocker arm.

Tools: Screwdriver. Feeler gauge.

1 Turn the engine until the fibre block is exactly on the crest of one of the 'humps' of the cam. A slight movement of the cam in either direction will give a false reading.

2 Slacken the screw or screws retaining the fixed-contact plate and move the plate by inserting a screwdriver blade in the slots in the plate and base-plate. Set the gap to 0.020 in. for used contacts and to 0.022 in. for a new pair (to allow for the initial bedding-down of the contact-breaker heel). Measure the gap with a feeler gauge while turning the screwdriver blade to reduce the gap or to increase it.

3 Tighten the securing screw. Re-check the gap.

4 Check the ignition timing (Section 12.12), as alteration of the gap will alter the timing.

12.10 Removing and refitting the distributor

Tools: Spanners. Scriber.

1 Remove the distributor cap and turn the engine until the rotor arm points to the position of the No. 1 cylinder plug lead segment in the distributor cap.

2 Scribe an alignment mark from the body of the distributor on to the clamp plate and a second mark from the clamp plate on to the crankcase.

3 Disconnect the vacuum advance pipe from the distributor when a vacuum control is fitted.

4 Disconnect the low-tension lead from the distributor terminal.

5 Remove the setscrew securing the clamp plate and remove the distributor. Providing that the pinch-bolt in the clamp plate is not loosened, the ignition timing will not be lost when the distributor is removed. However, the scribed lines are an added insurance.

6 When refitting the distributor, turn the rotor until the driving dog is felt to engage with the driving shaft. As a precaution, check the timing as described in Section 12.12, especially if new contact points have been fitted while the distributor was off the car.

12.11 Dismantling and reassembling the distributor

It should not normally be necessary to dismantle the distributor completely. When appreciable wear develops on the shaft and other components, the best plan is to fit a reconditioned, service-exchange unit. In the notes which follow it is assumed that the distributor has been removed from the car, as described in Section 12.10.

Materials: New centrifugal-advance weight springs. New pin for shaft. Any other replacement parts found to be necessary. Engine oil.

Tools: Screwdriver. Spanner. Long-nose pliers. Pin-punch. Hammer. No. 30 drill if new shaft assembly is to be fitted.

1 Remove the cap, rotor, the vacuum control, which is retained by a single screw, and the contact-breaker plate assembly which carries the contacts and condenser. Renewing the contacts is covered in Section 12.8 and checking the vacuum timing control in Section 12.7.

2 Drive out the retaining pin from the lower end of the distributor shaft and take off the tabbed thrust washer. Clean any burrs off the lower end of the shaft and withdraw the shaft and centrifugal weight assembly from the housing, complete with the upper thrust washer.

3 Remove the oil sealing ring and the clamping plate from the housing.

4 Take the springs off the centrifugal weights and fit new springs.

5 Check the distributor cap and the rotor as described in Section 12.5. Preferably fit a new rotor.

6 Check the fit of the shaft in the bushes in the housing.

7 Make sure that the contact-breaker upper plate moves smoothly on its lower plate, but with slight frictional resistance to the movement. The two plates must not be separated. If they are worn a new assembly must be fitted.

8 Before reassembling, note that an identification number is stamped on the underside of the lower plate of the shaft assembly. This is 25 for all engines.

9 Lubricate the shaft and the felts in the housing and cam with engine oil. If the original shaft assembly is being refitted, make sure that there are no burrs on it.

10 Fit the upper thrust washer to the shaft, insert the shaft in the housing and fit the tabbed thrust washer and a new retaining pin. With a feeler gauge check that the end-float between the tabbed thrust washer and the housing is within limits. This should be 0.002-0.005 in. for new parts and a maximum of 0.010 in. for a used distributor. If a new shaft is being fitted, it will be necessary to drill a hole for the retaining pin with a No. 30 drill, making sure that it is exactly at right-angles to the shaft and that when the pin and washer are fitted, the correct end-float will be obtained as described above. Perhaps a job best left to a Vauxhall dealer or an engineering workshop?

12.12 Checking and adjusting the ignition timing

The basic ignition timing can never be completely 'lost' if a special point is made of checking, *before* removing the distributor, the position of the distributor body in relation to the engine, and also the direction in which the rotor is pointing when the engine is set with No. 1 piston at top-dead-centre on the compression stroke and the timing marks are correctly aligned as described below –

There is a pointer on the rear flange of the crankshaft fan pulley, which lines up with two projections on the timing case. Viewed from the front of the engine, the right-hand projection indicates top-dead-centre, and the left-hand projection (as viewed from the front of the car), 9° before top-dead-centre.

So much for the timing indicator. To carry out the job if the distributor has been removed from the engine, follow operations 1-5 below. If the distributor has not been removed, only operations 1, 3, 4 and 5 are necessary.

Tools: Sparking plug spanner. Socket or set spanners. Timing light (optional). Torch or inspection lamp if required.

1 Remove the sparking plugs and the valve cover and turn the crankshaft clockwise (as viewed from the front of the engine), until both valves of No. 1 cylinder (nearest to the radiator) are closed – i.e. No. 1 piston is on the compression stroke. Align the timing mark with the pointer as described above. If you overshoot the correct position, turn the engine through another full revolution clockwise – don't turn it backwards, as the slack in the timing chain will give a misleading setting.

2 Slacken the bolt in the clamping plate. Rotate the distributor rotor so that the driving tongue on the shaft will engage with the slot in the pump spindle. Slide the distributor into place and fit the setscrew that secures

Fig. 12.6 Setting the timing. On both standard and low-compression engines the crankshaft pulley pointer **1** should be aligned with the 9° btdc pointer **2** on the timing case. Turn the distributor body clockwise to advance the timing

the clamp plate to the crankcase. The rotor should be pointing approximately in the direction of the position of the No. 1 sparking-plug lead terminal in the distributor cap.

3 Make sure that the centrifugal advance weights are not binding, by turning the rotor anti-clockwise and relasing it. Check that the contact-breaker baseplate is free to rotate slightly, if a vacuum control is fitted.

4 Set the timing by rotating the distributor body anti-clockwise until the contact points are just closed and then slowly turn it clockwise until they just separate. If the ignition is switched on, a small spark can be seen and heard to jump across the points as they separate.

A more accurate method of timing is to connect a side-lamp bulb, mounted in a suitable holder, across the two low-tension terminals on the top of the ignition coil. When the points are closed the lamp will light up. At the instant that they open, it will be extinguished. When checking the opening point, keep a light finger pressure on the rotor in a clockwise direction to take up backlash in the drive.

5 When the right timing has been obtained, tighten the clamping bolt to prevent the distributor body from rotating and then recheck the timing. *Do not over-tighten the bolt.*

12.13 Checking the timing on the road

The static setting should be regarded only as the starting point for a series of road tests during which the timing can be precisely adjusted by rotating the distributor a fraction of a turn at a time to suit the condition of the engine and the fuel that will normally be used.

Tools: Spanner. Stop-watch.

1 Make a series of tests on a level road. Note carefully, by stop-watch readings, the time taken to accelerate from 30 mph to 50 mph in top gear, with the throttle fully open in each case and over the same stretch of road. The best ignition setting is that which results in the shortest time to accelerate over the speed range. This will also give the most economical fuel consumption.

2 When altering the timing by the roadside, move the distributor by only a fraction of a turn. Be particularly careful not to over-advance the ignition.

13 The transmission
Clutch, gearbox, propeller shaft, rear axle

For the benefit of the novice it should perhaps be explained that the term 'transmission,' in the English rather than the American sense, applies to all the components in the drive-line between the engine and the rear wheels: the clutch, gearbox, propeller shaft and the rear axle, which includes the differential, final-drive gears and driving shafts. It is an unfortunate fact of life that overhaul of these components, or at least the key assemblies, calls for the use of special tools and gauges and it is for this reason that it is the practice, in many garages nowadays, to fit service-exchange assemblies, rather than to carry out major repairs to worn or defective units.

Similarly, a complete overhaul of a synchromesh gearbox is beyond the scope of the average owner. Special service tools will be needed to do the job properly, and it will probably be necessary to renew the majority of the parts in a worn gearbox – which is something that you will only find out, of course, after you have stripped the box!

As we suggest in Chapter 8, there may be little difference between the total cost of the spares needed and the price of an exchange gearbox, with everything in favour of the professionally-rebuilt unit.

Rear axles fall into the same category as gearboxes: special tools and gauges are needed, together with a considerable degree of skill, to ensure a quiet, long-lasting assembly.

The time factor

Where routine maintenance jobs such as topping-up a synchromesh gearbox or the rear axle are concerned, the time factor must obviously depend on whether or not the work can be done quickly and conveniently with the car over a pit or raised on a garage lift. The actual topping-up and waiting for the surplus oil to drain out takes only a few minutes.

As regards more ambitious work that is likely to be tackled at home, the following are some estimated times: adjusting the clutch cable, 15 min; fitting a new clutch driven plate and/or clutch cover assembly (including removing and refitting the gearbox), 3½ hr; removing and refitting a gearbox alone, 3 hr; removing and refitting the complete propeller shaft assembly, 45 min.

The clutch

The Borg and Beck clutch is shown dismantled in Fig. 13.2. The clutch cover assembly, which houses the pressure plate and a diaphragm spring, cannot be dismantled. If any part is worn or damaged, a new cover assembly must be fitted.

The driven plate is faced with friction material on both sides and is clamped between the pressure plate and the machined face of the flywheel by the diaphragm spring.

The release bearing acts at the centre of the fingers of the spring and is operated by a pivoted arm – termed the clutch fork – to which the lower end of the inner clutch cable is attached.

The outer cable seats in a rubber insulator in the clutch housing and is assembled at the upper end in a steel damper sleeve which locates in a collar in the engine bulkhead. Rubber grommets are used to insulate the damper from the outer cable and the dash panel, to prevent noise being transmitted into the car.

13.1 Adjusting the clutch-operating cable

If a free movement of ½ - ¾ in. (13-19mm) does not exist at the clutch pedal, the clutch-operating cable should be adjusted at the lower end, where it is connected to the clutch-operating lever (Fig. 13.1).

The release lever and the release bearing are shown in Fig. 13.3 The reason for rotating the bearing while carrying out adjustment as described below is that otherwise it is difficult to judge just when the bearing begins to apply pressure to the fingers of the diaphragm spring, which offer only a very low resistance during the first part of the clutch pedal travel.

Tools: Spanners.

1 Tighten the clutch-cable adjusting nut until the clutch release bearing is just nipped by the operating lever. This can be checked by inserting a finger through the unused clutch fork slot in the housing and spinning the bearing while tightening the adjusting nut.

2 Screw the lock-nut back from the adjusting nut to the extent of ¼ in. (6 mm).

3 Screw the adjusting nut back until it contacts the lock-nut and then lock the two together.

13.2 Clutch overhaul

As indicated earlier, the clutch cover assembly and the

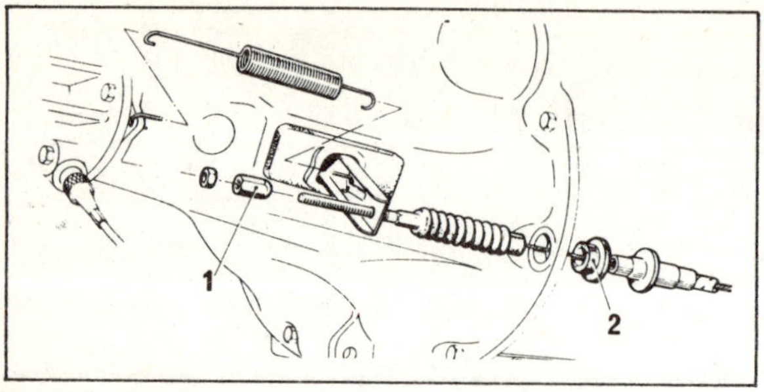

Fig. 13.1 The clutch-housing end of the clutch control cable. The adjusting nut is shown at **1** and the insulating bush at **2**

driven plate are not repairable and must be renewed as complete assemblies.

Although it is sometimes sufficient to renew a worn driven plate alone (if this has failed after a fairly low mileage, for example), in practice it is a worthwhile insurance against future trouble to renew both the plate and the cover assembly at the same time. It is also advisable to renew the clutch release bearing and to fit a new pilot bush in the flywheel.

The special tool Z8527 will be needed to remove the old bush and Z8566 to fit the new part. The pilot of this tool ensures that the internal diameter of the bush will be correct when installed, avoiding any risk of collapsing the porous bush when driving it home.

Before fitting the new bush, close one end with the forefinger, fill the bush with oil, place the thumb over the open end and squeeze until oil seeps out through the wall of the bush. Repeat the operation until the bush is saturated with oil.

To remove the housing and clutch assembly –

Materials: New parts as required. Paraffin. Rags. Marking paint or scriber.

Tools: Spanners. Pliers. Screwdriver. Special tool SE 768 or substitute (see text).

1 Remove the gearbox as described in Section 13.6.

2 If the clutch cover assembly is to be refitted, mark the flange of the cover and the flywheel to ensure reassembly in the same relative positions.

3 Unscrew the cover retaining screws progressively in a diagonal sequence to release the tension of the spring without distorting the cover flange. Remove the cover and driven plate.

4 Clean the driven plate and the clutch assembly, brushing or blowing out any clutch dust from the latter, but do not swill the cover in a paraffin bath, as this will remove the essential lubricant from the cover assembly.

5 Check the diaphragm spring in the cover assembly for any signs of wear or fractures and the driven plate for worn linings and loose or broken compression springs and worn hub splines. If oil has reached the driven plate, the rear main crankshaft bearing may be worn or the oil seal may be faulty. These items are normally dealt with during an engine overhaul. If the flywheel is scored, have it skimmed by a Vauxhall dealer or fit a new one.

6 When refitting the clutch, it is essential to centralize the hub of the driven plate, preferably by using service tool SE 768. Alternatively an improvised aligning tool can be made up from a length of wooden dowel, built up to the correct diameters to fit the spigot bearing in the flywheel and the bore of the clutch hub and clutch cover by wrapping it with insulation tape or masking tape.

7 With the aligning tool in place, and with the face of the clutch plate marked 'Flywheel Side' correctly assembled, refit the cover assembly. Before tightening the retaining screws progressively in a diagonal sequence, make sure that everything is properly lined-up, including the alignment marks if the old cover is being refitted.

8 Refit the gearbox, as described in Section 13.6.

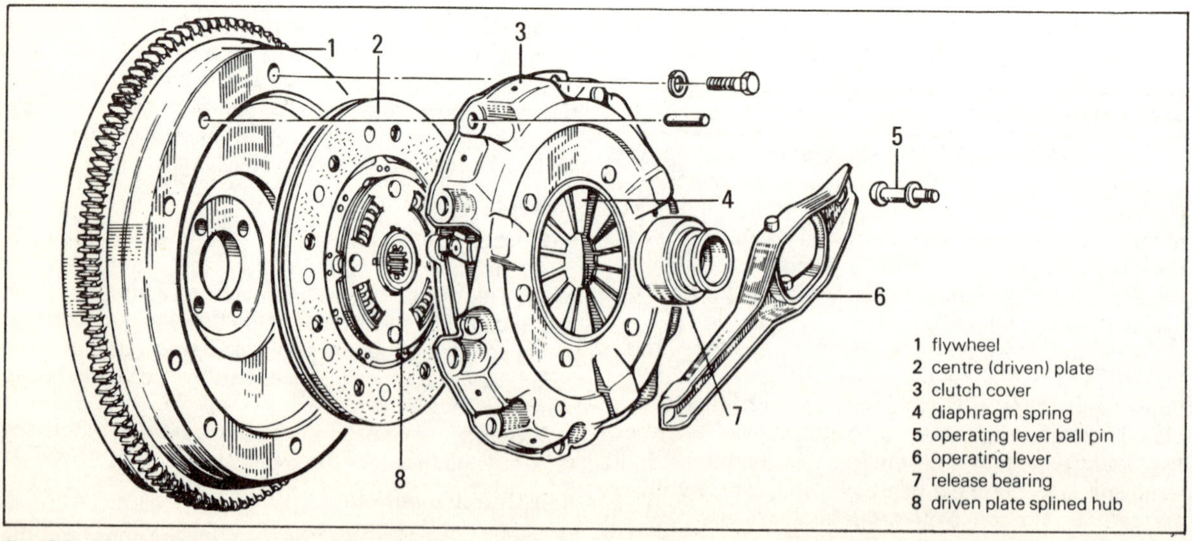

Fig. 13.2 The components of a Borg and Beck clutch

13.3 Fitting a new clutch release bearing

Materials and tools: as for gearbox removal (Section 13.6)

1 Remove the gearbox (Section 13.6)

2 Pull the fork off the ball pin on which it pivots and withdraw the fork and release-bearing assembly.

3 Detach the bearing and check it for wear. Do not wash it in petrol or paraffin, or degrease it, if it is to be refitted. The sealed bearing is packed with sufficient lubricant to last its life.

4 If the ball on the pivot-pin is worn, tap the pin out of the housing. When fitting a new pin, use a soft-faced hammer to avoid damaging the ball-end. Grease the ball.

13.4 Renewing the clutch cable

This is a straightforward job, except that it is not too easy to reach the eye on the end of the inner cable which fits over a hook on the clutch pedal.

Materials: New cable. Multipurpose grease.
Tools: Jack. Axle stands. Spanners.

1 Disconnect the inner cable from the clutch release lever, remove the corrugated gaiter and pull the outer cable out of the rubber insulator in the clutch housing. Release any clips along the length of the cable.

2 At the pedal end, pull the inner cable forward, unhook it from the clutch pedal and then detach the outer cable from the damper sleeve and the engine bulkhead.

3 When fitting a new cable, do not lubricate it with oil or grease. A special lubricant is used on the inner cable during assembly. The ball-end seating on the adjusting nut and operating lever should, however, be lubricated with grease.

4 Adjust the free travel of the operating lever as described in Section 13.1.

The synchromesh gearbox

A manual gearbox needs no attention, other than

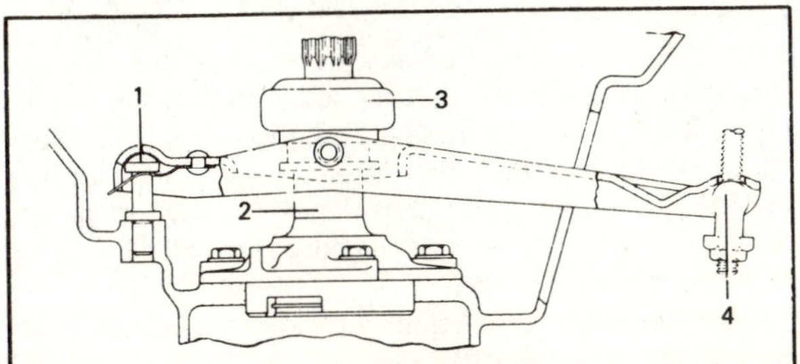

1 ball pin
2 transmission front cover sleeve
3 release bearing
4 clutch cable adjusting nut

Fig. 13.3 The clutch-operating lever and release bearing

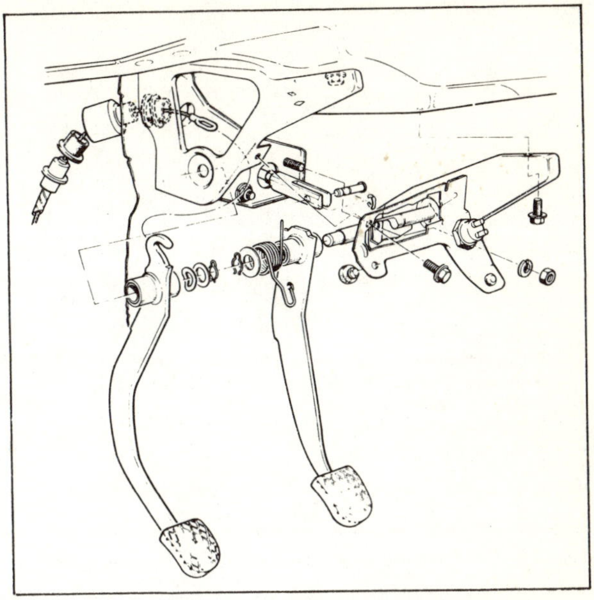

Fig. 13.4 The clutch and brake pedal assemblies. The clutch cable engages with the hook on the clutch pedal (shown on the left)

checking the oil-level during routine servicing and topping-up if necessary with the grade of oil specified in Chapter 17. Any oil leaks will be obvious while this is being done. If they are serious, ask your dealer for advice.

When trouble develops in the gearbox, considerable experience is needed to diagnose it with any degree of certainty. Excessive noise, or a tendency to jump out of gear, are usually caused by the cumulative effect of wear at a number of points, over a large mileage. Piecemeal replacements are seldom effective for very long; usually the most economical course is to fit a reconditioned gearbox, as recommended earlier.

13.5 Checking the gearbox oil level

The combined oil level and filler plug is screwed into the left-hand side of the gearbox and a $\frac{9}{16}$ in. Allen key is needed to remove and refit it. A Vauxhall dealer should be able to supply this.

To inject the oil it will be necessary to use a flexible-tube extension on one of the 'squeeze bottle' dispensers filled with 90EP gear oil.

If the car is over a pit or on ramps, the plug can be reached from below but it is easier to work from under the bonnet, without raising the car.

1 With the car on a level surface, unscrew the plug, after cleaning the area around it.

2 If oil does not flow from the opening inject oil until it overflows and allow time for the surplus oil to run out.

13.6 Removing and refitting a synchromesh gearbox

The gearbox must be removed from beneath the car,

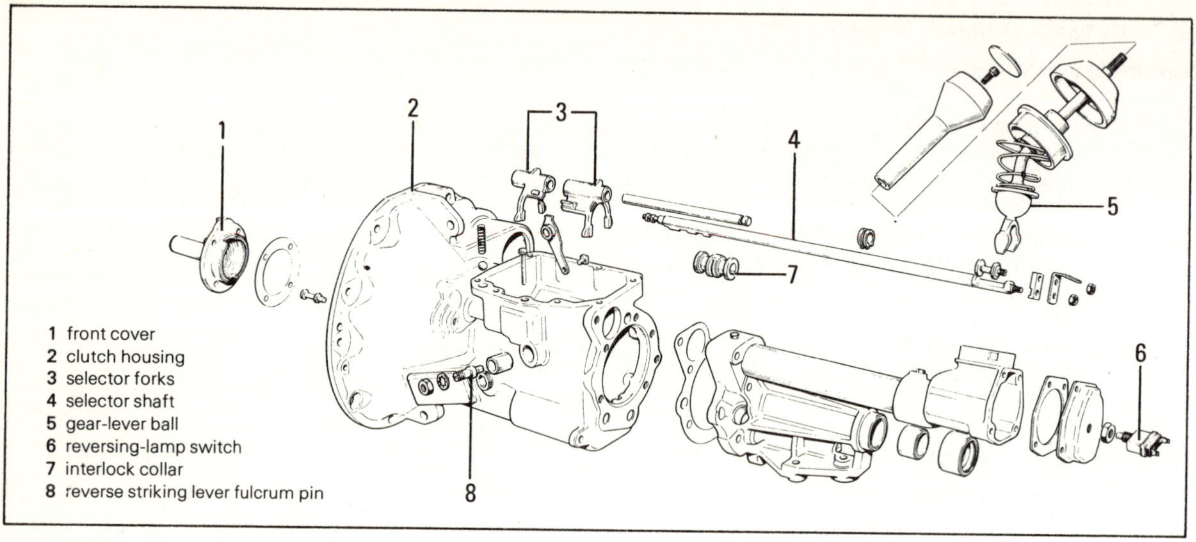

Fig. 13.5 The gear lever, selector mechanism and the gearbox casings

which means that if a garage hoist or a pit is not available it will be necessary to support the car securely on axle stands or to raise the wheels on secure blocks, to give a comfortable working height.

Materials: Paraffin. Rags.

Tools: Spanners. Screwdrivers. Pliers. Two jacks. Axle stands. Marking paint or scriber.

1 Remove the gear lever by pulling off the rubber seals, pressing down on the retaining cap at the base of the lever and twisting it clockwise.

2 Disconnect the clutch cable from the clutch-operating lever and withdraw it from the housing.

3 Working beneath the car, paint or scribe alignment marks on the flange of the universal joint on the front end of the propeller shaft and on the driving flange on the gearbox, to ensure reassembly in the same relative positions.

4 Remove the flange bolts and tie the shaft to one side to keep it clear of the gearbox. Plug the opening in the gearbox to prevent oil being spilt when the gearbox is tilted.

5 Disconnect the speedometer drive cable.

6 Take the weight of the engine and gearbox with a jack placed as far towards the rear of the engine sump as possible, using a length of wood to distribute the load, and remove the plate that connects the sump to the flywheel housing.

7 Remove the setscrews which retain the short cross-member which supports the gearbox — see Fig. 9.14 in Chapter 9.

8 Place a second jack beneath the gearbox to take the weight of this unit before disconnecting the clutch housing from the engine. To make it easier to remove the clutch housing front cover, slacken the transmission brace bolts at the engine sump bracket. Lower the two jacks carefully, keeping the gearbox in line with the engine, until the gearbox can be pulled rearwards to free the input shaft from the clutch. *At this stage it is very important not to allow the weight of the gearbox to be carried by this shaft.*

9 Refitting the gearbox is simply a reversal of the steps in removing it, but again the importance of not allowing the weight of the gearbox to hang on the input shaft must be emphasized, owing to the risk of bending the shaft or damaging the clutch. Make sure that the mounting cross-member is installed the right way round and that the washers are correctly fitted, if the mounting has been removed from the gearbox. Install spacers between the cross-member and the underbody, if these are not already fitted, as described in Section 9.14 of Chapter 9.

10 Before inserting the propeller shaft sliding sleeve, make sure that it is completely free from scores or burrs and smear the outside of the sleeve and the lip of the oil seal in the gearbox rear cover with Rocol anti-scuffing paste. Don't forget to install the spring in the bore of the sleeve and to fit new locking tabs to the coupling bolts.

11 When installing the gear lever, smear the ball and fork with grease and insert the lever so that the longer leg of the fork ends is on the left-hand side of the selector shaft. Fit the retaining cap and make sure that it is properly engaged. Also check that the rubber gaiters are properly fitted, as a displaced gaiter will allow a lot of noise to enter the car.

12 After assembly, adjust the clutch-operating lever free travel — Section 13.1.

13.7 Fitting a new oil seal to the gearbox rear cover

Oil leakage past the oil seal in the rear cover of the gearbox will be revealed by drips on the garage floor.

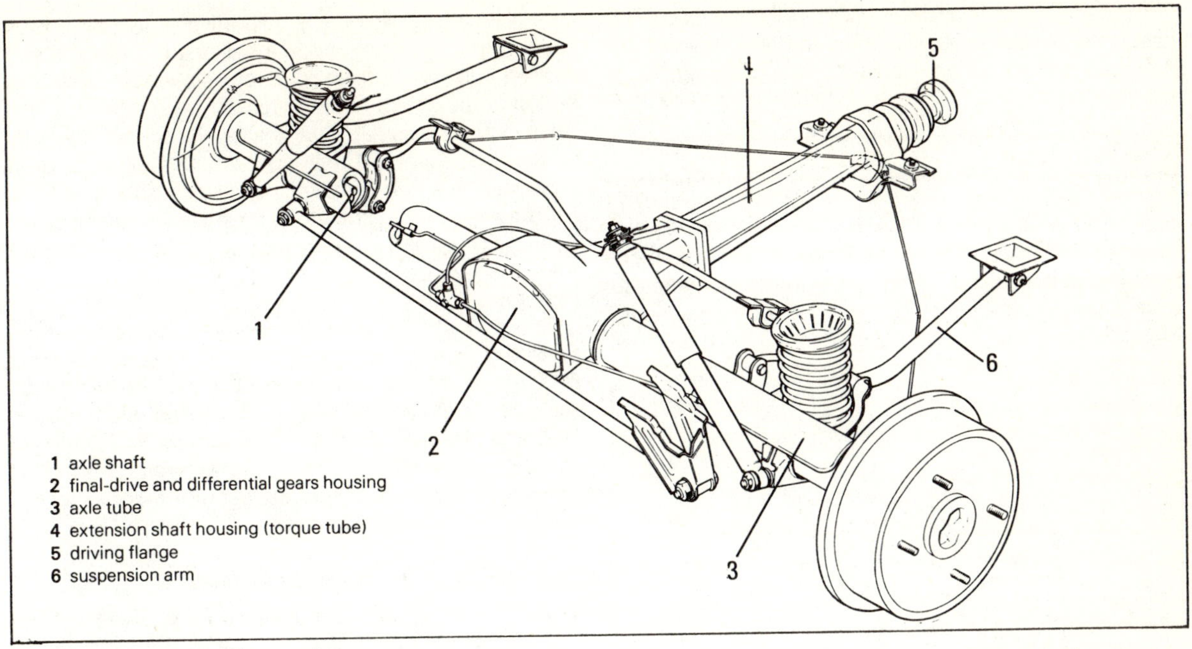

Fig. 13.6 The rear axle and its mountings

Oil will also be flung on to the underside of the car by the front propeller shaft universal joint.

To renew the seal –

Materials: New seal. Rocol anti-scuffing paste.

Tools: Sharp drift. Hammer. Spanners. Special tool Z8426 – not absolutely essential.

1 Disconnect the propeller shaft coupling after marking the flanges to ensure correct reassembly and withdraw the sliding sleeve from the gearbox.

2 Tap off the old oil seal, using a sharp drift alternately on each side of the seal.

3 Preferably use the special tool Z8426 to fit the new seal. If this is not available, be very careful not to distort the seal when fitting it.

4 Check that the outer surface of the sliding sleeve is completely free from burrs or scores, as these will result in a short life for the new seal.

5 Smear the lips of the seal and the surface of the sliding sleeve with Rocol anti-scuffing paste.

6 Install the spring in the bore of the sleeve and use new locking tabs when fitting the propeller shaft coupling flange bolts. The alignment marks on the coupling flanges must, of course, be correctly lined-up.

The propeller shaft

The drive is taken from the gearbox to the rear axle by a single propeller shaft which has a sliding sleeve coupling at its forward end which engages with the mainshaft of the gearbox.

The needle cups for the needle roller bearings in each universal joint are retained by staking-over the metal of the yoke. Replacement yokes, bearings or journal assemblies are not supplied as spares. When the universal joints are worn a new propeller shaft assembly, complete with joints, must be fitted.

Check the tightness of the bolts in the joint flanges during routine servicing. Also test the joints for wear by attempting to raise and lower the shaft at each end. Loose flange bolts and worn bearings can cause pronounced transmission vibration at higher road-speeds and a knock when accelerating, decelerating and starting from a standstill.

13.8 Removing and refitting the propeller shaft

Removal and refitting the shaft is quite straightforward, provided that the following points are borne in mind –

Tools: Spanners. Scriber or marking paint. Axle stands.

1 If the original shaft is to be refitted, it is essential to mark the flanges before dismantling. If the shaft is assembled with the joints 'out of phase' severe vibration will be set up. If a new shaft is to be fitted, make sure that the yokes of the joints are in the same relationship to one another as in the original shaft.

2 After withdrawing the propeller shaft from the gearbox, plug the opening in the gearbox rear cover to prevent loss of oil.

3 It is particularly important that the exterior of the sliding sleeve at the front end of the shaft is free from burrs or scores. Otherwise the oil seal in the gearbox will have a short life. While the shaft is off the car, it is advisable to protect the sleeve by wrapping it with insulating tape or masking tape.

4 Before installing the sleeve smear its outer surface,

and the lip of the oil seal, with Rocol anti-scuffing paste. Remember to fit the spring inside the sleeve. Use new locking tabs when fitting the rear coupling flange bolts.

The rear axle

The rear axle is what is termed a semi-floating hypoid type. The final-drive gears and the differential pinions are carried in taper roller bearings in a single-piece housing, to the nose of which an extension is bolted to form a torque tube which helps to locate the rear axle. This tube encloses an extension shaft which is splinted to the pinion shaft of the final-drive assembly and is supported at its front end in a ball bearing, carried in a rubber cushion housed in a cross-member which is bolted to the underside of the car.

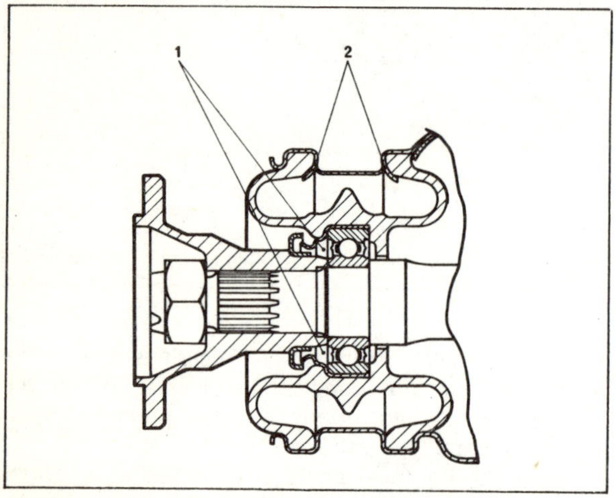

Fig. 13.7 The rubber-cushioned bearing at the forward end of the rear-axle extension shaft. The space **1** is packed with grease which is harmless to rubber and the rubber cushion is retained by the tabs **2**

As explained earlier, rear axle repairs are not normally within the scope of the do-it-yourself owner. Even renewal of the hub bearings, which incorporate oil seals for the axle shafts, should be left to a Vauxhall dealer. The work involved is described in Chapter 14, where we treat the hub bearings as being part of the suspension system.

The only routine attention required by the rear axle, therefore, is to check the oil level in the axle casing at 6000-mile intervals. It is not necessary to drain and refill the axle — except, of course, during an overhaul. An 'extreme pressure' or 'hypoid' oil with an SAE viscosity of 90EP or 140EP must be used to avoid any risk of breakdown of the oil film between the highly-stressed teeth of the final-drive gears.

13.9 Checking the rear axle oil level

The combined oil filler and level plug is screwed into the rear face of the axle casing and a $\frac{5}{16}$ in. Allen key will be needed to unscrew and refit it. As in the case of the gearbox, a flexible extension for the oil-can or a squeeze pack filled with gear oil will make the job of topping-up much easier. The car must be on a level surface.

1 Wipe the area around the plug and unscrew the plug.

2 If oil does not flow out, inject a small quantity and allow the overflow to cease before refitting the plug.

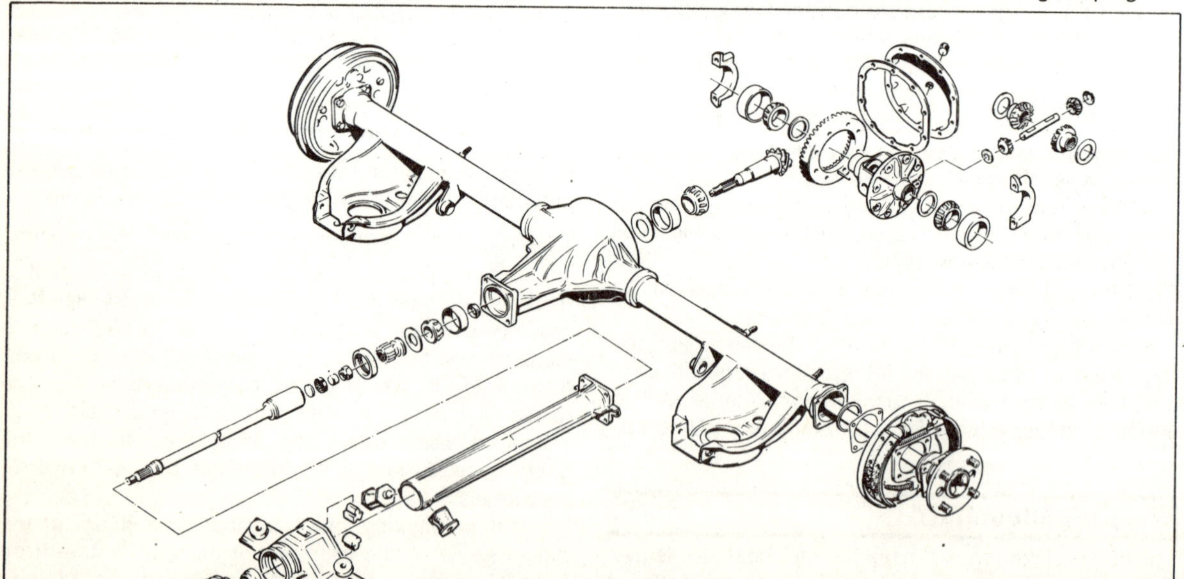

Fig. 13.8 The rear axle fully dismantled. Normally, stripping and reassembly of the axle should be left to a Vauxhall dealer or a specialist firm

14 The suspension and steering

A glance at Trouble-shooting Chart 8 will show that the steering, roadholding and controllability of a car depend on a number of closely-related factors, in which it is difficult to draw a firm dividing line between some steering and suspension components.

In this chapter, however, we shall deal with the swivel ball-joints of the front suspension and the front and rear-wheel hub bearings, in the first section, treating them as suspension items. The rack-and-pinion steering unit, tie-rods and ball-joints are covered in the second section dealing with the steering gear – a rather arbitrary, but fairly logical division which works out quite well in practice.

First, however, a word of warning: if you have a Chevette GL, a point to remember is that the special styling of the road wheels is achieved by bonding a rigid polyurethane insert to the outer face of the wheel, with a raised centre boss which carries the Vauxhall medallion.

With this type of wheel, if a tyre is changed by using a garage tyre-fitting or bead-breaking machine which clamps on to the centre boss, the styling insert can be damaged – so make sure that the mechanic uses conventional tyre levers to remove and refit the tyre.

The time factor

Suggested times for the more important jobs are: Servicing front-wheel hub bearings (one side), 40 min; removing and refitting steering knuckle ball joints,

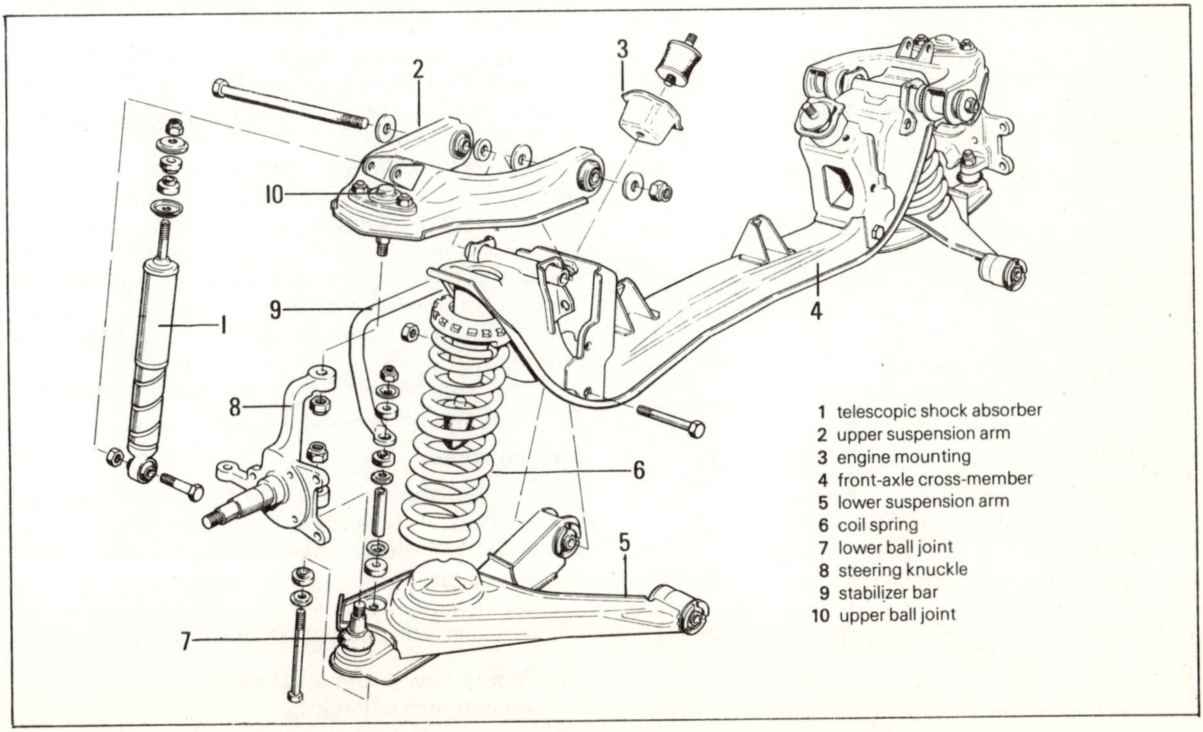

Fig. 14.1 The components of the coil-spring independent front suspension

1½ hr; dismantling and reassembling a suspension arm, 1 hr; removing and refitting a rear spring, 45 min; removing and refitting a rear axle shaft, 1 hr; removing and refitting a front shock absorber, 1 hr; removing and refitting a rear shock absorber, 30 min; renewing a tie-rod outer ball joint, 20 min; removing and refitting the steering rack assembly, 1 hr.

The front suspension

The independent front wheel suspension takes the form of a coil spring on each side of the car, fitted between upper and lower suspension arms which are pivoted at their inner ends to a cross-member. Each lower arm incorporates an outrigger which positions the suspension in a fore-and-aft direction.

At their outer ends the arms are coupled by ball joints to swivelling steering knuckles which carry the wheel hubs and brake calipers.

A telescopic hydraulic shock absorber is fitted between each upper arm and the bodywork and a stabilizer or anti-roll bar is connected between the two lower arms.

The front suspension needs no routine maintenance, apart from checking the ball joints and rubber bushes for wear, making sure that the various attachment nuts and bolts are kept tight, and servicing the wheel hub bearings as described in Section 14.1.

14.1 Servicing the front-wheel hub bearings

During the 12 000-mile service the front-wheel hub bearings should be removed for inspection and repacked with grease.

The sequence in servicing the bearings is as follows –

Materials: Lithium-base grease. New oil seals and bearings, if required. Rocol anti-scuffing paste if seals are renewed. New caliper retaining bolts. Castrol-Girling Universal brake and clutch fluid.

Tools: Spanners. Screwdriver. Soft-faced hammer. Brake bleeding equipment.

1 Remove the wheel and prise off the hub dust cap, which is a push-fit in the hub.

2 Remove the brake caliper, after first taking out the brake pads (see Chapter 15) and unscrewing the brake pipe union on the bracket in the steering knuckle. Plug both the end of the pipe and the union to prevent the entry of dirt or grit.

3 Withdraw the split-pin, remove the nut retainer, unscrew the hub-retaining nut and pull off the hub.

4 Wash all parts in paraffin. Look for any broken rollers, scored or pitted tracks or signs of 'blueing' caused by overheating. Any of these faults will, of course, call for new bearings.

5 Check the condition of the oil seal and renew it if necessary. If the outer track of the inner roller bearing needs to be removed the seal will, or course, have to be extracted and a new seal installed after the bearing has been reassembled.

6 Insert the seal with its lip facing into the hub and carefully tap it home with a suitable tubular drift or block of wood, until its shoulder just contacts the hub.

7 Make sure that the seat for the seal on the stub axle is perfectly clean. If any trace of corrosion is not polished off, the effective life of the seal will be reduced. Lip-type oil seals should be lubricated during assembly with Rocol anti-scuffing paste, which can be obtained from a Vauxhall dealer.

8 Pack the bearings and the hub half-full with clean grease and reassemble. *Do not* fill the hub completely. Space must be left for expansion as the hub warms up during normal running.

9 Adjust the bearings. Tighten the hub-retaining nut with a tubular spanner until a slight drag is felt when the hub is rotated. Slacken back the nut, remove the tommy-bar and retighten the nut by using hand pressure only to turn the spanner until one of the slots lines-up with the split-pin hole in the end of the stub axle. Fit a new split-pin, bend over the ends and refit the dust cap.

10 Refit the brake caliper, reconnect the brake pipe and bleed the brakes as described in Chapter 15.

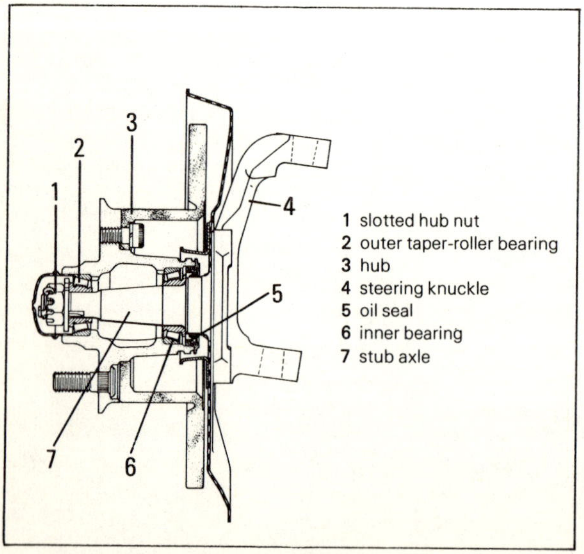

Fig. 14.2 Section through a front-wheel hub

Special notes

If the wheel bearings are too tightly adjusted the hub will overheat. If there is too much play, the brake-pad piston will be knocked back into the caliper, giving excessive pedal travel.

Support the caliper, or tie it to the suspension arm while the hub is off, to avoid straining the brake hose.

14.2 Fitting new upper and lower suspension arm ball joints

The ball joints which attach the suspension arms to the

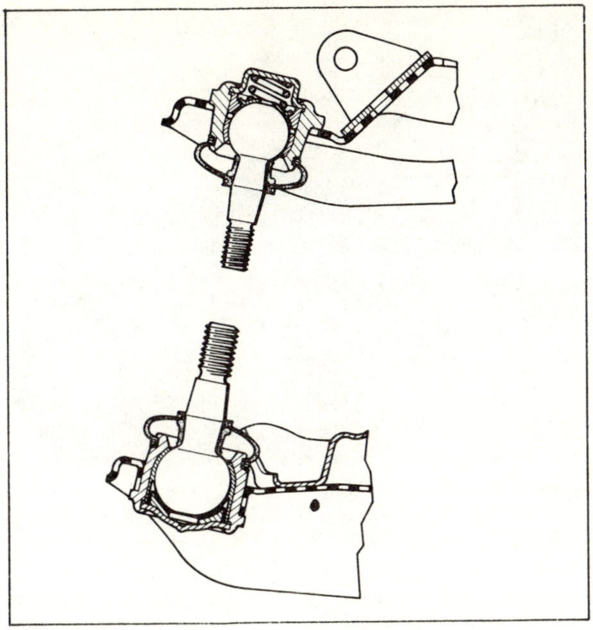

Fig. 14.3 The upper ball joint is bolted to the suspension arm. The socket of the lower joint is splined and pressed into the lower arm

steering knuckles are preloaded to eliminate vertical clearance and there should be no trace of slackness in them.

The best way to check these joints for wear is to jack-up and support the front of the car under the lower suspension arms and hold the upper and lower joints in turn while rocking the road wheel vertically. Any slackness due to wear can be easily felt, calling for renewal.

The upper joints are bolted to the suspension arms. The lower joints are splined externally. In production they are pressed into plain housings in the arm, broaching corresponding splines which will also fit the splines in replacement joints.

To renew the joints –

Materials: Set of new joints. Paraffin. Rags.
Tools: Ball-pin extractor (Vauxhall tool 817 or similar). Hammer. Tubular drift. Jack. Axle stands. Spring compressor VR2219 – not essential, see text.

1 Raise and support the car under the underframe. Place a jack under the lower suspension arm and raise the arm until the spring is partly compressed. Alternatively, use the special Vauxhall spring compressor if this can be borrowed or hired.

2 Disconnect the steering tie-rod ball-joint from the steering arm, using the Vauxhall tool 817 or a ball-pin extractor. If this is not available, refit the nut to the ball pin to protect the threads and tap the joint off its taper.

3 Remove the nuts from the upper and lower suspension arm ball joints and release the joints from the steering knuckle, again using the extractor or by tapping them free. At this stage slacken the nut on the upper arm pivot bolt and tie or wire the upper arm against the bump stop to prevent any risk of straining the brake hose.

4 Lower the jack slowly to allow the spring to expand, taking the greatest care not to allow the jack to tip while the spring is still under compression. If the special spring compressor is being used, slacken this off.

5 To renew the upper ball joint, first note the position of the joint before unscrewing the retaining nuts. The new joint must be installed the same way round as the old joint, in order to retain the correct camber angle.

6 To renew the lower ball joint, disconnect the stabilizer bar and with the spring partly compressed as just described, detach the ball pin from the steering knuckle, using a ball-pin extractor. Ideally, the special Vauxhall press assembly should be used to remove the joint, but as the old joint is to be discarded it can be tapped downwards out of the arm. The press is also used to install the new joint, after engaging the splines on the socket with those in the suspension arm but the joint can be carefully tapped home, using a tubular drift which will bear on the flange of the socket – *not* on the sealing disc.

7 After reassembling the suspension, lower the car on to its wheels before fully tightening the nut on the upper suspension arm pivot bolt.

14.3 Removing and refitting the steering knuckles

Materials: Any new parts required. Brake fluid if disc brakes or Lockheed drum brakes are fitted (see text).
Tools: Spanners. Spring compressor (not essential – see Section 14.2). Jack. Axle stand. Ball-pin extractor. Circlip pliers. Hammer. Tubular drift.

1 Jack-up and support the front of the car under the lower suspension arm.

2 Remove the wheel hub and disc (Section 14.1).

3 Disconnect the upper and lower suspension arm ball joints as described in Section 14.2.

4 After reassembly, bleed the brakes as described in Chapter 15 if the pipeline has been disconnected.

14.4 Removing and refitting the upper and lower front suspension arms.

This is a straightforward job after the steering knuckle has been removed as described in Section 14.3 and the shock absorber disconnected – Section 14.10. If the bushes are worn, the following points are important –

1 The front bush in the upper arm incorporates inner and outer sleeves, whereas the rear bush does not have an outer sleeve.

2 The arm can be removed after the fulcrum bolt has been withdrawn.

3 The bushes can be pressed out by using suitable tubular distance pieces and a vice, but a support must be placed between the two flanges of the arm (see Fig. 14.4) to prevent these being distorted when pressure is applied. It is therefore really advisable to leave this job to a Vauxhall dealer.

4 The front and rear bushes should be pressed in from the front of the arm. When fitting the rear bush, smear it with soap solution. Again, a support must be used.

5 When refitting the arm, make sure that the spacers between the upper arm and the cross-member are installed correctly and that the mating tapers of the ball pin and the steering knuckle are clean and free from grease. Tighten the nut on the pivot bolt with the weight of the car on the tyres, to ensure that the bushes take up the correct 'neutral' position.

6 The bush in the straight section of the lower suspension arm can be removed and refitted in the same way as with the upper arm. Renewal of the bush in the outrigger of the lower arm, however, is really a job for a Vauxhall dealer as it is difficult to do the job properly at home without the correct tools.

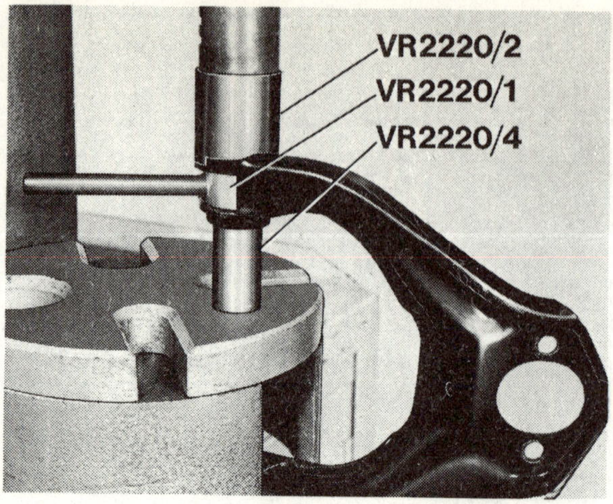

Fig. 14.4 Pressing a bush out of an upper suspension arm, using the support VR2220/2 and the remover VR2220/4. It is important to insert the spacer VR2220/1 to prevent distortion of the flanges of the arm

14.5 Removing and refitting a front spring

The front coil springs are of the same length and may be interchanged from side to side, but make sure that you get the correct grade of springs for your particular model. For safety reasons we suggest that a proper spring compressor – preferably the Vauxhall tool VR2219 – should be used when removing and refitting a spring.

Materials: New spring if required.

Tools: Ball-pin extractor. Spanners. Spring compressor, Vauxhall tool VR2219 or universal type of compressor obtainable from an accessory shop. Hammer. Jack. Axle stands.

1 Before fitting the spring compressor, slacken the nuts on the pivot bolts for the lower suspension arm and the outrigger and disconnect the stabilizer bar from both lower arms.

2 Compress the spring, with the hooks of the compressor located over approximately seven coils. If the Vauxhall tool is used, the hook and the end of the drive plate painted red should be to the right, as viewed from the side of the vehicle.

3 Remove the nut from the lower ball joint pin and release the taper, using a ball-joint extractor.

4 To avoid straining the brake hose, wedge or tie the upper arm and steering knuckle away from the lower arm and the spring.

5 Remove the fulcrum bolt and withdraw the lower arm, complete with the spring if the Vauxhall tool is used, or the arm and spring separately.

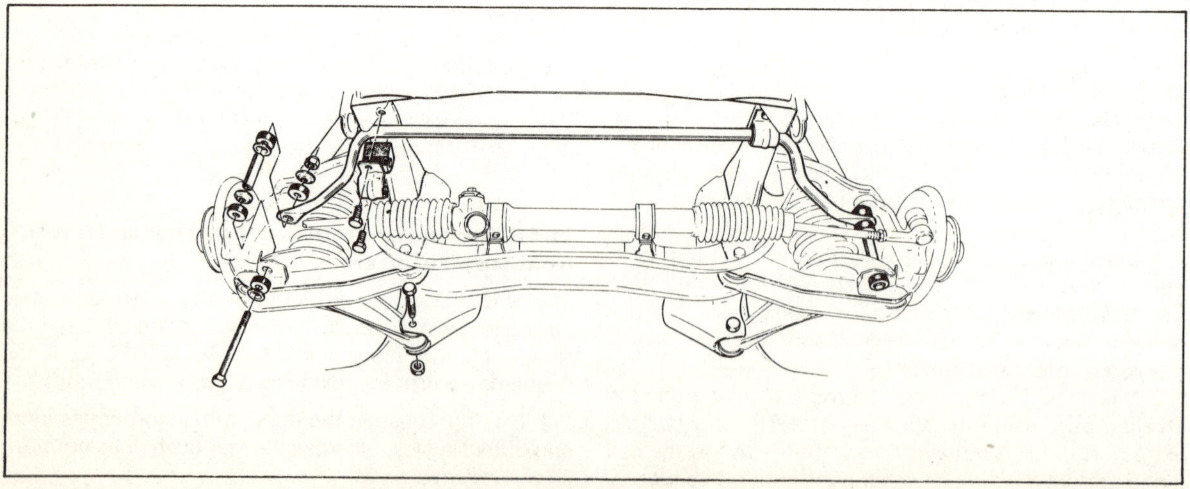

Fig. 14.5 The front stabilizer bar is connected to links to the brackets on the lower arms and secured to the underbody by metal straps and insulating rubbers

6 When refitting the spring, the straight portion of the bottom coil must be seated correctly in the recess in the lower arm. Make sure that the insulator is correctly fitted to the upper end of the spring.

7 The mating tapers of the ball joint and steering knuckle must be clean and free from grease.

8 Tighten the nuts on the suspension arm and outrigger pivot bolt when the weight of the car is on the tyres, so that the bushes will be in the neutral loaded position.

14.6 Removing and refitting the front stabilizer bar

The bar is retained by metal straps and insulator rubbers and is linked to brackets on the lower arms, by insulated bushes.

When refitting the bar, the identification marking shown in Fig. 14.6 must be upwards and the split in the insulator rubbers must be towards the front of the car.

Smear the rubbers with Dow Corning oil (obtainable from a Vauxhall dealer) before installing them and tighten the nut on the retaining bolt until the dimension A in Fig. 14.6 is 1.5 in. (38 mm).

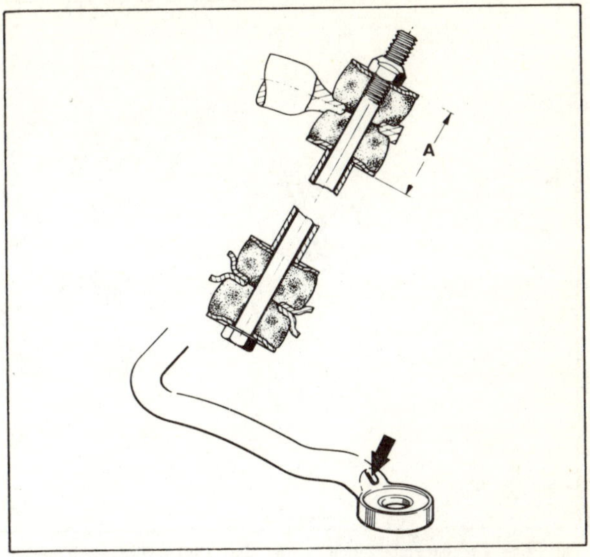

Fig. 14.6 When installed the marking shown by the arrow on the front stabilizer bar must be upwards and the splits in the insulating rubbers in the brackets must be towards the front of the car. The nuts should be tightened until the dimension A is 1.5 in. (38 mm)

The rear suspension

The simple layout of the rear suspension is shown in Fig. 14.7. The rear axle is supported by coil springs, fitted with upper and lower rubber insulators, and is located by the pinion shaft extension housing - or torque tube — and by a pair of pivoted arms.

A transverse Panhard rod helps to locate the axle laterally and a stabilizer bar is attached to the axle tubes by links and to the underbody by U-shaped clamps.

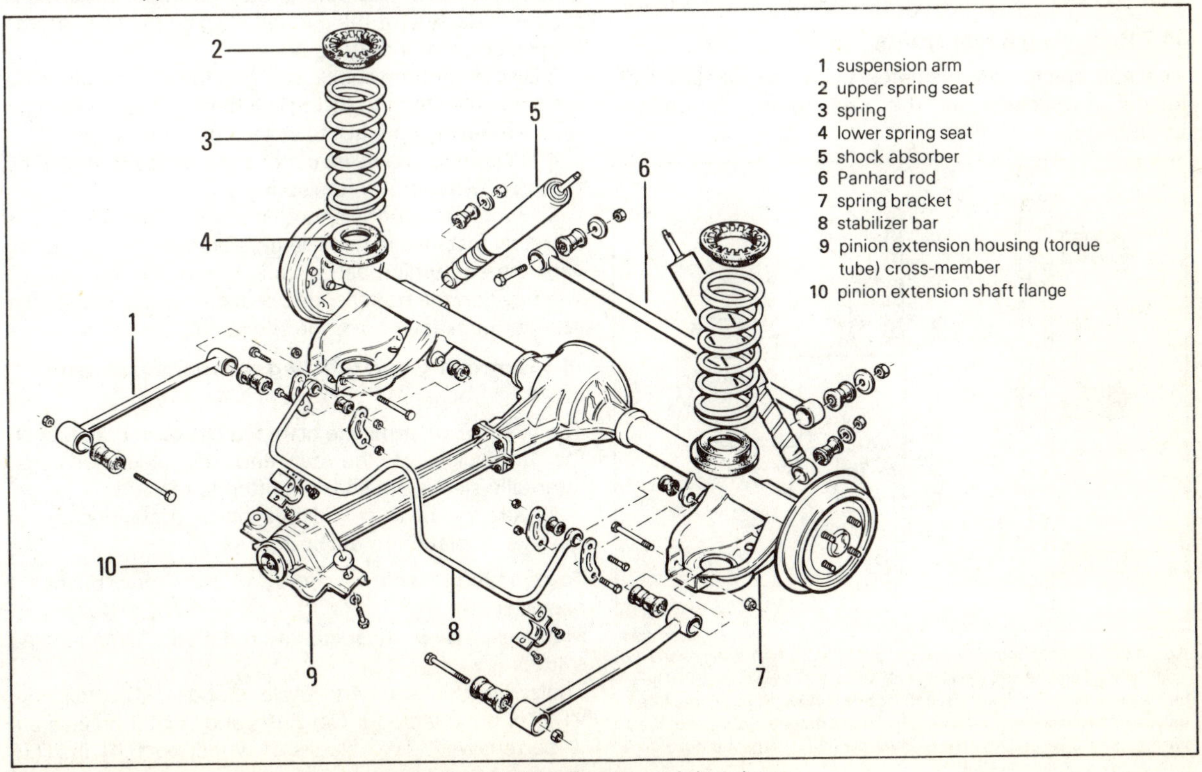

Fig. 14.7 The rear axle is of the torque-tube type and is carried on coil springs and pivoted arms

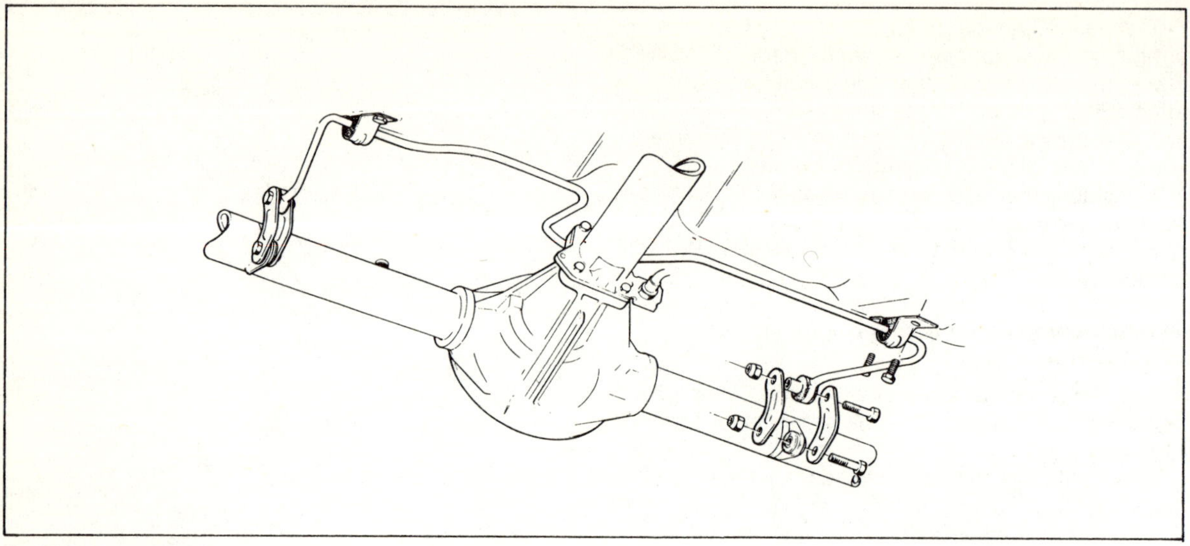

Fig. 14.8 The rear stabilizer bar is attached by links which are bolted to the axle tubes and secured to the underbody by U-shaped clamps with rubber insulators

Double-acting tubular hydraulic shock absorbers are fitted between the axle and the underside of the car. These also act as rebound stops.

The rear suspension requires the minimum of routine maintenance, attention being confined to occasional checks on the condition of the rubber bushes and shock absorbers, and the tightness of the various nuts and bolts.

14.7 Removing a rear spring

The rear springs are insulated by rubber seats which locate in brackets on the axle tube and on the underbody.

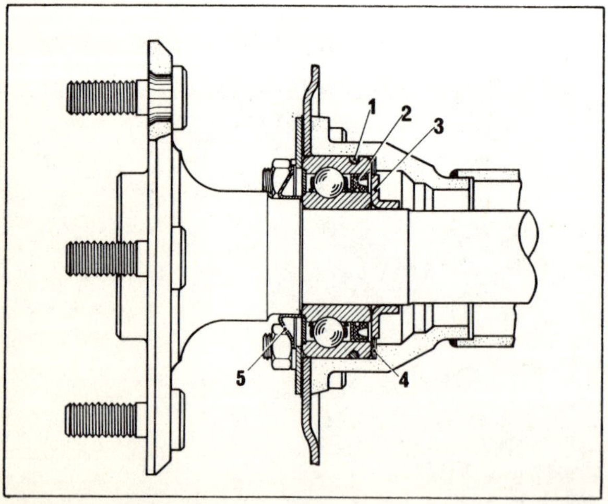

Fig. 14.9 A section through a rear hub. The axle shaft is supported by a ball bearing embodying a sealing ring **1** and a lip-type oil seal **2**. The bearing is retained by the pressed-on flanged ring **3**. Shims **4**, are fitted between the bearing and the axle tube counterbore to ensure that the bearing is held securely by the retainer plate **5**. A separate dust shield is pressed on to the axle shaft

To avoid any risk of straining a brake hose, a spring should be removed from one side at a time.

To remove and refit a spring –

Tools: Spanners. Jack. Axle stands.

1 Jack-up the rear of the body and support it on stands. Then take the weight of the axle with the jack.

2 Disconnect the stabilizer bar from both mountings on the underside of the car and slacken the nuts on the suspension arm mounting bolts.

3 Disconnect the shock absorber lower mountings on the side on which the spring is to be removed and lower the axle, taking care not to stretch the brake hose.

4 The spring and its insulator can then be removed by pulling downwards on the spring.

5 When refitting the spring, make sure that the seat is correctly installed in the axle tube bracket. Fit the spring with the end which has a straight end coil downwards and position the upper spring seat so that the step in the seat contacts the end of the spring coil.

14.8 Removing and refitting the rear suspension arms

The suspension arms are clamped between brackets on the underside of the car and the axle housings. Internally-sleeved bushes are fitted to the arms.

An arm can be removed irrespective of the position of the axle in relation to the body.

To remove and refit an arm, and install new bushes if necessary –

Materials: New bushes, if required. Liquid soap solution.

Tools: Jack. Spanners. Axle stands. Vauxhall tool VR2221 or suitable tubular drifts and vice, if bushes are to be renewed. Two blocks of wood, each 4½ in. (115 mm) long.

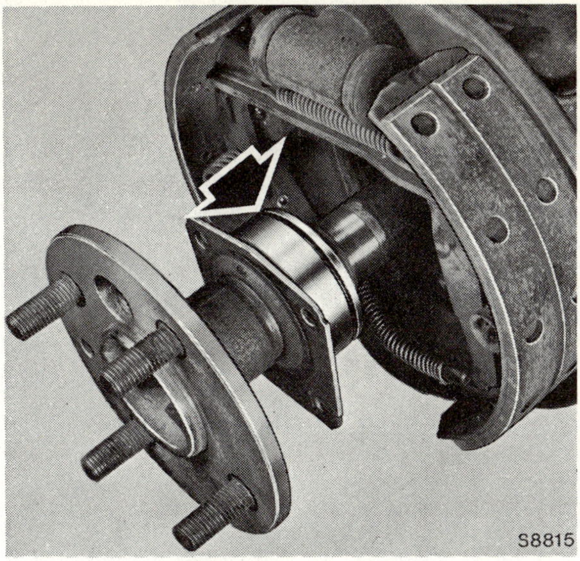

Fig. 14.10 When fitting an axle shaft make sure that the sealing ring is located in the groove in the bearing and lubricate the ring and the bore of the housing with oil to make it easier to fit the ring

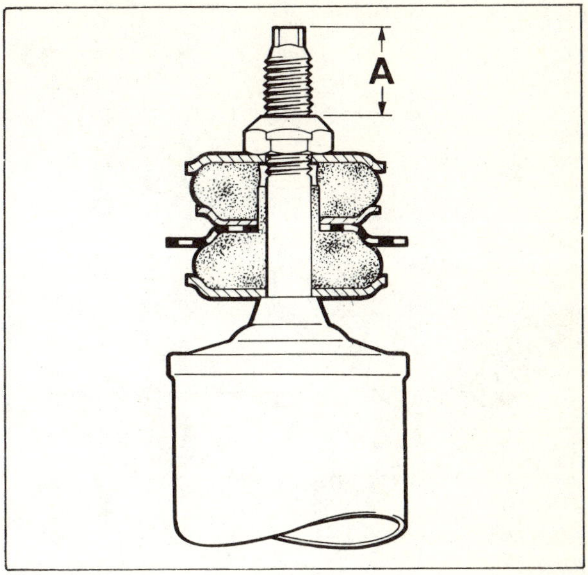

Fig. 14.11 When fitting a front shock absorber, the upper nut must be tightened until the distance A is 0.8 in. (20 mm) in order to compress the bushes correctly.

1 Jack-up and support the rear of the car and also support both sides of the rear axle.

2 Disconnect the handbrake cable guide from the clip on the arm, remove the nut from the pivot bolt at each end of the arm and withdraw both bolts.

3 If the bushes in the arm are worn, preferably use the Vauxhall tool VR2221 to press each bush out and to fit the new replacement. Smear the rubber with liquid soap solution to make it easier to insert the bush.

4 When fitting the arm, the handbrake cable clip should be towards the rear and facing downwards.

5 To ensure that the bushes will be in the correct 'neutral' position when the springs are loaded, insert two blocks of wood, 4½ in. (115 mm) long, between the axle and the underside of the car, adjacent to each bump stop and load the rear of the car until the blocks contact the underbody. Then tighten the nut on the pivot to a torque of 50 lb ft (67 Nm).

14.9 Renewing the rear-wheel hub bearings and oil seals

If a rear-wheel bearing is worn, or the oil seal is faulty — check for leakage from the oil drain hole in the brake backplate - the most satisfactory course is to ask a Vauxhall dealer to fit a new bearing and new seals. The bearing is a tight fit on the shaft and is retained by a pressed-on flanged ring. It is located in the axle tube by a bolted-on retaining plate and it is this plate, plus the tight fit on the bearing and the retaining ring on the shaft, that prevents the shaft pulling out, complete with the wheel and brake drum.

A press must be used to remove the bearing and fit a replacement, several tons pressure being needed for the operation.

A d.i.y. owner can reduce the labour charge, however, by withdrawing the axle shaft, complete with the bearing, and taking it to his local dealer for attention. The following is a brief summary of the work —

Materials: New oil sealing ring for bearing outer race. Rear axle oil.
Tools: Socket spanners with extension bar. Drift. Hammer. Jack. Axle stand.

1 Raise the rear of the car and support it on stands.

2 Remove the road wheel and the brake drum (Chapter 15).

3 Undo the nuts which secure the bearing-retaining plate by passing a socket spanner through the holes in the axle flange.

4 Pull out the axle shaft, complete with the bearing. If it is tight, tap the inner side of the flange. Don't use levers, owing to the risk of distorting the brake backplate. A Vauxhall dealer will use a special slide hammer to extract the shaft, but a d.i.y. owner is unlikely to have this tool.

5 Before refitting the shaft, check that the oil drain hole in the brake backplate beneath the axle tube is clear. Fit a new oil sealing ring to the groove in the bearing and lubricate this and the bore in the axle tube with oil to enable the seal to slide in without damage. Also oil the whole of the length of the shaft to prevent any risk of corrosion.

6 Tighten the bearing retainer nuts to the torque specified in Chapter 17 and check the axle oil level, if necessary topping-up with the correct lubricant.

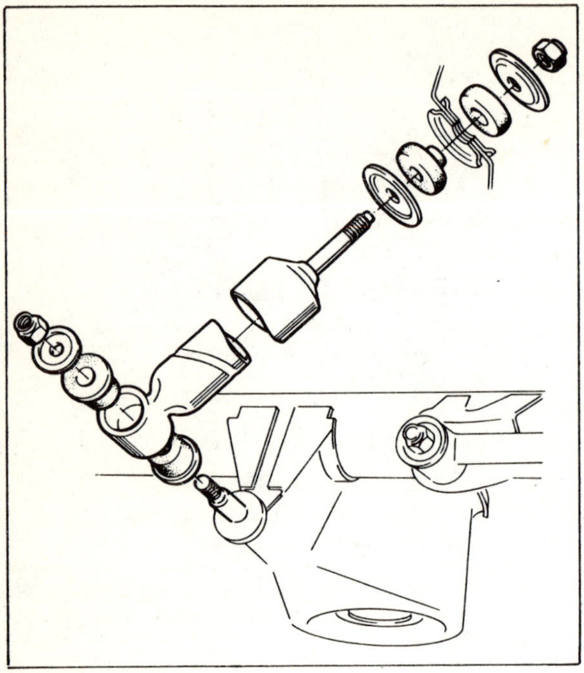

Fig. 14.12 The rear shock absorbers are attached at the upper and lower ends of rubber-bushed mountings

The shock absorbers

The front and rear shock absorbers do not, of course, have an unlimited life. When they become worn they will affect the steering, roadholding and the comfort of the ride. After about 30 000 miles (48 000 km) it is as well to have the shock absorbers checked by a dealer, preferably using a special test rig which enables their effectiveness to be accurately measured and recorded. Weak shock absorbers should be renewed without delay. They could cause a fatal accident.

14.10 Fitting a new front shock absorber

Removal of a front shock absorber is quite straightforward, but don't attempt to do this with the front wheels raised unless a support is placed under the suspension lower arm, since the shock absorbers control the rebound, and therefore the extension, of the front springs.

Materials: New shock absorber and rubber bushes.
Tools: Spanners.

1 Remove the pivot bolt from the lower mounting eye of the shock abosrber.

2 From inside the engine compartment, unscrew the nut that retains the upper mounting bushes and washers.

3 When fitting a new shock absorber, use new mounting bushes. The upper mounting nut must be tightened down until the top of the nut is 0.8 in. (20

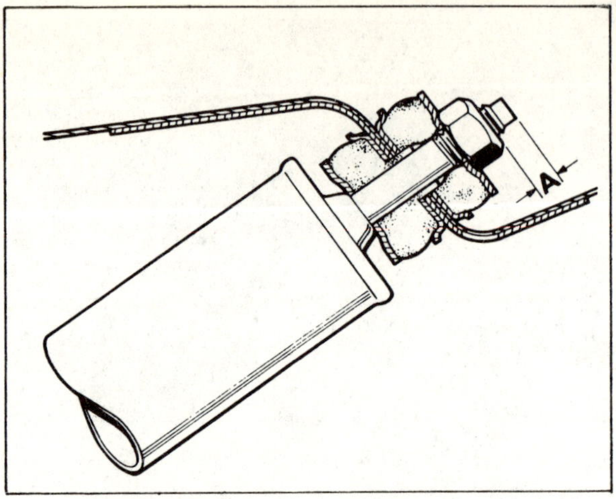

Fig. 14.13 When fitting a rear shock absorber the nut must be tightened to give a distance A of 0.3 in. (8 mm) to provide the correct compression on the bushes

mm) below the end of the mounting stud to provide the correct compression of the bushes.

14.11 Fitting a new rear shock absorber

The rear shock abosrbers are attached at their lower ends by rubber bushes to studs on the brackets on the rear axle tubes and at their upper end are retained by nuts on studs which are accessible from inside the loading area or boot, after removing the carpet and floor panel.

Materials: New shock absorbers and bushes.
Tools: Spanners. Jack. Axle stand.

1 Jack-up and support the rear of the car. Then transfer the jack to beneath the rear axle to prevent the shock absorber from extending fully, since it controls the rebound and extension of the spring.

2 Remove the nuts from the upper and lower mounting studs and withdraw the shock absorber.

3 When assembling, tighten the upper mounting nut until the top of the nut is 0.3 in. (8 mm) below the end of the stud to provide the correct compression on the bushes.

The steering gear

The rack-and-pinion steering gear is mounted on the front-axle cross-member. Rotation of the steering wheel is transmitted by the steering column, through a flexible coupling, to the pinion of the steering unit, which moves the rack from side to side. This movement is transmitted to the steering arms on the steering knuckles by adjustable tie-rods.

The ball joints which couple the inner ends of the tie-rods to the steering rack are lubricated from the rack itself and are protected by corrugated rubber bellows. The outer joints are lubricated on assembly and are

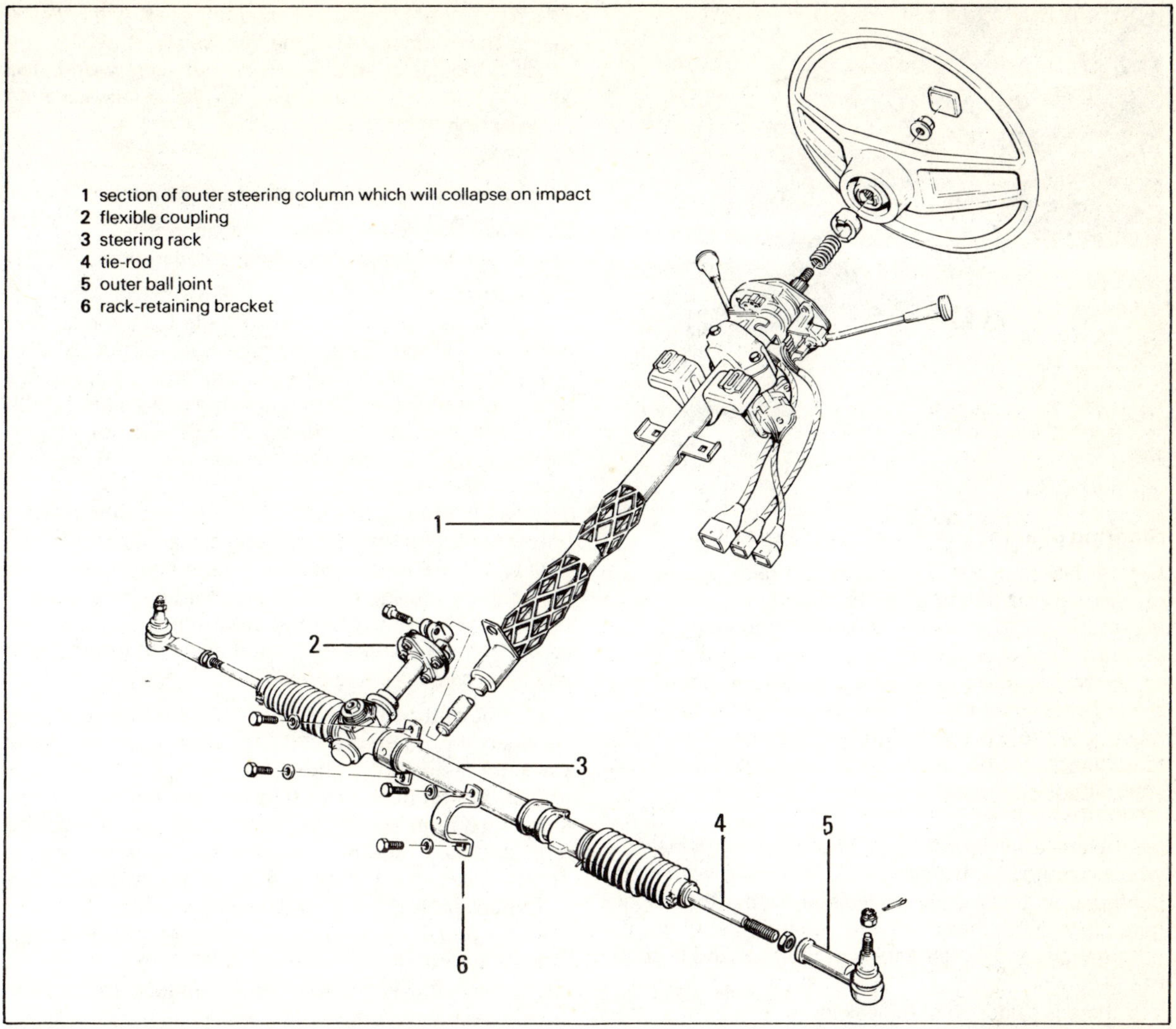

Fig. 14.14 The layout of the rack-and-pinion steering gear

protected by gaiters. They do not need further lubrication during their normal life. When they develop wear, they must be renewed.

The rack bellows and the gaiters on the joints should, however, be inspected during routine servicing. Apart from allowing lubricant to escape, a damaged gaiter or bellows will also allow water and grit to enter the joint or the rack, quickly rendering it unserviceable.

One-third of a pint of SAE 90 hypoid oil is poured into the rack housing when it is assembled and the rack should not require further lubrication unless a gaiter has been damaged or a clip has slackened off, allowing oil to escape. The steering gear should on no account be completely filled with oil, as this will result in a pressure build-up which could burst the gaiters or blow them off the ends of the rack.

Even when the gear contains the correct amount of oil, never swing the roadwheels quickly from lock to lock while the car is jacked-up, as this may generate sufficient hydraulic pressure to damage or to dislodge the gaiters.

Wheel balancing

Wheel-wobble and quite severe vibration at about 60-80 mph (100-130 kph), and sometimes at lower speeds, can be caused by unbalanced wheels and tyres. It is advisable to have the balance checked by a properly equipped garage every 3000 miles (5000 km), preferably with the aid of a dynamic balancer which allows the degree of unbalance to be checked electronically when the wheel is spun without removing it from the front hub.

The rear wheels should be balanced at the same time. They can not only cause vibration, but may also cause a rear-end steering effect if they are badly out of balance.

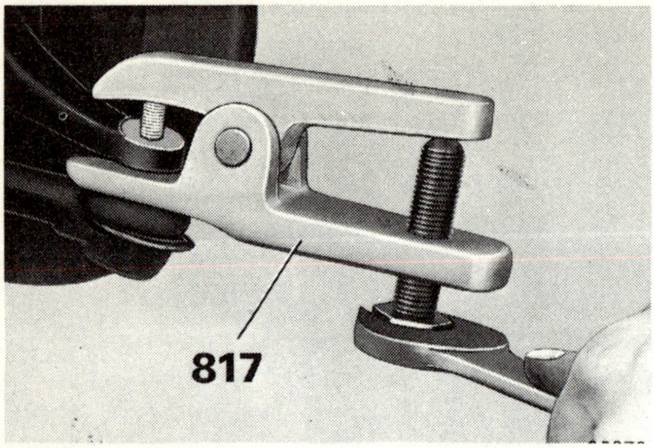

Fig. 14.15 Using a steering ball joint extractor to separate the taper on a ball pin. The Vauxhall tool 817 is a typical example of tools of this type

Steering gear repairs

Before dealing in detail with steering-gear repairs, one or two general points must be mentioned. The most important is that many steering troubles can be attributed quite simply to incorrect wheel alignment, the wrong pressures, or unbalanced front wheels and tyres. Steering alignment checks and wheel balancing must be left to a properly equipped garage. It is useless to attempt to do these jobs without the aid of specialized equipment.

There have been cases in which the steering rack has been blamed for heavy steering or knocking when the wheel is turned from lock to lock, when the trouble has been due, in fact, to the oil leaking from a torn rubber gaiter. When checking the gaiters, stretch the corrugations and look for splits at the tops and bottoms of the convolutions.

If there is evidence of oil leakage – say from a loose gaiter clip – but the gaiter itself is sound, centralize the steering rack, take off the gaiter retaining clip on the driver's side, inject not more than $\frac{1}{3}$ pint of SAE 90EP oil into the gaiter, refit the clip and turn the steering from side to side to distribute the oil in the housing.

When the steering rack-and-pinion is badly worn, the safest plan is to fit a reconditioned assembly. Stripping and reassembly calls for the use of special tools and a stock of adjusting shims that are not likely to be found in the home garage.

A final point concerns the difficulty that is experienced in removing the tapered ball pins of the steering ball-joints from their housings. The only satisfactory method is to use a simple ball-joint extractor. One often sees it stated that a joint can be parted by striking both sides of the housing simultaneously with heavy hammers. While this may sometimes be effective it often results only in the expenditure of a lot of hard work and bad language, and possibly damage to the ball pin or the seal. The almost contemptuous ease with which a proper screw-type extractor deals with the job makes the modest cost of the tool well worthwhile. The official tool is Remover 817, but screw-operated extractors of a similar type can be obtained quite cheaply from most accessory shops.

14.12 Renewing tie-rod outer ball-joints

Materials: New joints. Paraffin. Clean rags.
Tools: Service tool 817 or similar ball-pin extractor. Set of spanners. Wire brush.

The outer ball-joints have nylon seats for the balls and are spring-loaded. By applying leverage it is possible to move the socket in line with the stud, against the pressure of the spring, but if any free movement can be felt simply by pushing and pulling on the joint by hand, this indicates wear or a broken spring, which calls for renewal of the joint.

When tightening or slackening the nut on the tie-rod, prevent the joint rotating by using a spanner on the two flats which are machined on it. There have been cases of the joint housing being so distorted by a strong pull on the locking nut when this precaution has not been taken that the ball has become detached from the joint while the car was being driven.

1 Remove the retaining nuts and break the taper joint between the ball pin and its housing, using a special extractor – see notes above.

2 Count the number of threads showing beyond the lock-nut on the tie-rod, or paint a mark on the tie-rod registering with the face of the lock-nut, to ensure approximately correct wheel alignment on reassembly.

3 Slacken the lock-nut and unscrew the ball-joint from the end of the tie-rod.

4 When refitting the joints (or fitting new ones), check that the same number of threads is showing behind each lock-nut.

5 Have the wheel alignment checked by a Vauxhall dealer or a garage which has precision wheel aligning equipment.

14.13 Removing the steering rack assembly

A flexible coupling at the base of the steering column is attached to the pinion shaft of the steering gear by a split clamp, tightened by a pinch bolt which passes across a groove which is machined on the pinion shaft. On right-hand-drive models this clamp is an integral part of the coupling but it is worth mentioning that on left-hand-drive cars the clamp is a separate item.

If the coupling will not slide off the shaft easily after the clamping bolt has been withdrawn, do not try to hammer it off. There are plastic injections in the steering column shaft which allow the column to collapse in an accident and these can be damaged by any shock-load on the shaft, calling for the fitting of a new shaft.

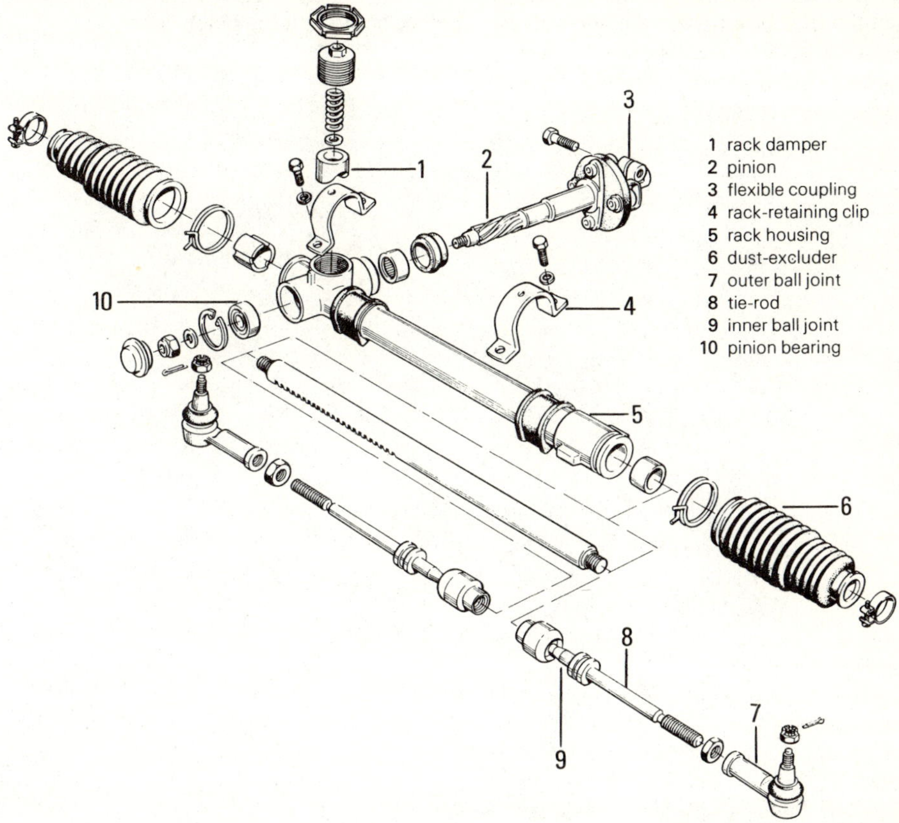

Fig. 14.16 The steering rack fully dismantled

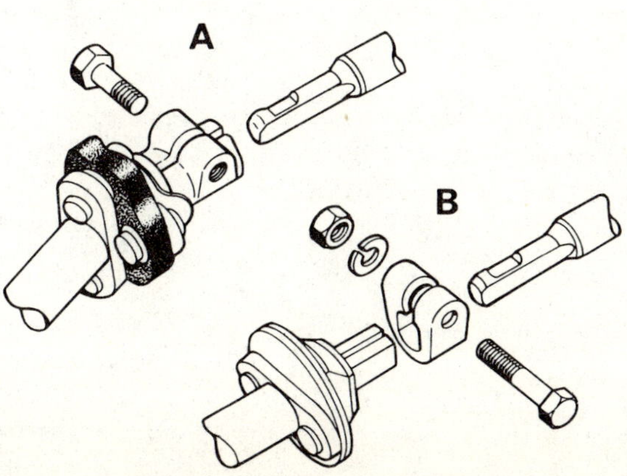

Fig. 14.17 Steering column flexible couplings. On right-hand-drive cars the clamp is an integral part of the coupling, as shown at A. On left-hand-drive models (B) the clamp is separate from the coupling and the pinch bolt is assembled from the left-hand side of the car

To remove the steering gear –

Materials: New rack-and-pinion assembly if required.
Tools: Spanners. Ball-pin extractor. Jack. Axle stand.

1 Jack-up and support the front of the car.

2 Unscrew and remove the bolt from the split clamp in the coupling.

3 If the coupling is tight on the shaft after removing the clamping bolt it can be freed by turning the steering wheel in each direction.

4 Disconnect the steering tie-rod ball-joints from the steering arms (Section 14.12). Undo the nuts and bolts which secure the rack assembly and lift it away.

14.14 Refitting the steering rack assembly

Tools: Spanners. Jack. Axle stand.

Reverse the instructions for removing the rack assembly in the previous section, paying particular attention to the following points –

1 Set the road wheels in the straight-ahead position.

2 Centralize the rack by counting the number of turns of the pinion shaft which are needed to move the rack from one end of its travel to the other and then move the rack back through half this number of turns.

3 Make sure that the steering wheel spoke is horizontal and that the groove for the clamping bolt on the pinion shaft is uppermost. Install the pinch bolt and tighten it to 13 lb ft (17 Nm). The mounting bolt for the steering gear should not be overtightened, to avoid distorting the rack housing. The recommended torque is 15 lb ft (20 Nm).

4 Tighten the bolts which retain the steering gear before tightening the pinch-bolt.

15 The braking system

All Chevettes have disc brakes at the front and drums at the rear. A dual-line braking system, which provides separate hydraulic circuits for the front and rear brakes, ensures that if one circuit should be put out of action for any reason, it will still be possible to stop the car. If a circuit does fail, a warning light is illuminated on the instrument panel.

Because disc brakes call for higher operating pressures than drum brakes (owing to the relatively small area of friction pad that is pressed against the disc), a vacuum-servo, which reduces the effort required on the brake pedal, is provided as standard.

The servo piston, operated by the partial vacuum which exists in the inlet manifold of the engine, acts on the hydraulic piston in the master cylinder and boosts the pressure in the brake lines by a ratio of about 2:1.

Practical pointers

As with other components of the car, 'repair by replacement' is assuming increasing importance where braking systems are concerned. Service-exchange sets or relined brake shoes from a reputable supplier are a better proposition than attempting to reline existing shoes. Similarly, it is preferable to fit new master and slave cylinders instead of installing new rubber seals in the old components. Brake manufacturers, in fact, tend increasingly to supply only new or reconditioned assemblies, instead of repair kits.

But before committing yourself to a fairly expensive item, check-out the more obvious causes of unsatisfactory braking, using Trouble-shooting Chart 9.

These considerations will explain why we have not included in this chapter detailed instructions for stripping or repairing the hydraulic units concerned.

A final word of warning if you do intend to service any of the hydraulic components yourself – metric brake fittings are used on these cars and *it is essential to fit only metric replacements.*

Metric unions, union nuts, hose ends and bleed screws are coloured black and most of them also have the letter M stamped on them. Apart from the difference between Unified and metric screw threads, the design of some of the parts is also different. For example, a metric hose connector seals against the *bottom* of the threaded hole – not against a flange. There should therefore be a small gap between the hexagon on the hose and the face of the brake cylinder or caliper when the hose has been screwed fully home.

The time factor

A complete check on the braking system can be carried out comfortably in a morning. Typical times for other individual jobs are: fitting new brake shoes to two drum brakes, 1½ hr; fitting set of disc brake pads, 30 min; bleeding brakes, 45 min.

Routine servicing

15.1 Topping up the brake fluid reservoir

The brake master cylinder may have a single reservoir, or two separate reservoirs, clipped together and closed by a single cap, which incorporates two diaphragms to seal the fluid against dirt or moisture from the air. The upper surface of each diaphragm is vented to the atmosphere so that as the fluid level drops the diaphragm deforms and is drawn down into the reservoir.

The 6000-miles check on the fluid levels is largely a precautionary measure. If frequent topping-up is needed, look for leakage from the pipelines, unions or hydraulic cylinders.

To top-up the system –

1 Before removing the filler cap, clean the cap and the reservoir or reservoirs with methylated spirits. Do not use paraffin or petrol as these may contaminate the brake fluid.

2 When a single reservoir is fitted, top-up the fluid to the maximum level marker with Castrol Girling universal clutch and brake fluid. If twin reservoirs are fitted, pull off the cap and remove the rubber diaphragm assembly. Check that the diaphragm is in good condition and that it has resumed its normal shape. Bring the fluid level up to the maximum level marker on each reservoir. When refitting the diaphragm, insert the free end of the tab in the slot in the reservoir body.

3 If the fluid level has fallen appreciably, ask an assistant to depress the brake pedal firmly while you check all the pipelines and unions for any sign of leakage.

15.2 Changing the brake fluid

Brake fluid (and particularly the disc-brake type) absorbs moisture from the air. Some moisture can also be drawn in past the wheel-cylinder seals. Since this moisture seriously lowers the boiling point of the fluid, 'brake fade,' or complete brake failure, can result when the fluid boils in the wheel cylinders under heavy or prolonged braking conditions.The diagnosis is confirmed if normal braking is restored when the brakes cool down. The water in the fluid also corrodes the internal parts of the hydraulic components. The fluid should therefore be changed after 24 000 miles, or two years, in service.

Obviously, fluid should never be stored in an unsealed container; the old fluid that has been bled from the system must not be re-used.

Materials and tools: As for bleeding the brakes—see Section 15.3

The fluid is changed by opening the bleed screw on each wheel cylinder in turn, fitting a tube to the nipple, with its lower end in a suitable container, and pumping the brake pedal to expel the old fluid. The process is the same as for bleeding the brakes (Section 15.3) but all the fluid in the system is pumped out and replaced by new fluid.

Fig. 15.1 The rear-brake automatic adjusters can be backed-off, to make it easier to remove the drum, by turning them in the directions shown by the arrows

15.3 Bleeding the brakes

This is *not* a routine job. It should be necessary to expel air from the system only if any of the unions have been undone or new parts have been fitted, but air can be drawn in past worn wheel-cylinder or master-cylinder seals — in which case renewal of the parts is obviously indicated.

The brake-bleeding procedure is the same as for changing the fluid, but it is necessary only to pump the pedal until air bubbles no longer issue from the bleed pipe. The reservoir must be topped-up at frequent intervals to prevent air entering the system.

A nipple which incorporates an air-bleed valve will be found on the backplate of each rear brake and on each front brake caliper. On right-hand-drive models there is a further bleed screw in the pressure-reducing valve — see Section 15.10.

You will need the help of an assistant to do the job properly unless you use one of the several 'easy-bleeding' devices which can be bought from accessory shops and which make brake bleeding a simple, one-man job.

Materials: Tin of Castrol Girling universal clutch and brake fluid.

Tools: Brake bleed valve spanner. Length of rubber or plastic tube to fit bleed nipple. Container for fluid bled from system. 'Easy-bleed' device, if available.

1 Pump the brake pedal several times to exhaust the vacuum in the servo.

2 Attach the bleed tube to the nipple on the wheel which is furthest from the brake master cylinder. Pass the tube through a box or ring spanner that is a good fit on the bleed nipple and submerge the free end of the tube in a little brake fluid in a clean container.

3 Open the bleed screw one complete turn and ask your assistant to depress the brake pedal with a slow, full stroke and then allow it to return unassisted. Top-up the fluid level in the master cylinder reservoir and then repeat the pumping stroke.

5 Watch the flow of fluid into the container and continue pumping until no further air bubbles appear. Tighten the bleed screw while the pedal is held down. *Do not overtighten the screw.* It is comparatively easy to shear it off.

6 Bleed the other brakes in the same way, working back progressively towards the master cylinder. Finally, bleed the pressure-reducing valve.

15.4 Brake adjustment

The front disc brakes are self-adjusting and require no attention during the life of the friction pads, provided that the checks described in Section 15.9 are carried out at 6000-mile intervals.

The rear brakes are also self-adjusting. Two pivoted adjusters, mounted on the backplate, have pins which

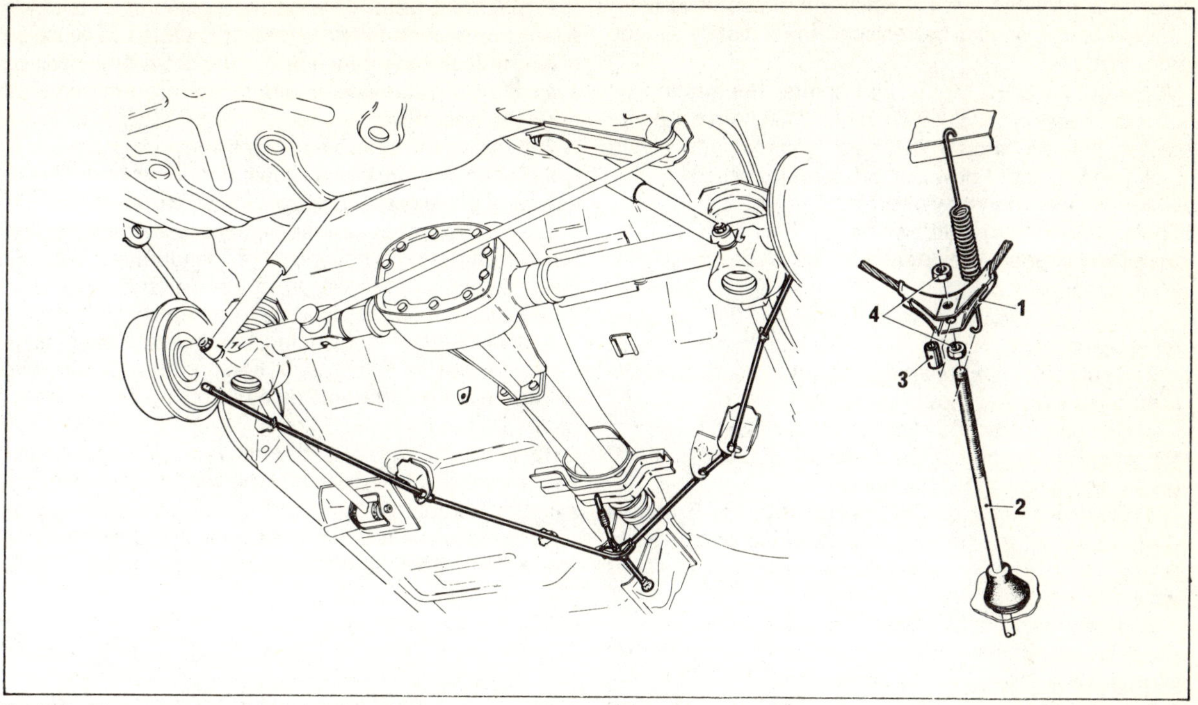

Fig. 15.2 The arrangement of the handbrake cable. On the right is shown the equalizer **1**, which is secured to the relay rod **2** by a spacer **3** and two nuts **4**, which allow the cable to be adjusted

engage with slots in the brake shoes so that the adjusters are moved outwards as the shoes wear.

The adjusters are preloaded by wave-washers, however, and when the brakes are released the correct shoe-to-drum clearance is maintained because the tension of the shoe-return springs is not sufficient to overcome the preloading on the adjusters.

When it is necessary to remove the drums the adjusters can be turned back by applying a spanner to the bolts shown in Fig. 15.1, which project from the brake backplate.

The adjusters should not be lubricated and no attempt should be made to remove them from the backplate. The method of checking the preloading is described in Section 15.6.

15.5 Handbrake cable adjustment

Normally, correct adjustment of the rear-brake shoes will eliminate any excessive free movement on the handbrake lever. In time, however, the handbrake cable will stretch and it will be necessary to take up the slack by shortening the cable. Be careful not to adjust the cable too tightly, as this will cause the rear brakes to bind.

The one-piece handbrake cable incorporates an equalizer which is attached to the handbrake relay rod. Nylon cable guides are held in brackets which are welded to the underbody and to the lower rear suspension arms.

A cable guide on each rear brake backplate also acts as a stop for the cable return spring.

To adjust the handbrake cable –

Tools: Spanners to fit adjusting nut and lock-nut.

1 Chock the front wheels securely and support the rear of the car.

2 Slacken the nut on the handbrake relay rod in front of the equalizer and screw the rear nut along the rod to eliminate all slackness in the cable.

3 Check that both rear wheels rotate freely. If one brake is binding slightly, apply the handbrake hard to equalize the tension on both brakes, release the lever and recheck the wheels for freedom. To avoid any risk of the brakes binding it is best to set the adjustment so that the handbrake lever can be pulled up by one notch without the shoes contacting the drums, but a firm pull should raise it by four notches and apply the brakes fully.

15.6 Servicing a drum brake

A drum brake service consists of checking the thickness of the lining remaining on the brake shoes, cleaning out accumulations of brake dust and road grit, and checking the operating cylinders, adjusters and the handbrake lever for binding and the cylinder seals for fluid leakage.

The brake shoes fitted, and replacements supplied by Vauxhall dealers, have a groove around the centre of the linings. When the linings are worn down so that the groove is no longer visible, they are almost level with the rivets and should be replaced immediately — see item 6 below.

Materials: Paraffin. Methylated spirits. Penetrating oil or rust-releasing fluid. Clean rags. Duckham's Keenol grease. For a complete overhaul: replacement relined brake shoes; set of new pull-off springs; possibly, new wheel cylinders and new backplates.

Tools: Spanners. Screwdriver. Pliers. Hammer, preferably copper- or hide-faced. Jack. Axle stand.

To remove the shoes –

1 Jack-up and support the rear of the car and remove the wheel.

2 Slacken off the brake adjusters fully by turning the nuts in the direction shown in Fig. 15.1.

3 Remove the spring clips which are fitted to two of the wheel studs and pull off the drum. If it sticks, tap it gently with a soft-faced hammer.

4 Clean out all the brake dust and grit from inside the drum and from the components mounted on the backplate. *Be careful not to inhale the dust as it contains asbestos, which can harm the lungs.*

5 If the brake linings have not worn down so that the rivets are near the surface, and the drums are not badly scored (light scoring is inevitable) the brake is fit for a further period of service, until the next routine inspection becomes due. Otherwise, continue the stripping as described in the following sections. But before refitting the drum ease the shoes outwards and lubricate the pads with Keenol grease. This can be applied with a thin strip of metal. Be careful not to pull the shoes outwards more than necessary, as this may displace the handbrake lever mechanism. Use only a smear of grease to avoid any risk of contaminating the brake linings.

6 Make a careful note of the positions of the two springs in relation to the shoes. It is wisest to work on only one brake at a time so that the other brake will be available for reference if difficulties are encountered during reassembly.

7 Remove the shoe steady pins and springs.

8 To remove the brake shoes, unhook the handbrake cables and release the front shoe from the lower pedestal. The shoes can then be collapsed together and the return spring removed. The handbrake operating lever cannot be removed from the rear shoe, the lever and the shoe being supplied as an assembly.

9 If no further dismantling is required, check each piston for seizure in its bore. Then tighten a loop of wire or string across the end of each piston to prevent it being ejected from the cylinder.

10 If a piston has seized, remove the wheel cylinder. First rotate the adjusters until the shoes are clear of the cylinder pistons. Disconnect the fluid pipeline and plug the pipe to prevent the fluid being lost and dirt entering the system. Remove the retaining screws to release the cylinder assembly.

11 If it is required to fit new rubber seals to the pistons, push them out of their bores, clean the interior of the cylinder with methylated spirits and if there is the slightest sign of pitting or scoring, reject it. *If the bore is in perfect condition,* fit new seals, following the instructions included with the repair kit.

12 If the automatic adjusters do not appear to have been operating correctly, check the preloading on each adjuster by applying a spanner to the bolt on the backplate. A torque of 27-35 lb in. (1-3.9 Nm) should be needed to move the adjusters.

Note that this torque is measured in lb in. — not lb ft. As it is unlikely that you will have a torque wrench

Fig. 15.3 When installing the rear brake shoes the larger hooked end of the return spring must be fitted to the rear shoe, which incorporates the lever which is operated by the handbrake cable

Fig. 15.4 The eccentric-type automatic adjusters for the rear shoes are mounted on the brake backplate and have pins which engage with slots in the brake shoes. The adjusters are friction-loaded by wave washers to prevent them slackening off

reading in these low values, the easiest way to check the torque is to measure the pull on the end of a spanner, using a spring balance. For example, a pull of 5 lb on a spanner 6 in. long, or at a distance 6 in. away from the centre of the adjusting nut, represents a torque of 30 lb in. The specified torque range therefore represents a pull of $4\frac{1}{2}$-$5\frac{3}{4}$ lb at a 6 in. radius.

If the adjusters are not working properly a new backplate must be fitted as described in Section 15.8, since the parts are not supplied separately.

15.7 Reassembling a drum brake

Materials and tools: as for Section 15.6. If a wheel cylinder has been removed and refitted, brake bleeding equipment (Section 15.3) will also be needed.

1 Carefully inspect the brake shoes and renew them if they are worn down so that the rivet heads are nearly flush with the surface, or if the linings have been contaminated by oil or hydraulic fluid.

2 Preferably fit new pull-off springs. If doubtful, compare one of the old springs with a new spring.

3 Clean the backplate thoroughly and smear the shoe contact pads on the wheel cylinder, pedestal and backplate with Duckham's Keenol grease, but be careful, of course, to keep the grease away from the linings.

4 Assemble the shoes with the strut as shown in Fig. 15.3 and fit the larger hooked end of the spring in the rear shoe, which incorporates the handbrake operating lever.

5 If the brake pipe has been disconnected, bleed the system (Section 15.3).

6 Smear the axle shaft spigot with grease before refitting the brake drum. Push the spring retaining clips on to two opposing wheel studs, hard up against the drum.

7 Operate the adjusters by depressing the brake pedal several times to reset the brake shoes to the correct clearance.

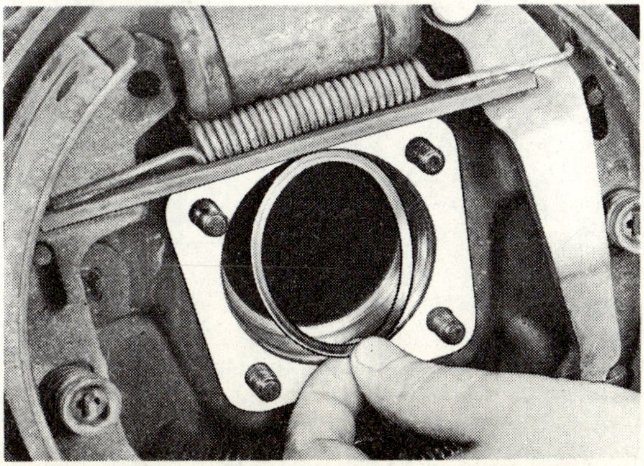

Fig. 15.5 It may be necessary to change the shims fitted between the rear-wheel hub bearing and the axle tube if a new brake backplate is fitted

15.8 Fitting a new brake backplate

If the automatic brake adjusters are not operating properly, they cannot be dismantled or serviced. Instead a new backplate must be fitted.

When a new plate is installed it is important to ensure that the hub bearing retaining plate is in contact with the outer race of the axle shaft bearing, to eliminate end-float. This is done by fitting the correct number of shims between the axle shaft bearing and the counterbore in the axle tube.

As this job calls for the use of an accurate depth gauge and a supply of shims of different thicknesses, it is advisable to leave the adjustment to your Vauxhall dealer, but there is no reason why you should not dismantle and reassemble the rear brake as described in Section 15.7 and then take the car to your dealer to have the adjustment checked.

15.9 Renewing disc brake pads

Fitting new friction pads to a disc brake is a simple process, for which no special tools are needed. It is not necessary to dismantle the calipers. *In fact, this must never be done except under workshop conditions.* If the piston seals are leaking, it is best to have them replaced by a Vauxhall dealer.

The pads should be renewed when the friction material has worn down to a thickness of 0.06 in. (1.5 mm).

To avoid any risk of fluid overflowing from the brake reservoir when the pads are forced back into the caliper, it is advisable to reduce the level to the half-full mark.

Materials: Paraffin. Methylated spirits. Clean rags. Disc brake fluid. Copper-based lubricant. If the pads are worn, those in both front brakes must be renewed, otherwise unbalanced braking will result. For this reason the friction pads are supplied as kits for two caliper assemblies.

Tools: Pliers. Strong screwdriver. Jack. Wheel-nut spanner.

To change the pads –

1 Remove the wheel.

2 Remove the clips that lock the retaining pins, pull out the pins and remove the pad-retaining spring.

3 Grip the outer edge of one pad with a pair of pliers, rock it slightly to free it and withdraw it from the caliper with the anti-squeal shims. Deal with the other pad in the same way.

4 If the pads are likely to last until the next service is due (previous experience will show the rate at which they are wearing), clean off all rust and grit before replacing them.

5 Thoroughly clean the inside of the caliper and the exposed face of each operating piston. Rust can cause a piston to bind. To check this, insert a piece of wood between the end of each piston and the disc to act as a

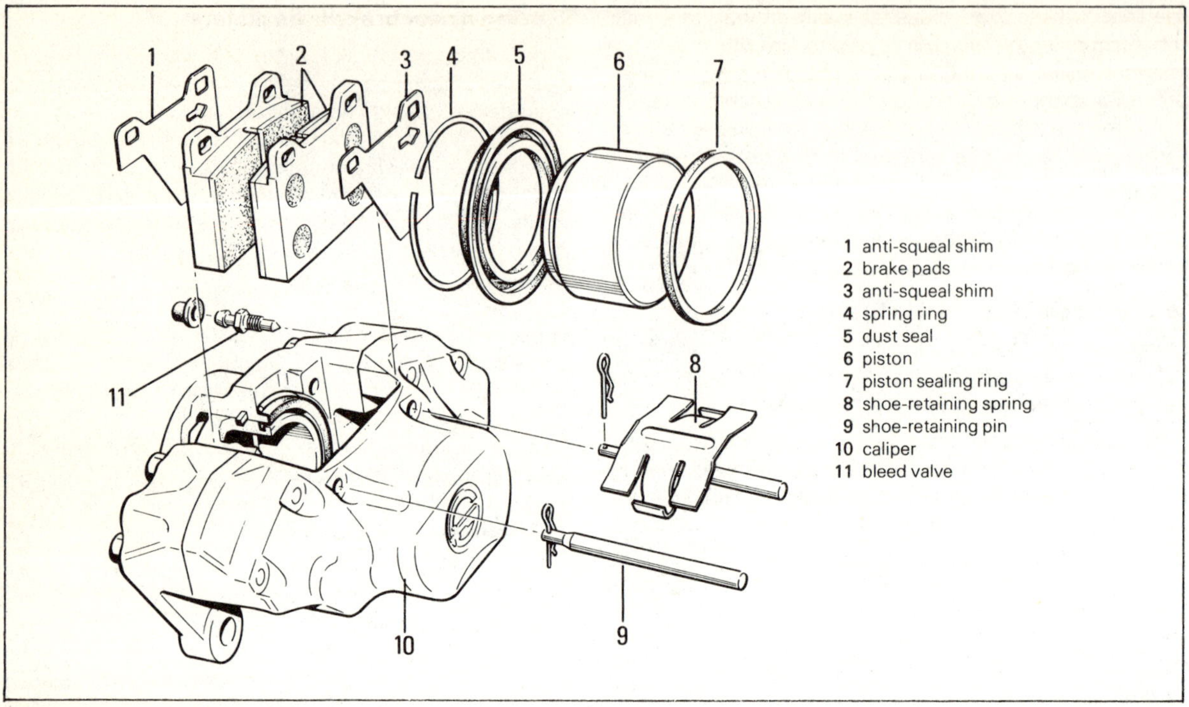

Fig. 15.6 A front disc-brake caliper fully dismantled

distance piece. If the wood is about $\frac{1}{8}$ in. (3.2 mm) less in thickness than the gap, the pistons can be pushed out, by pumping the brake pedal, sufficiently to allow their ends to be inspected, but without the risk of ejecting them from their bores. Clean the pistons, but do not rotate them in their bores. If there is any sign of fluid leakage it is best to have the caliper checked by a Vauxhall dealer, since the cylinder bores may be corroded, which would call for the fitting of a new caliper.

6 If a piston has seized in its bore, it will not move when the brake pedal is pumped with the spacing block in place. Also, the brake disc will probably be rusted on that side. If the piston cannot be freed a new caliper may be needed. Again, consult your dealer.

7 Check the brake disc for signs of deep scores. Some scoring is inevitable in normal service, but a badly scored or corroded and pitted disc, or one that appears to have excessive run-out at the edge when rotated, should be inspected by a Vauxhall dealer.

8 Check the wheel bearings for excessive 'shake' before fitting the new brake pads. Wheel bearing wear is dealt with in Chapter 14. Excessive wear will result in the pads being knocked back from the disc, causing increased brake pedal travel.

9 Slacken the brake bleed valve and lever each piston back into its bore with a strong screwdriver. Surplus fluid should flow from the bleed valve when this is done, but also check that there is no risk of the fluid overflowing from the master cylinder.

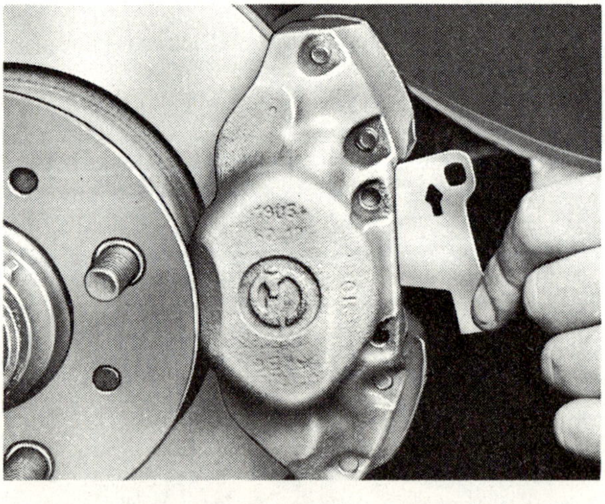

Fig. 15.7 When fitting the front brake pads the anti-squeal shims must be installed with the arrow in the direction of forward rotation of the disc

10 Refit the pads and the anti-squeal shims, with the arrows in the shims pointing in the direction of normal rotation of the wheel. Before fitting the pads and shims to the caliper, smear a small amount of high-melting point copper-based grease such as Copaslip or Cuprysil on the backplate of the pad, on the contact areas on the edge of the pad backplate and on both sides of the shims. This will help to prevent brake squeal, *but use only a copper-based lubricant — not ordinary grease.*

Check that each pad moves easily in the caliper. If there are any high spots, these should be filed off.

11 Replace the pad-retaining spring, pins and clips. Make sure that the retaining spring is fitted as shown in Fig. 15.6.

12 Close the bleed valve, top-up the master cylinder and press hard on the brake pedal to force the pads into contact with the disc.

15.10 The brake-pressure reducing valve

To reduce the risk of the rear wheels locking under heavy braking conditions, a pressure-reducing valve is mounted on the master cylinder support bracket. This prevents any further rise in the pressure applied to the rear-brake cylinders when a safe maximum has been reached.

This 'brake pressure conscious' valve is controlled by the pressure in the front brake pipelines. If a failure should occur in the front brake hydraulic circuit, however, the valve is bypassed and full pressure is applied to the rear brakes.

The valve cannot be repaired or serviced and must be renewed if it is faulty. It must be connected as shown in Fig. 15.8.

15.11 Servicing the brake hoses

During routine servicing the brake hoses should be inspected for signs of leakage, chafing or general deterioration. They should in any case be renewed after 40 000 miles or every three years, whichever occurs first.

Scrupulous cleanliness is vital when removing and refitting the hoses.

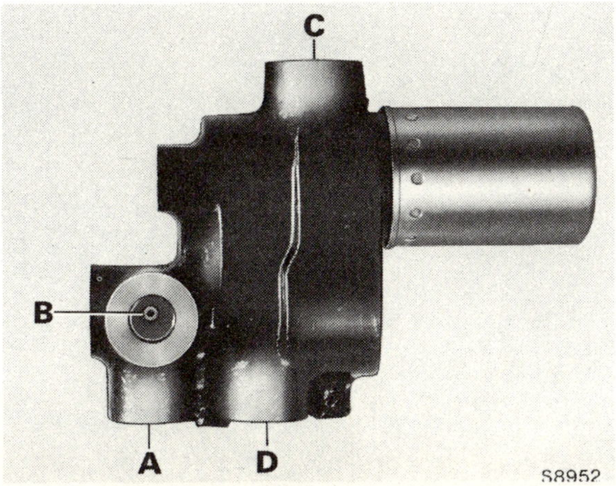

Fig. 15.8 The 'brake-pressure conscious' pressure-relief valve. On right-hand-drive cars a bleed screw is installed in the port B and front-brake fluid pressure is sensed through the port A. Fluid pressure to the rear brakes enters through port C and the modified pressure leaves the valve through the port D

Fig. 15.9 Removing a clip which retains a brake hose to the body or axle bracket. The clip must always be fitted with the bent tag away from the flexible hose

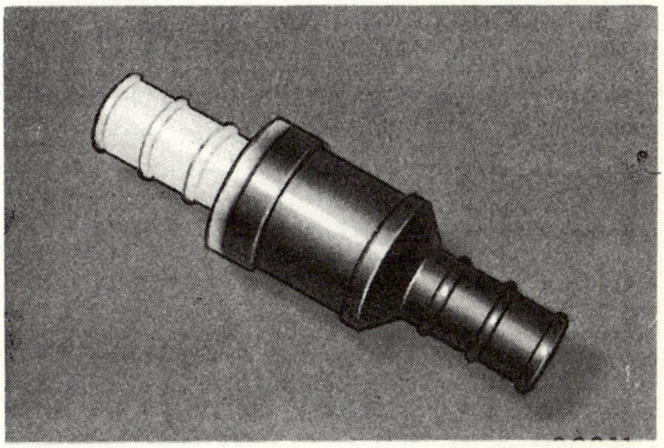

Fig. 15.10 The vacuum-check valve which is fitted in the hose between the inlet manifold and the vacuum servo. It must be installed with the white section towards the servo

The vacuum servo

The vacuum-operated servo is mounted in the engine compartment and acts directly on the primary piston in the hydraulic master cylinder.

If the servo does not operate, or seems to lack power, first check that there is no leakage at the unions in the hose connecting it to the inlet manifold, and that the hose itself has not perished or collapsed.

If all seems to be in order here, the vacuum check valve which maintains a vacuum in the servo body may be faulty. This valve cannot be serviced and must be renewed if it is suspect. It must be installed with the arrow on the valve body towards the inlet manifold and the white section towards the servo.

If a new valve does not improve matters, have the servo checked by a Vauxhall dealer. Like many modern components it is not repairable and must be replaced if it develops a fault.

Should the servo fail for any reason, fluid can still flow through it to the brakes, but a considerably heavier pressure on the brake pedal will be required to obtain the same braking power.

If the trouble is simply due to interruption of the vacuum supply, such as the engine stalling or a faulty hose or union, the reserve of vacuum in the servo allows the brakes to be applied two or three times. The system is designed to stop the car safely if the pedal is held down, but pumping the pedal will reduce the reserve each time the pedal is applied and released.

15.12 Renewing the servo air filter

A plastic-sponge ring on the servo rod that is linked to the brake pedal filters the air that enters the servo. It can be renewed only after the servo has been taken off and the mounting bracket and rubber boot have been removed.

The most convenient time to renew it, therefore, is when the servo is given a service check, which should preferably be done by a Vauxhall dealer after the servo has been in service for about 36 000-40 000 miles.

16 The electrical system

No special electrical knowledge, or expensive test instruments, are needed for normal maintenance of the electrical equipment, nor should simple fault-tracing and first aid measures present any problems. If any serious troubles crop-up, however, it is best to take advantage of the service-exchange scheme operated by your dealer, under which a faulty component is replaced by a reconditioned, guaranteed unit at a fixed charge (this subject is discussed in more detail in Chapter 8).

A point to remember when removing and replacing the battery, or when working on the system, is that the negative battery terminal is earthed. As there will be both positive-earth and negative-earth systems in use for some years to come, special care must also be taken when ordering and installing replacement equipment and accessories such as a transistor-operated car radio or tape-player, which will be seriously damaged if it is connected so that its polarity is reversed.

The time factor

The maintenance checks and simple servicing work described in this chapter do not normally call for pre-planning, minor jobs taking only a few minutes each. Suggested times for more ambitious work are: removing and refitting the dynamo or alternator, 45 min; removing and refitting the starter motor, 1 hr; overhauling a dynamo, 1½ hr; overhauling a starter motor, 2 hr.

16.1 Topping-up the battery cells

Check the level of the liquid in the cells at weekly intervals and don't allow the electrolyte to fall below the tops of the separators between the plates, or the perforated separator guard, as the case may be.

Distilled or 'purified' water is obtainable quite cheaply from chemists. Tapwater and rainwater may contain impurities that will shorten the life of the battery. In an emergency, water from the drip-tray of a refrigerator which has been defrosted can be used, but *not* the water obtained by melting ice cubes.

Never use a naked flame when inspecting the fluid level. An explosive mixture of hydrogen and oxygen is produced when the electrolyte begins to bubble, as the battery becomes fully charged.

16.2 Battery maintenance

The tops of the cells must be kept clean and dry, to prevent corrosion of the terminals and leakage of current.

The battery-retaining clamp should be just sufficiently tight to prevent movement of the battery on its mounting. Overtightening it may crack or distort the battery case.

Scrape any corrosion off the terminals. Replace the connectors and tighten the retaining screws. Smear the terminals and posts with petroleum jelly to protect them against corrosion.

Don't overlook the connections at the earthed end of the battery earthing strap, at the starter motor and at the solenoid switch, mounted on a bracket beside the battery. These connections must be clean and secure.

16.3 Ignition and alternator warning light

A red warning light on the instrument panel glows whenever the generator is not producing an adequate supply of current. Although this lamp is usually termed the ignition warning light (because one of its functions is to remind you not to leave the ignition switched on when the engine is not running) it has the equally important function of warning that the generator is not charging. It should therefore be regarded as an *ignition and no-charge* warning light.

If the light does not go out, or glows faintly whenever the engine is speeded-up above idling speed, the battery is not receiving a charge and will quickly become discharged if the trouble is not put right without delay. First check that the fan belt is intact and correctly tensioned (Chapter 10). Then have the generator and regulator checked by an electrical specialist, or make the tests described in Section 16.18.

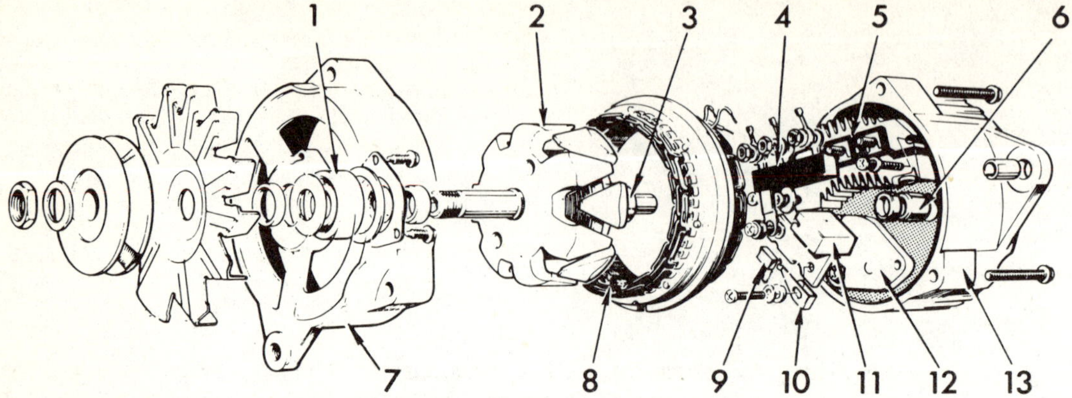

1 drive-end bearing
2 rotor
3 slip rings
4 diode trio
5 rectifier
6 slip-ring end bearing
7 drive-end bracket
8 stator
9 brush
10 brush lead clip
11 brush-holder
12 regulator
13 slip-ring end bracket

Fig. 16.1 The Delco-Remy DN460 alternator

16.4 Servicing an alternator

An alternator requires no routine maintenance, except for keeping the terminals and the end-plate free from deposits of dust and grease. There are, however, several practical points to be remembered when dealing with an alternator which may be overlooked by an owner who has previously dealt only with dynamos.

If the battery has been removed, when refitting it, first connect the negative battery terminal to the earth strap and then fit the positive terminal connector. *Never disconnect the battery when the engine is running.*

Care must be taken not to earth the 'live' connector in the moulded socket if it is removed from the alternator. Never run the engine with the main output cable from the alternator disconnected.

If a charger is to be used to charge-up a flat battery, first isolate the alternator by disconnecting both battery terminals.

If the charging circuit gives trouble, or the alternator requires routine servicing, the work should always be done by a fully-qualified auto-electrician.

16.5 Starter motor servicing

An inertia-engaged starter is fitted as standard – that is, the pinion runs along a threaded sleeve into engagement with the flywheel starter ring when the starter motor rotates. Cars exported to some countries have pre-engaged starters, on which the pinion is moved into engagement positively, by a solenoid-operated lever, before the motor begins to rotate.

The starter should be serviced at reasonable intervals say, every 36 000 miles (60 000 km) - when it should

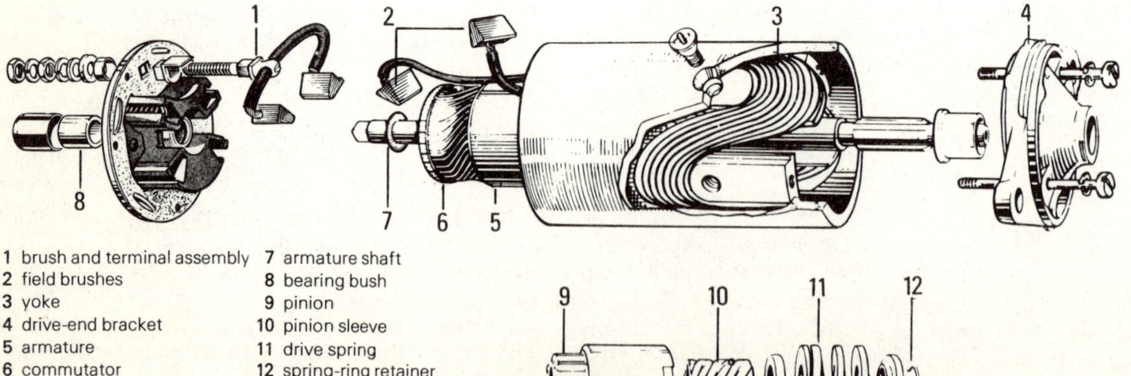

1 brush and terminal assembly
2 field brushes
3 yoke
4 drive-end bracket
5 armature
6 commutator
7 armature shaft
8 bearing bush
9 pinion
10 pinion sleeve
11 drive spring
12 spring-ring retainer

Fig. 16.2 The Lucas M35J/1 starter motor dismantled. This is an inertia-drive type

be removed from the car and dismantled so that the commutator, brushes and the pinion-drive components can be inspected and cleaned.

The dismantling that is needed to service these parts is quite straightforward, but make a careful note of the order in which the parts are removed, especially when dealing with a pre-engaged drive mechanism.

To remove the starter motor –

Materials: Paraffin. Clean rags. Loctite 270 (AVV).

Tools: Jack. Axle stands. Spanners. Special wrench VR2217. $\frac{5}{16}$ in. hexagon key adaptor if pre-engaged starter is fitted.

1 Before the starter can be taken off, it is necessary to remove the right-hand engine mounting. After taking off the air cleaner, raise and support the front of the engine, with suitable wooden packing to protect the sump.

2 Remove the nut from the securing bracket of the right-hand engine mounting, raise the front of the engine, remove the three bolts that attach the bracket to the engine and after withdrawing the bracket remove the mounting and the impact cup, using the Vauxhall wrench VR2217.

3 After disconnecting the starter feed wire, take out the starter securing bolts and withdraw the starter beneath the alternator. The retaining bolts for a pre-engaged starter are of the socket-headed type and a $\frac{5}{16}$ in. hexagon key adaptor and extension bar for the socket set will be needed to remove and refit them.

4 When refitting the starter and the engine mounting, thoroughly clean the bolts which attach the bracket to the crankcase and smear them with Loctite 270 (AVV) to prevent them working loose.

To overhaul the starter –

Materials: New brushes and drive parts, as needed. Paraffin. Clean cloth. Solder and flux.

Tools: Screwdriver. Pliers. Soldering iron. Drive spring compressor, if starter has an inertia-engaged drive.

1 Remove the solenoid-operated engagement mechanism if the starter is the pre-engaged type.

2 Remove the long through-bolts.

3 Take off the drive-end bracket and the commutator-end bracket, being careful not to damage the brushes and leads.

4 Clean the commutator and if it is badly scored, have it reconditioned by an auto-electrician.

5 New commutator-end bracket brushes are supplied as an assembly with the terminal, in a kit which also includes two field-winding brushes. To fit these, cut off the original brush leads about 0.3 in. (8 mm) away from the aluminium tag, make sure that the long and short leads are correctly located and solder them in position.

6 To dismantle an inertia drive, compress the spring (a special tool can be bought from accessory shops) and remove the circlip from the end of the shaft. When reassembling the drive, do not lubricate the parts.

7 Before reassembling a pre-engaged starter check the drive parts for wear and the switch contacts for signs of bad burning, renewing any items as necessary. Lubricate the helix of the armature shaft, the moving parts of the engagement lever, the outer surface of the roller clutch housing and the lip of the seal in the drive-end bracket with grease. For temperate and cold climates use Shell SB2628 and for hot climates, Shell Retinax A.

1 field brushes
2 yoke
3 solenoid
4 drive-end bracket
5 pinion
6 engagement lever
7 armature
8 field brushes
9 commutator-end brush-holder

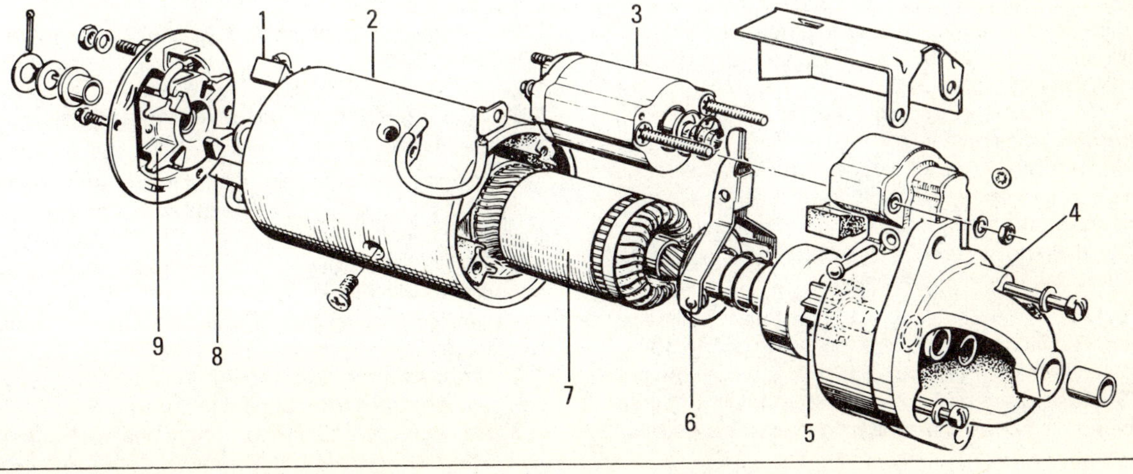

Fig. 16.3 Lucas 5M90/PE pre-engaged starter motor

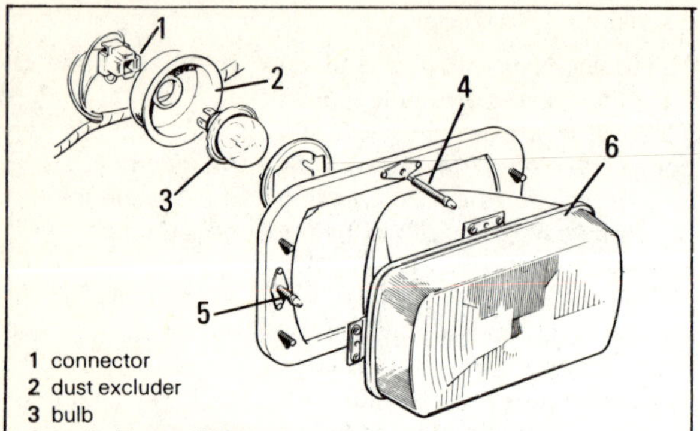

1 connector
2 dust excluder
3 bulb
4 vertical beam alignment screw
5 horizontal beam alignment screw (one each side)
6 reflector and lens assembly

Fig. 16.4 A Cibié rectangular headlamp. This differs only in detail from the Lucas type shown in Fig. 16.5

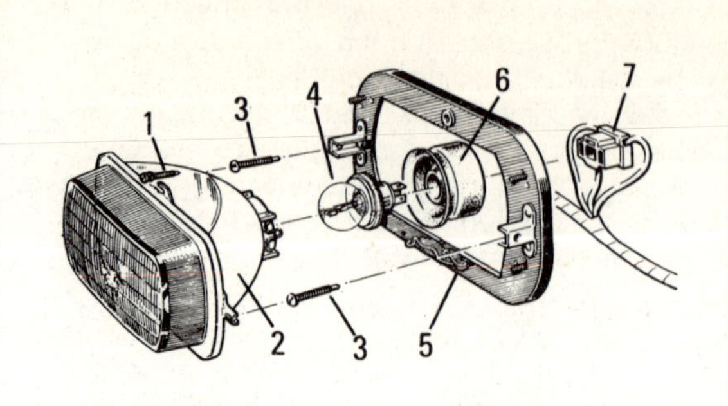

1 vertical beam alignment screw
2 reflector and lens assembly
3 horizontal beam alignment screws
4 bulb
5 retaining clip
6 dust excluder
7 connector

Fig. 16.5 A Lucas headlamp dismantled

16.6 Adjusting the headlamp beam

It is particularly important that the headlamp beams should be correctly aligned. Most garages today have optical beam-setting equipment which enables the lamps to be precisely adjusted.

Each unit has three beam-adjusting or trim screws (Fig. 16.6). One screw raises or lowers the beam and the others swing it from side to side. The screws extend into the engine compartment. It is preferably to use the special Vauxhall tool VR2103 to rotate them if you intend to align the lamps yourself, although this is not essential.

16.7 Removing and refitting the headlamp bulbs or light units

Either Cibié or Lucas headlamps may be fitted, the difference between the two types being in the method of attaching the light unit and the fact that the Lucas lamp has a plastic reflector.

On Cibié lamps plastic retaining inserts, which are riveted to the light unit, clip over the tapered ends of the beam trim screws. A Lucas lamp is held in contact with the trim screws by a retaining spring in the bottom of the mounting plate.

If it is necessary to remove the complete reflector assembly, after taking off the headlamp surround the Cibié unit can be eased off the trim screws. The Lucas unit can be removed by releasing the retaining spring and easing the bracket out of the top trim screw.

Normally, of course, it is necessary only to change the headlamp bulb. To do this—

1 From inside the engine compartment pull back the rubber cover and disconnect the wiring connector.

2 Prise the spring clips back and withdraw the bulb.

3 When fitting a bulb, notice that the flange is located by a projection which engages with a slot in the reflector body.

4 Never handle the glass of the bulb with the bare fingers. Traces of oil or skin acid will be burnt on to the bulb by the heat of the filament and will reduce the light output. Use a clean cloth or a tissue when removing or fitting a bulb.

16.8 Removing and refitting side-lamp and direction-indicator bulbs

Removing and refitting these bulbs is straightforward, the lens being retained by two screws.

16.9 Removing and refitting the rear-lamp bulbs

The indicator, tail/stop-lamp and reversing-lamp bulbs are accessible when the two screws which retain the rear-lamp have been removed.

16.10 Changing the rear number plate bulb

The wedge-base, capless bulb is fitted in a holder which is clipped into the lamp body. To change it—

1 Remove the screws which retain the lens, ease the lens downwards and disengage the rear end from the body.

2 Pull the bulb holder out of its clips and remove the bulb.

16.11 Changing the instrument-illumination and warning-lamp bulbs

To change the instrument-illumination and warning lamp bulbs the instrument assembly must be withdrawn from the panel.

1 Detach the bayonet-type speedometer cable connector by reaching up behind the instrument panel. On right-hand-drive cars it will first be necessary to remove the windscreen demisting duct.

2 The instrument assembly is retained by clips and can be pushed out from behind the panel.

3 Squeeze the clips which retain the warning-lamp bulb carrier and withdraw the carrier. After disconnecting the instrument feed plug and the clock and

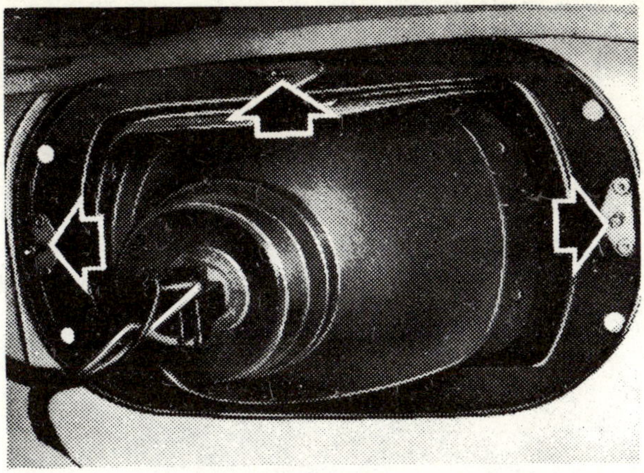

Fig. 16.6 The three beam aligning screws on a typical headlamp assembly are indicated by the arrows

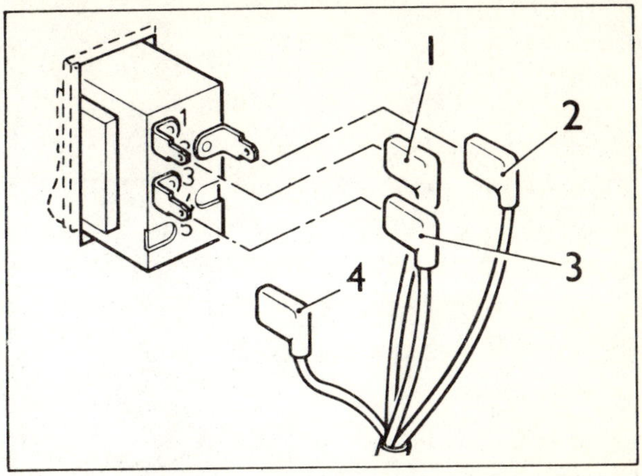

Fig. 16.7 Connections to lighting switch, 1, Blue. 2, Brown/blue. 3, Red/green. 4, Red/blue (This wire is connected to fog lamp switch for fog rear guard)

instrument lamp wires, the instrument assembly can be lifted away.

16.12 The brake-pressure and handbrake warning lamp switches

The brake-pressure warning lamp in the instrument assembly is controlled by a switch in the master cylinder. This is operated by a piston which moves away from the central position if pressure is lost in the front or rear brake pipeline. A pin in the switch then touches a contact and completes the circuit to earth, illuminating the warning lamp.

As a check that the warning lamp is serviceable, a spring-loaded switch is attached to the handbrake ratchet plate. With the brake applied and the ignition switched on, the warning light should be illuminated, but it should be extinguished when the handbrake is released – unless, of course, pressure has been lost in one half of the braking system.

To change the switches–

1 The contact head of the pressure-warning lamp switch can be unscrewed from the brake master cylinder without loss of fluid, after the wire has been disconnected.

2 To detach the switch from the handbrake lever, the lever itself must first be removed. This entails taking out the left-hand front seat and raising the carpet to give access to the lever mounting bolts. The switch is retained by a single screw and is not repairable.

16.13 The windscreen wiper

The electrically-operated wiper normally requires no attention, other than renewal of the wiper blades at least once a year.

If the blades do not sweep through satisfactory arcs, or fail to park neatly when the wiper is switched off (they are self-parking), the arms may have been incorrectly fitted to the driving spindles. They can be withdrawn by depressing the spring catch that clamps the arm to the splined section of the spindle. Refit the arm in the desired position and push if fully home.

Wet the screen before checking the sweep and the parking of the blades. A test on a dry screen will give misleading results, owing to excessive friction between the blades and the glass.

Either SWF or Trico arms and blades may be fitted.

1 To change an SWF blade, depress the spring catch and withdraw the blade towards the pivot end of the wiper arm.

2 To change a Trico blade insert a screwdriver between the leaf spring and the arm and then tilt the outer end of the blade attachment sleeve towards the windscreen.

16.14 Direction indicators

The flashing indicator lamps are fed with current from a sealed control unit. Failure or erratic action of the indicators may be caused by a blown bulb, dirty contacts in the indicator switch or in the lamp units, or by faulty wiring or a blown fuse. If checks on these points

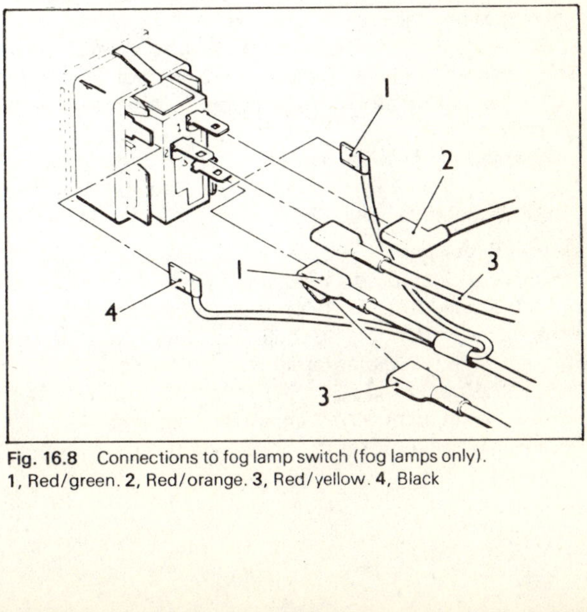

Fig. 16.8 Connections to fog lamp switch (fog lamps only). 1, Red/green. 2, Red/orange. 3, Red/yellow. 4, Black

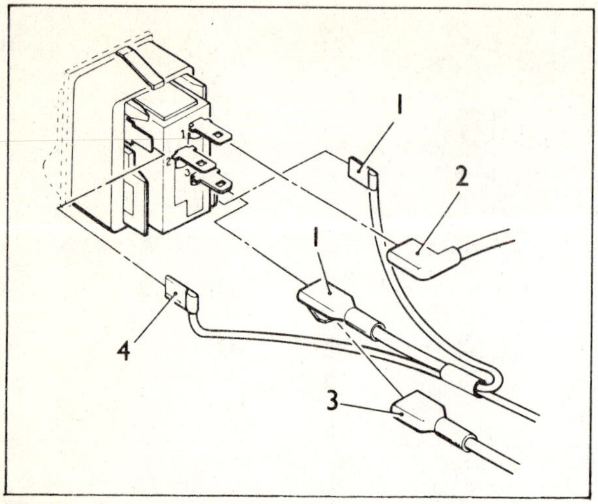

Fig. 16.9 Connecting to fog lamp switch (fog rear guard lamps only). 1, Red/green. 2, Red/orange. 3, Red/blue. 4, Black

do not reveal any faults, the flasher unit is probably the culprit and must be replaced, since it is not repairable.

There are two types of flasher unit — the vane type, which is normally fitted, and the hot-wire type. A Lucas vane-type unit is rectangular, the Magnatex unit drum-shaped. A hot wire unit is cylindrical and is manufactured by Lucas.

It is therefore easy to identify the type of unit that is fitted if it is necessary to diagnose possible causes of trouble, as indicated in the table below.

The unit is clipped to the steering column brace and when a hazard warning system is fitted the flasher unit for this is clipped to the brace beside the normal indicator unit.

The following notes will help in diagnosing possible causes of trouble in the indicator circuit—

Vane-type unit

One indicator bulb defective. The other bulb on the same side, and the respective warning lamp bulb, will remain on (not flashing), with no audible warning from the unit, when the switch is operated.

Both turn indicator bulbs on the same side defective. The warning lamp bulb will remain on (not flashing), with no audible warning from the unit, when the switch is operated.

Warning lamp bulb defective. The indicator bulbs flash at a slightly lower frequency and audible warning remains operative.

Hot-wire type unit

One indicator bulb defective. When the switch is operated the other bulb on the same side and the respective warning lamp bulb will flash at a faster frequency with audible warning from the unit.

Both indicator bulbs on the same side defective. The warning lamp bulb will remain on (not flashing), with no audible warning from the unit, when the switch is operated.

Warning lamp bulb defective. The indicator bulbs and the audible warning will operate normally when the switch is operated.

16.15 Testing and renewing a faulty brake stop-light switch

The switch is mounted behind the shank of the brake pedal, contact being made as soon as the pedal moves away from the plunger of the switch.

To check the circuit—

1 If the stop lights flicker or do not come on when the brake pedal is depressed, check the lamp bulbs, holders and wiring and fuse.

2 If everything seems to be in order, disconnect the wires from the stop-lamp switch, switch on the ignition and touch the terminals on the wires together. If the stop-lamps then light up, either the stop-lamp switch is faulty or the leads were making poor contact with the terminals on the switch. If the stop-lamps do not come on when the wires are short-circuited, there must be a fault at some point in the wiring or the fuse has blown (see Section 16.16).

To change the switch—

1 Pull off the wiring connections.

2 Depress the brake pedal and remove the pedal-stop rubber from the switch plunger.

3 Unscrew the hexagonal retaining nut and withdraw the switch from the bracket.

4 Fit the new switch and adjust it so that with the ignition on, the stop lamps are illuminated when the brake pedal is depressed by about $\frac{3}{4}$-1 in. (20-25 mm).

16.16 Fuses and protection against short-circuits

The electrical system is protected against overloading or short-circuits in two ways: by six fuses, housed in a plug-in connector on the engine bulkhead; and by either one or two fusible links — a sort of super-fuse which is connected into the main battery feed, and which protects the entire electrical circuit with the exception of the starter.

If a fuse burns out, find the cause and rectify the fault before fitting a new fuse having the same rating, which is shown on a coloured slip of paper inside the fuse. Always fit a fuse of the correct rating and *never be tempted to bridge the fuse-holder clips with ordinary wire,* as this can lead to a fire in the wiring, or a burnt-out component.

If a fusible link burns out, refer to Section 16.17. Normally, however, one of the 35-amp fuses in the fuse box below the instrument panel on the right-hand side of the steering column, will fail first.

The fuses can be seen when the pull-down cover is opened. They are numbered from 1 to 6, the number being behind each fuse. The circuits protected are—

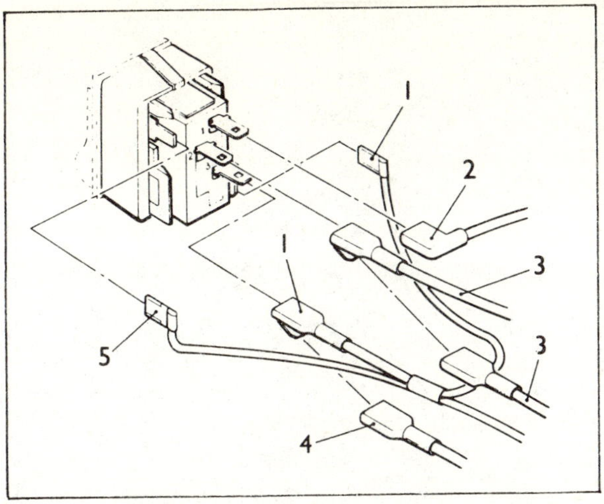

Fig. 16.10 Connections to fog lamp switch (fog lamps and fog rear guard lamps). 1, Red/green. 2, Red/orange. 3, Red/yellow. 4, Red/blue. 5, Black

Fuse No.	Circuits protected
1	Right-hand side and tail lamps, instrument lamps and where applicable cigar lighter bulb, fog lamps and fog rear guard lamps.
2	Left-hand side and tail lamps, number plate lamp and where applicable engine compartment lamp.
3	Interior lamp, horn, headlamp flasher and where applicable hazard warning system and clock.
4	Heated rear window and reverse lamps.
5	Stop lamps, direction indicator lamps and warning lamps, oil and alternator warning lamps, voltage stabilizer, fuel and temperature gauges, heater motor and brake-pressure warning system.
6	Windscreen wiper and wash and where applicable headlamp wash/wipe, radio, cassette player and cigar lighter element.

16.17 Renewing a fusible link

The two fusible links are connected into the main battery feed at the starter solenoid switch, mounted on a bracket beside the battery.

The links protect the whole of the electrical system with the exception of the starter, and are designed to burn-out if a heavy overload occurs – due to a short-circuit, for example, or a similar fault.

One link protects the lighting switch and the feed to numbers 1 and 2 fuses. The other supplies the ignition switch, ignition system and the feeds to fuses 3, 4, 5 and 6.

To renew a link the service repair kit shown in Fig. 16.16 must be used. In this illustration some of the other wiring to the starter solenoid switch has been omitted.

1 Cut away the burnt-out fusible link from the soldered junction on the harness at the points A and B in the illustration.

2 Strip back the insulation from the new link to bare about ¾ in. (20 mm) of the wire and double the wire back. Similarly strip the insulation from the harness cable or cables for approximately ½ in. (12 mm). In each case scrape the wires to give a clean, bright surface.

3 Insert the bared ends of the wires into the butt connector and crimp the connector to secure them.

4 Fit the ring terminal of the new link to the solenoid switch terminal.

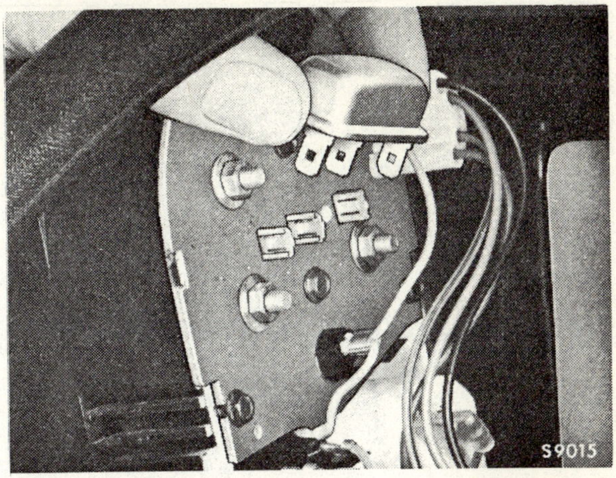

Fig. 16.11 The voltage stabilizer which supplies current to the petrol and water-temperature gauges is plugged into the printed circuit at the back of the instrument assembly

Simple fault-tracing

A thorough diagnosis of an ailing electrical system calls for the use of proper fault-tracing equipment, or at least, an accurate moving-coil voltmeter. Ideally, a special Automotive Electrical Instrument Tester should be used to check the fuel and temperature gauges, so this sort of work is outside the scope of the average owner.

There are, however, some simple tests that can be

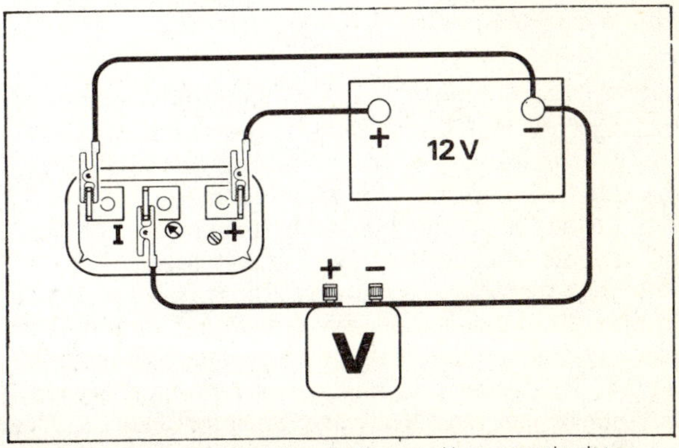

Fig. 16.12 The voltage stabilizer can be tested by connecting it to a battery and voltmeter as shown. When the unit has warmed-up the voltmeter should record regular pulsations in voltage, with an average reading of 10 volts midway between the minimum and maximum readings. A faulty stabilizer cannot be repaired

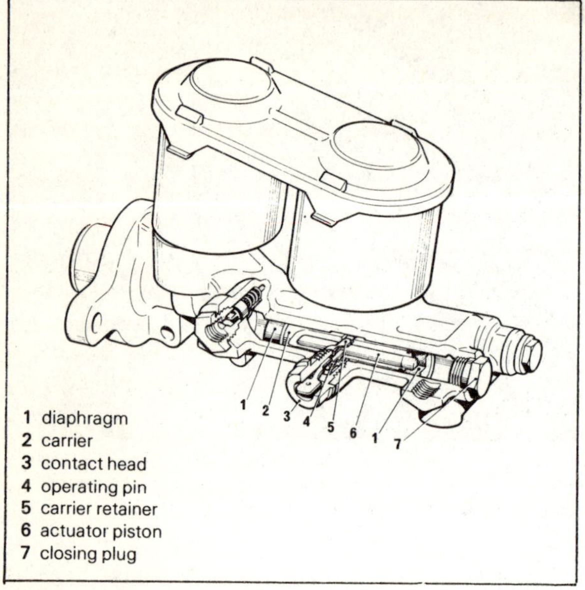

Fig. 16.13 The brake-pressure warning light switch is incorporated in the brake master cylinder. The contact head can be unscrewed without loss of brake fluid

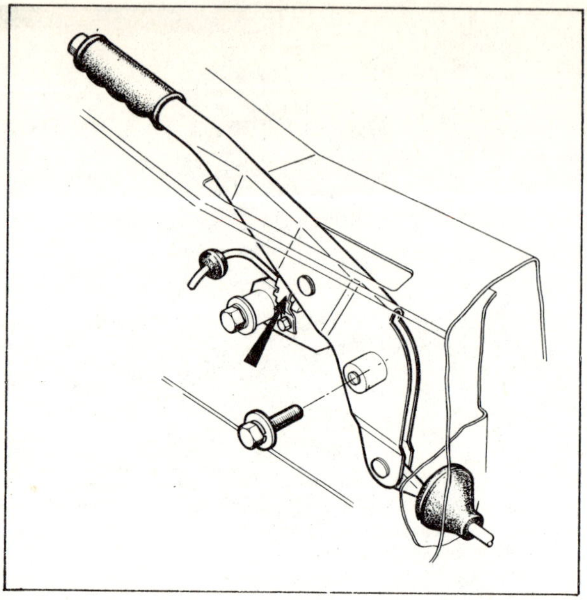

Fig. 16.14 The handbrake warning light switch, indicated by the arrow, is attached to the mounting bracket of the handbrake and actuated by the lever pawl

made when it is suspected that the generator is not giving its full charge, or when the starter motor does not turn the engine.

16.18 Testing the generator and charging system

The following tests, for which only a voltmeter is required, are sufficient to show whether or not all is well with the alternator and the charging system. A moving-coil type of meter is to be preferred, but any good-quality instrument can be used, as the checks depend on comparative readings, rather than on exact voltages. They are based on the fact that the battery voltage varies according to the state of charge, and is always higher when the cells are receiving a charge from the generator.

To make the test—

1 Clip the voltmeter leads to the battery terminals, making sure that the surface of the metal has been pierced. If the battery is sound and well charged, a reading of 12-12.5 volts should be obtained.

2 Switch on all the lights. The reading should now fall to approximately 11-11.5 volts.

3 Start the engine and speed it up to the equivalent of about 20 mph in top gear, but do not race it. The reading should now be about 13.5 volts, and the voltmeter needle should be steady. If it flickers, there may be trouble in the diodes or in the regulator circuit.

4 If voltage readings roughly equal to those quoted are obtained, it can be assumed that the battery and charging system are sound. If the voltage across the battery does not rise by 1 volt when the engine is speeded-up above idling speed, there is a fault somewhere in the charging system, probably one of those just mentioned. If the increase exceeds about 1.5 volts, either the regulator or the battery is faulty. Do not try to check the regulator. Leave this sort of work to a qualified auto-electrician.

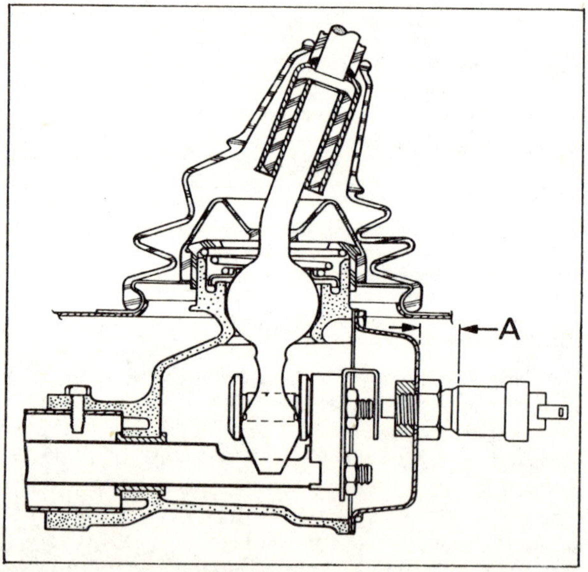

Fig. 16.15 The reversing lamp switch in the gear-lever housing must be screwed in until the distance A is 0.3 in. (7.5 mm). Jointing compound must be used on the threads but not be allowed to run on to the switch plunger

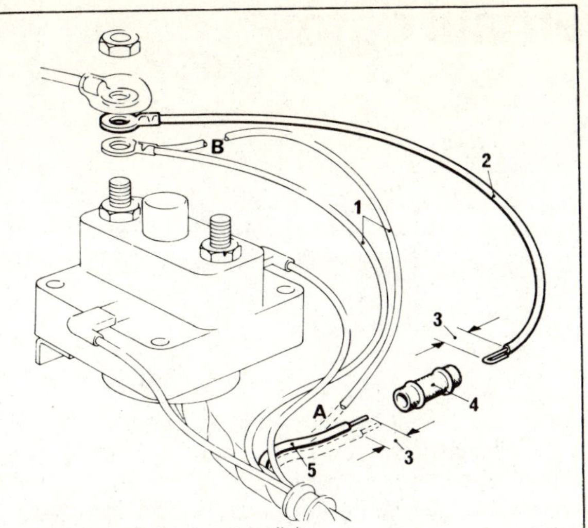

A and B Cuts made in burnt-out link
1 original links
2 replacement link
3 approximately ½ in. (12 mm)
4 butt connector
5 Two cables, colour-coded brown, or single cable coded brown/blue (part of existing harness)

Fig. 16.16 The method of fitting a new fusible link is described in the text. In this illustration some of the wires connected to the starter solenoid switch have been omitted for clarity

16.19 Testing a faulty starter motor

1 Switch on the lights and press the starter switch. If the solenoid switch clicks and the lights go dim, but the starter does not operate, either the battery is discharged or current is flowing through the windings of the starter but for some reason the armature is not rotating. Probably the starter pinion is jammed in mesh with the flywheel starter ring. This fault is usually confined to inertia-engaged starters.

2 The easiest way to free a jammed starter pinion when a synchromesh gearbox is fitted is to switch off the ignition, engage *top gear* and rock the car *forwards*. Do not rock the car backwards and forwards, as this may jam the pinion more firmly in mesh with the flywheel ring-gear teeth.

3 If the lamps remain bright, the starter switch may be faulty, but first check for loose or corroded connections on the ignition switch or on the electromagnetic solenoid starter switch itself, which is mounted on the engine or next to the battery on the starter motor itself when a pre-engaged starter is fitted.

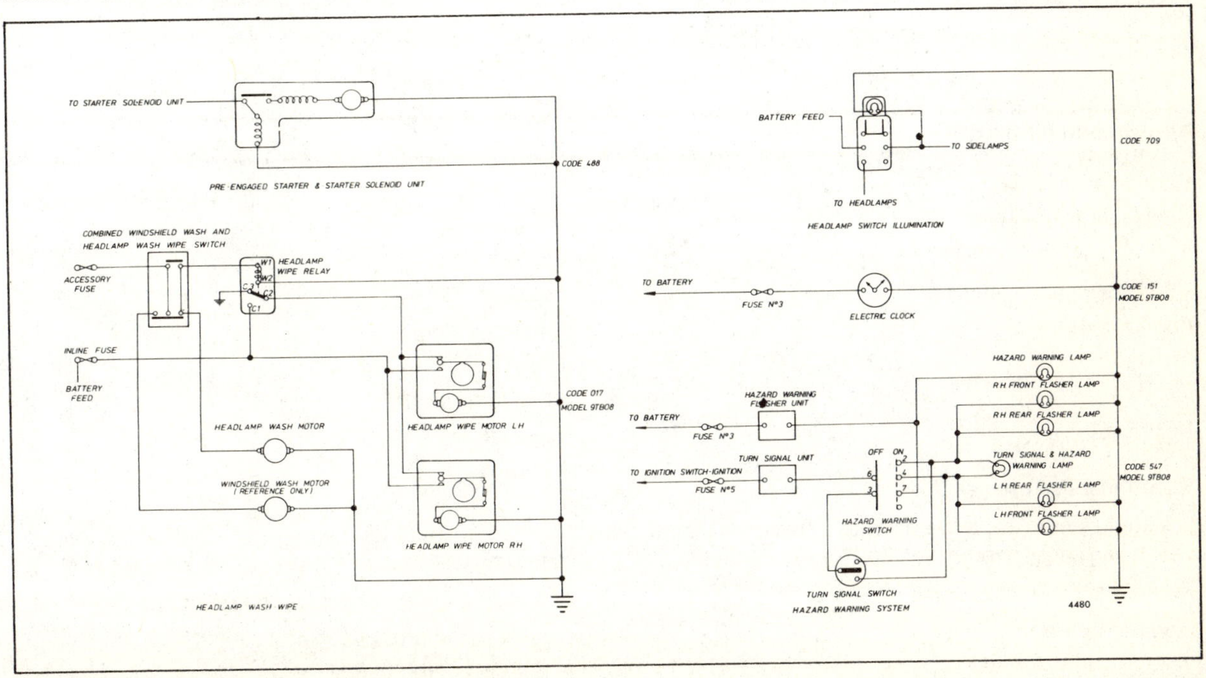

Fig. 16.17 Theoretical wiring diagram for optional equipment

17 Specifications and overhaul data

In this chapter we have included specifications and data which will be needed to carry out adjustments, overhauls and replacements which are within the scope of a d.i.y. owner.

We have avoided giving elaborate lists of fits, clearances and engineering tolerances, however, since internal and external micrometers, depth gauges and other precision measuring equipment are not likely to be found — or needed — in the average home garage.

As we recommend in Chapter 8, highly-skilled work of this sort should be left to a Vauxhall dealer or to a specialist who is best qualified to handle it. Alternatively, it is often possible to fit a reconditioned, service-exchange component at a cost which shows a considerable saving over the price of a new part.

As emphasized in other chapters, it is advisable to tighten some of the more important nuts and bolts to a specified torque figure, expressed in lb ft and Nm, in order to obtain the correct tightness without risking overstressing a bolt or nut or distorting a part. The correct tightening torques for the more critical components have therefore been included in the data tables.

When self-locking nuts (stiff nuts) are fitted, these should not be re-used if their self-locking effect has been reduced or if they are of the deformed-thread type and the lacquer coating has been affected. They should not be degreased. As a precaution, it is better to fit new nuts.

Top-up and fill-up data

Capacities (approx.)

Fuel tank: hatchback	8 gal (38 litres)
saloon and estate	10 gal (45 litres)
Cooling system, with heater	10.2 pints (5.8 litres)
Engine sump: total, dry engine	5.5 pints (3.13 litres)
refill, with filter element change	5 pints (2.84 litres)
Gearbox	1.1 pints (0.62 litre)
Rear axle	1.15 pints (0.65 litre)

Recommended fuel grades

It is important to use a fuel that has a sufficiently high octane rating to prevent detonation ('pinking') under load, which can cause overheating and may damage the pistons and engine bearings.

Standard compression-ratio engine (9.2:1)	97 octane, minimum (4-star rating in UK)
Low compression-ratio engine (7.3:1)	90 octane, minimum (2-star rating in UK) or 94 octane (3-star rating in UK)

Oil consumption

A reasonable consumption for a worn engine is about 500-750 miles per pint, but a new or reconditioned engine which has been properly run-in may require only a negligible amount of oil between changes.

Recommended lubricants (temperate climates)

Engine	Multigrade oil 10W/50 or 20W/50
Ignition distributor shaft, contact-breaker pivot, automatic timing control	Engine oil
Carburettor damper	10W/30 engine oil
Synchromesh gearbox and rear axle	SAE 90EP, 85W/140EP or 90/140EP hypoid gear oil
Front-wheel hub bearings	Multipurpose grease

Engine — see Chapter 9

All models are four-cylinder, overhead-valve units, with push-rod operation of the valve gear.

Technical specifications

Capacity	1256 cc (76.6 cu. in.)
Cylinder bore	80.97 mm (3.188 in.)
Stroke of crankshaft	60.96 mm (2.40 in.)
Standard compression ratio	9.2:1
Low compression ratio	7.3:1
Brake-horse power at standard compression ratio	58.5 bhp (DIN) at 5600 rpm
Firing order	1, 3, 4, 2.

Engine lubrication

Oil filter	Full flow, replaceable element
Oil pressure hot, at 3000 rpm	55-65 lb/sq. in. (3.8-4.5 kg/cm² or bars)

Engine maintenance and repair

Valve clearances, hot: inlet and exhaust	0.008 in. (0.2 mm)
Valve seat angle on valve head	44°
Valve seating angle in cylinder head	45°
Valve stem clearance in guide: Inlet	0.0005-0.0020 in. (0.013-0.051 mm)
Exhaust	0.0013-0.0028 in. (0.033-0.071 mm)
Compression pressure at cranking speed (hot) and throttle open:	
Standard compression engine	140 lb/sq. in. (9.7 kg/cm² or bars), minimum
Low compression engine	120 lb/sq. in. (8.3 kg/cm² or bars), minimum
Maximum permissible variation between cylinders	20 lb/sq. in. (1.4 kg/cm² or bars)
Piston clearance in cylinder bore	0.009-0.0014 in. (0.023-0.036 mm)
Piston-pin fit in connecting rod	Interference fit
Piston-pin clearance in piston bosses at 20°C	0.00025-0.00045 in. (0.006-0.011 mm)
Connecting-rod bearing diametrical clearance	0.001-0.0029 in. (0.025-0.074 mm)
Connecting-rod bearing side clearance	0.004-0.010 in. (0.10-0.25 mm)
Main journal clearance in bearing	0.001-0.0025 in. (0.025-0.064 mm)
Crankshaft end-float	0.002-0.008 in. (0.05-0.20 mm)
Camshaft end-float	0.002-0.009 in. (0.05-0.23 mm)

Torque-wrench settings	lb ft	Nm
Connecting-rod bolts	25	34[1]
Crankshaft main bearing bolts	82	111[1]
Flywheel bolts	30	41[2]
Cylinder head bolts	49	66
Oil filter bolt	14	19
Engine front mountings and nuts	29	39
Engine rear mounting:		
Mounting to transmission bolt	32	45
Cross-member to body bracket bolts	28	40

[1] Oiled threads [2] Sealed threads

Cooling system — see Chapter 10

Type	Pressurized system with belt-driven pump and a viscous-coupling fan
Filler cap: nominal pressure	15 lb/sq. in. (1.055 kg/cm² or bars)
opening pressure	13½-17½ lb/sq. in. (0.94-1.21 kg/cm² or bars)
Thermostat valve opening temperature	88°C (190°F)
Torque-wrench setting: fan securing screw	14 lb ft (20 Nm)

Carburettor and petrol pump — see Chapter 11

Carburettor type	Zenith/Stromberg 150CD-SEV
Metering needle	BIDV
Jet orifice	2.54 mm
Air valve piston spring colour	Natural
Engine idling speed	800-850 rpm
Petrol pump	AC mechanical

Ignition system — see Chapter 12

Sparking plugs	AC 42XLS (or latest recommendation by Vauxhall dealer)
Sparking-plug gap	0.040 in. (1 mm)
Distributor	AC Delco
Contact-breaker gap: new contacts	0.022 in. (0.55 mm)
used contacts	0.020 in. (0.50 mm)
Cam dwell angle	35-37°
Ignition timing	9° btdc
Torque-wrench setting: sparking plugs	25 lb ft (34 Nm)

Clutch, gearbox, propeller shaft, rear axle — see Chapter 13

Clutch type	Borg and Beck single dry plate, diaphragm spring type, operated by cable
Free travel at operating lever	½ in. (13 mm)
Gearbox	Four-speed synchromesh

Torque-wrench settings	lb ft	Nm
Clutch to flywheel bolts	14	20
Gearbox mounting to transmission bolt	32	45
Gearbox cross-member to body bracket bolts	28	40
Axle shaft bearing retainer plate nuts	19	26*
Wheel nuts	48	65*
Pinion extension housing to axle housing bolts	20	27
Pinion extension shaft flange nut	18	25

* Clean dry threads

Suspension, steering, wheels and tyres — see Chapter 14

Steering gear	Rack-and-pinion type
Steering ratio	3.5 turns lock-to-lock

Checks on the steering geometry — castor, camber and steering pivot inclination angles — call for the use of special equipment and this work must therefore be carried out by a Vauxhall dealer. This also applies to the front-wheel alignment which must be within the following limits — 0.16-0.24 in. (4-6 mm) toe-in at wheel rims.

Front-wheel bearing end-float	0.001-0.004 in. (0.02-0.1 mm)

Torque-wrench settings	lb ft	Nm
Front suspension		
Upper arm fulcrum bolts	47	64
Lower arm fulcrum bolts	49	66
Lower arm outrigger fulcrum bolts	49	66
Axle inner mounting bolts	47	64
Axle outer mounting bolts	55	74
Upper ball joint retaining nuts	30	40
Stabilizer bar mounting bolts	15	20
Shock absorber lower mounting bolts	30	40
Rear suspension		
Panhard rod to body mounting bolt	72	98
Panhard rod to axle nut	47	64
Suspension arm bolts	50	67
Pinion extension housing to cross-member bolts	15	20
Shock absorber lower mounting nuts	32	43
Steering		
Wheel nuts	69	94
Steering coupling pinch bolt	13	17
Tie-rod inner ball joint to rack	66	90
Steering gear mounting bolts	15	20

Wheels Rim Size 13 x 5J

Tyres

The pressures given on page 108 are average figures only. The latest recommendations by the manufacturers of the tyres fitted to your car should always be checked, as there are sometimes variations between different makes. Most garages and tyre specialists should have this information.

	Tyre size	Pressures — lb/sq. in. (kg/cm² or bars)			
		With driver and two passengers		With maximum loading	
		Front	Rear	Front	Rear
Saloons — E models	5.60x13	22(1.55)	22(1.55)	24(1.69)	30(2.11)
Hatchbacks and saloons	155SRx 13 or 175/70SRx13	21(1.48)	25(1.76)	22(1.55)	29(2.00)
Estates	155SRx13	21(1.48)	25(1.76)	24(1.69)	34(2.39)

Braking system — see Chapter 15

Dual hydraulic braking system, with tandem-piston master cylinder, separate circuits to front and rear brakes. Disc front brakes. Leading-and-trailing shoe automatically-adjusted rear brakes. Vacuum servo and pressure-conscious reducing valve for rear brakes fitted as standard.

Minimum permissible thickness of friction material

Disc brake pads	0.06 in. (1.5 mm)
Rear shoe linings	Linings are unserviceable when worn down to depth of groove
Brake fluid	Castrol Girling universal brake and clutch fluid

Torque-wrench settings

	lb ft	Nm
Brake caliper to steering knuckle bolts	72	98
Brake disc to hub bolts	30	40
Rear brake backplate nuts	19	26
Rear brake adjuster preload	27-35*	3.1-3.9

*lb in

Electrical system — see Chapter 16

Type	12-volt, negative terminal of battery earthed
Battery: standard	40 amp hour at 20-hour rate
large capacity	55 amp hour at 20-hour rate
Generator	Delco-Remy alternator
Starter motor: standard equipment	Inertia type Lucas M35J/1
heavy-duty option	Pre-engaged type Lucas 5M90/PE
Alternator drive belt tension	¼ in. (6 mm) deflection under thumb pressure applied midway between alternator and water pump pulleys

Weights and measures — approx.

Overall length: hatchback	12 ft. 11¼ in. (3.944 m)
saloon and estate	13 ft. 9 in. (4.190 m)
Overall width	5 ft. 2 in. (1.575 m)
Unladen height: hatchback and saloon	4 ft. 3½ in. (1.308 m)
estate	4 ft. 4 in. (1.324 m)
Wheelbase	7 ft. 10¼ in. (2.39 m)
Track, front and rear	4 ft. 3¼ in. (1.30 m)
Ground clearance, minimum	5¼ in. (130 mm)
Turning circle between kerbs	30 ft (9.144 m)

Kerb weight: hatchback L	16¾ cwt (851 kg)	saloon 2-door E	16¼ cwt (826 kg)
GL	17 cwt (864 kg)	4-door E	16¾ cwt (851 kg)
GLS	17½ cwt (889 kg)	2-door L	16½ cwt (838 kg)
estate	17½ cwt (889 kg)	4-door L	17 cwt (864 kg)
		4-door GLS	17¼ cwt (876 kg)

For maximum stability and safety when towing, it is recommended that the loaded weight of a caravan or trailer should not exceed three-quarters of the kerbside weight of the car.

Index